Praise for *The Latinization of U.S. Schools*

"Articulating what many know from experience but do not find reflected in the studies on Latino education, Jason Irizarry and his high school coauthors provide readers an insightful, inspiring, and powerful view of the capabilities—and often brilliance—of Latino students in America today. Breaking the mold of presenting Latino/a students as a group incapable of academic success and riddled with deficiencies, *The Latinization of U.S. Schools* confirms that what students need most is the belief in their unique abilities and the support to achieve their goals. Teachers and schools would do well to heed this message."
—Sonia Nieto, University of Massachusetts, author of *Dear Paulo: Letters from Those Who Dare Teach* (Paradigm 2008) and *Why We Teach* (2005).

"*The Latinization of U.S. Schools* illustrates the potency of participatory action research that intimately involves high school students in knowledge creation that surrounds their own lives and experiences. With eloquence, passion, and ringing clarity, Jason Irizarry and the youth from his research collaborative articulate a vision of schooling in which getting educated is synonymous with retaining their cultural, linguistic, and community-based identities. This is a courageous, inspiring, and life-saving book that truly succeeds in raising the heretofore silent voices of Latino students."
—Angela Valenzuela, University of Texas at Austin; author of *Leaving Children Behind: How "Texas-Style" Accountability Fails Latino Youth* (2004) and *Subtractive Schooling: U.S.-Mexican Youth and the Politics of Caring* (1999).

THE LATINIZATION
OF U.S. SCHOOLS

Series in Critical Narrative

Donaldo Macedo, Series Editor

University of Massachusetts Boston

NOW IN PRINT

The Hegemony of English
  by Donaldo Macedo, Bessie Dendrinos, and
    Panayota Gounari (2003)
Letters from Lexington: Reflections on Propaganda
  New Updated Edition
  by Noam Chomsky (2004)
Pedagogy of Indignation
  by Paulo Freire (2004)
Howard Zinn on Democratic Education
  by Howard Zinn, with Donaldo Macedo (2005)
How Children Learn: Getting Beyond the Deficit Myth
  by Terese Fayden (2005)
The Globalization of Racism
  edited by Donaldo Macedo and Panayota Gounari (2006)
Daring to Dream: Toward a Pedagogy of the Unfinished
  by Paulo Freire (2007)
Class in Culture
  by Teresa L. Ebert and Mas'ud Zavarzadeh (2008)
Dear Paulo: Letters from Those Who Dare Teach
  by Sonia Nieto (2008)
Uncommon Sense from the Writings of Howard Zinn (2008)
Paulo Freire and the Curriculum
  by Georgios Grollios (2009)
*Freedom at Work: Language, Professional, and Intellectual
Development in Schools*
  by María E. Torres-Guzmán with Ruth Swinney (2009)
*The Latinization of U.S. Schools: Successful Teaching and Learning
in Shifting Cultural Contexts*
  by Jason G. Irizarry (2011)

THE LATINIZATION OF U.S. SCHOOLS

SUCCESSFUL TEACHING AND LEARNING IN SHIFTING CULTURAL CONTEXTS

JASON G. IRIZARRY

with Project FUERTE

Paradigm Publishers

Boulder • London

Copyright © 2011 Paradigm Publishers

Published in the United States by Paradigm Publishers, 2845 Wilderness Place, Suite 200, Boulder, CO 80301 USA.

Paradigm Publishers is the trade name of Birkenkamp & Company, LLC, Dean Birkenkamp, President and Publisher.

Library of Congress Cataloging-in-Publication Data

Irizarry, Jason G.
    The Latinization of U.S. schools : successful teaching and learning in shifting cultural contexts / Jason G. Irizarry.
        p. cm. — (Series in critical narrative)
    Includes bibliographical references and index.
    ISBN 978-1-59451-958-1 (hardcover : alk. paper) — ISBN 978-1-59451-959-8 (pbk. : alk. paper)
    1. Hispanic Americans—Education. 2. Hispanic Americans—Education—Social aspects. 3. Hispanic American students—Social conditions. 4. Multiculturalism—Study and teaching—United States. I. Title.
    LC2669.I75 1997
    371.829'68073—dc23

                                                                    2011018054

Printed and bound in the United States of America on acid-free paper that meets the standards of the American National Standard for Permanence of Paper for Printed Library Materials.

Designed and Typeset by Straight Creek Bookmakers.

15 14 13 12 11   1 2 3 4 5

For Katie, Javier Jay, and Alex Emilio Irizarry
and in loving memory of Lydia Rivera,
mi abuela y mamá de crianza

CONTENTS

⊸

ACKNOWLEDGEMENTS

This book represents a collective journey that would not have been possible without the support of more individuals than I can name here. I could write an entire volume crediting all those who have touched my life and my work in some meaningful way. With sincere apologies to anyone I may have left out, I would like to thank the following people.

First, this book would have never been written if not for the the students who contributed to it. To the student-researchers in Project FUERTE, thank you for allowing me into your lives and for your commitment to the project—which has, I hope, proven to you that you are all indeed brilliant. Your zest for life and ability to laugh, even in the face of adversity, are contagious. I will forever be grateful to you all and wish you the best. *Mil gracias!*

To Katie, my wife and life partner, thank you for your indefatigable love and support. You have made countless sacrifices to allow me to pursue my dreams; the words on this page cannot begin to capture my appreciation. To my sons, Javier Jay and Alex Emilio: you constantly provide me with inspiration and remind me of those things that are most important in life. With your regular assurances that I'm "not a real doctor!" I will always remain grounded. I am truly blessed and thankful for you all.

My grandmother, Lydia Rivera, was a huge presence in my life, and the lessons I learned from her permeate this book. I hope you are proud, Ma. My parents taught me separate but equally important lessons. My passion for *latinidad* and all things Puerto Rican was nurtured by my mother, Roslyn Rivera. My father, Milton, demonstrated in his own life that it is never too late to accomplish wonderful things. I also derive great inspiration from my brother, Brandon, who always "keeps it 100."

I have been fortunate to have a wonderfully supportive extended family as well. A special thanks to all of my *tias* and *tios*—most notably Sara, Angel, Ramona, Frank, Gladys, Sammy, Liz, Celestino, Ana, Dorcas, Franklin, Eva, Robert, Julia, Awilda, Millie, Irma, Marina, Maria Inez, Lupe, and John. Thanks to all my cousins, especially Samuel ("Giz"), Laura, Emily, Angel, Judy, Ivette, Celestino, Candice, and Angie. I was fortunate to inherit wonderful in-laws, Gary and Sue Campbell, on whom I can always count on for support, encouragement, and desserts that are worth driving two hours for. To my friend Enrique Figueroa, thanks for introducing me to "the plight of the migrant worker" way back during our HEOP summer in 1992 and reminding me to keep social justice at the forefront of my consciousness ever since.

As I began this line of research, I was fortunate to have the support of the 2006–2008 cohort of the Cultivating New Voices (CNV) Among Scholars of Color Fellowship from the National Council of Teachers of English (NCTE). I am grateful to my colleagues: Benji Chang, Marcelle Haddix, Rochele Dail, Tambra Jackson, Kafi Damali Kamasi, David Kirkland, Django Paris, Detra Price-Dennis, Mary Alexandra Rojas, Mariana Souto-Manning, and Veronica Valdez. I am also indebted to all the CNV mentors, especially Maria Torres Guzmán, for their insights into various phases of this project. It is a great privilege and honor to have been included among such a distinguished group of scholar-activists.

I owe a special debt of gratitude to Sonia Nieto, my graduate advisor, friend, and mentor, whose work and words of encouragement continue to be source of inspiration and motivation. Thanks to my frequent writing partner, John Raible, and fellow writing group member Patty Bode for being "critical friends" and for their willingness to challenge me over the years through their feedback on my ideas and written work. Christine Clark, Rich Milner, and Tara Brown have all been great friends and colleagues.

I would also like to thank my colleagues and friends in the Neag School of Education, the Institute for Puerto Rican and Latino Studies, and the Center for Education Policy Analysis at the University of Connecticut. I am especially grateful to Scott Brown for taking a chance on hiring a post-doc with more ambition than research experience and for providing the support and guidance I needed to develop as a junior scholar. While I was developing this manuscript, I also benefited from interacting with the brilliant and dedicated individuals associated with the National Latino Education Research Agenda Project (NLERAP). The passion for improving the education of Latino youth through research, education, and advocacy displayed by participants in this collaborative often inspired me to write and work through the lulls that arose during the book's development.

There are several individuals who worked tirelessly behind the scenes to provide additional layers of support for the student-researchers in Project FUERTE. Most notably, Aja LaDuke went above and beyond the requirements of her part-time graduate assistantship and made a full-time commitment to the youth. Without her efforts the project and thus the completion of this manuscript would have been compromised severely. Scott Bonito and Kat Fairchild were two of the best interns ever to grace the halls of the Neag School of Education, and Deana Semeaza was vital in helping students navigate the college application process.

Finally, I thank Donaldo Macedo, the editor of the Series in Critical Narrative, for his helpful feedback and willingness to include my manuscript in the series alongside texts from an array of icons in the field, many of whom have shaped my worldview and profoundly influenced my professional trajectory. Thank you, as well, to Jason Barry and the staff at Paradigm Publishers for their comments on early drafts of the manuscript and assistance throughout the publication process. While many have helped to nurture this book along the way, in the end, I alone take full responsibility for any shortcomings in the text.

Jason G. Irizarry

INTRODUCTION

TEACHING AND LEARNING IN SHIFTING
CULTURAL CONTEXTS
PA' QUE LO SEPAS

As a faculty member in teacher education beginning a tenure-track position, I grappled with how I was going to remain connected with urban youth and schools after transitioning into life as an academic in the ivory tower, particularly at a land grant institution located in a rural area of the state. After much deliberation, I decided to teach a course, in addition to my responsibilities at the university, at a high school serving a large percentage of students of color from urban communities. I piloted the course with a group of high school seniors at a magnet school during the 2007–2008 academic year and moved the course to a more traditional comprehensive high school dealing with the urban condition the following year.[1] Here I enlisted a group of eleventh-grade Latino students who committed to participating in the course for two academic years.[2]

I entered my first day at Rana High School (a pseudonym) with my nervousness tempered by optimism resulting from the success of the class the previous year. The students in that group had grappled with difficult topics and developed inspiring action research projects that impressed hundreds of audience members at the numerous conferences and professional meetings where they presented their work. All of the student-researchers had graduated and enrolled in institutions of higher education, a rate of academic success that far exceeded national averages for youth of color. After the customary introductions, I began to share some of the background of the course and several of the accomplishments of the previous cohort with this new group of students. While I was speaking, I saw that I was losing one of the students as she fidgeted in her chair, staring at the floor and occasionally shaking her head disapprovingly.

Perhaps fed up with my unabashed enthusiasm for the course and my praise of the growth that I had witnessed among members of the previous cohort, Taína, a fifteen-year old Puerto Rican girl, looked up from the floor and stared at me. Her large brown eyes reflected a profound sense of sadness. I paused in mid-sentence, waiting for her to speak. The awkward silence, which felt like it lasted an eternity, was finally broken as Taína, filled with hurt, anger, and frustration cultivated over years of educational neglect and marginalization within schools, exclaimed, "Mister, what are you doing this for? We are not smart and that's it!"

"What do you mean?" I responded, unable to conjure up a more profound response to her query about my intentions and her sweeping proclamation about the academic abilities of the class.

"Latinos are not smart; we are just not smart!" she responded.

"She's right, Mister," several of her classmates added, and without exception they all collectively defended her claim and asserted their alleged genetically predisposed lack of intellect.

Our conversation set off a fiery debate, as I challenged them to provide evidence to support their disquieting supposition. "We are in the lowest classes," "We don't talk right," "Teachers tell us we are not smart," and "We are not like the white kids" were common responses in a threaded conversation that would span an innumerable number of classes, reemerging at various points throughout the year. The students' assertions, although shocking and disconcerting, are understandable given the negative assault that has taken place historically against Latinos in U.S. schools and in society at large. Schools have been, and continue to be, used as vehicles for assimilation, often exalting Anglo values and norms and forcing Latinos to shed their cultural identities for a chance at school success (Valenzuela, 1999).

In addition to limiting quality educational opportunities, this assault on Latino youth also has a psychological impact. The students' internalization of the negative messages and shortsighted appraisals of their academic capabilities offered by many of the educators they have encountered throughout their schooling experiences and per-petuated throughout the popular media had resulted in what Frantz Fanon (1967, p. 13), the psychiatrist, revolutionary, and influential scholar in postcolonial studies and critical theory, referred to as the "epidermalization of inferiority," referencing the highly racialized aspects of internalized oppression.[3] According to Fanon:

> Sometimes people hold a core belief that is very strong. When they are presented with evidence that works against that belief, the new evidence cannot be accepted. It would create a feeling that is extremely uncomfortable, called cognitive dissonance. And because it is so important to protect the core belief, they will rationalize, ignore and even deny anything that doesn't fit in with the core belief (p. 119).

The fact that Taína and her classmates were asserting the intellectual inferiority of Latinos to a Latino university professor with a doctorate was inconsequential to them. Their years in public schools had taught them one thing—"Latinos are not smart."

THE "BROWNING" OF U.S. SCHOOLS

Taína is one of approximately 11 million Latino youth enrolled in K–12 schools in the United States. They are a diverse group, with unique identities and distinct histories here in the United States and in their countries of origin. When collectively grouped together, Latino students constitute the largest group of minoritized students in schools and the fastest-growing population in the country.[4] One in every five children currently attending school is Latino. It is estimated that by the year 2050, the Latino school-age population will grow by more than 150 percent and Latino youth will then account for more than half of all public school students (Pew Hispanic Center, 2008). Although Latino population growth is evident across the country, the most rapid increases have been in areas that have not had a long-standing Latino presence, such as communities on the outskirts of Atlanta and Chicago and in the Pacific Northwest (Stamps and Bohon, 2006).

Fueled largely by significant increases in the Latino population, the racial/ethnic and linguistic texture of the United States is changing rapidly. A host of media personalities and politicians, including Lou Dobbs, Glenn Beck, Bill O'Reilly, Newt Gingrich, and Pat Buchanan, among many others, portray the Latinization of the United States as something to fear, demonizing immigrants and attempting to veil their xenophobia in calls to preserve "American values." For some, this fear mongering gains credibility in the work of reactionary scholar and late Harvard history professor Samuel Huntington, who forewarned whites of the fracturing of the United States as a result of what he referred to as "The Hispanic Challenge" (Huntington, 2004). Occurring simultaneously with the browning of the United States and the so-called challenges presented by it is the "graying" of the aging baby boom generation. More than 85 percent of senior citizens in the United States are white, whereas youth of color account for close to half of children under the age of eighteen (Vincent and Velkoff, 2010). The growing population of Latinos in the United States has raised the ire of many older Americans. Contrasting needs, values, and worldviews between older whites and a more youthful Latino population are evident in a surge in legislation over the last decade aimed at curbing the rights of and stifling opportunities for Latinos. Nowhere are the implications of these demographic shifts more evident than in schools. Although Arizona's State Bill 1070, which would allow law enforcement officials to arrest and detain suspected undocumented immigrants without a warrant, has received significant national attention, the proposed elimination of ethnic studies in Arizona and the controversy raised by changing the content related to youth of color in textbooks used in Texas schools, which has far-reaching implications for the texts used in schools across the country, have been less publicized. Also problematic are the racial/ethnic and generational patterns that emerged in recent school budget elections. In 2010, school budgets were defeated in many communities with large percentages of students of color and sizable populations of older whites, including the community where my student coresearchers attended school, where the budget was voted down three times before passing. These voting patterns support the findings from a 2007 study conducted by the Population Reference Bureau, which found that states in which the majority of voters were white and whose public schools served a majority of students of color often spent less on education than states in which the racial/ethnic texture of the voting population was more congruent with that of the students (Cohn, 2007). These trends highlight the power of a large, predominantly older white electorate to shape public policy that will undoubtedly affect the opportunity structure for an increasingly brown school-aged population.

Dramatic population growth among Latinos in the United States has not been accompanied by similar sizable gains in the academic achievement of this group. Data regarding the academic achievement of all Latino students are disheartening. Estimates suggest that approximately half of Latino students fail to complete high school, and too few enroll in and complete college. Statistics for Mexican/Mexican-American and Puerto Rican youth—the two largest groups of Latino students, accounting for almost three-quarters of the Latino population in the United States (64 percent and 9 percent respectively)—are even more disturbing. If current trends continue, 5.5 million of the 11 million Latinos currently enrolled in U.S. schools will not earn a high school diploma and will be effectively cut off from any chance of achieving the American dream. Of the half of Latinos who are able to successfully complete high school, only 2.8 million will attend college, with most of these students attending community colleges, not four-year institutions. Of those that attend college, only 770,000 of the 11 million, or less than 7 percent, will be awarded bachelor's degrees, and fewer than 250,000 will go on to earn master's degrees. As the education pipeline continues to narrow, less than 1 percent will go on to earn a doctorate.[5] These statistics pale in comparison to those for white students, who complete high school and attend and graduate from college at three times the rate of Latinos (U.S. Census, 2007). Because of the aforementioned demographic shifts, the education—or more accurately stated, undereducation—of Latino youth presents significant implications not only for Latinos but also for the U.S. population as a whole.

Such a sea change undoubtedly presents significant challenges for educators, the majority of whom have very little, if any, professional preparation to help them work more effectively with Latino students and families. Given the grim data regarding student achievement for this group, the need for policies and approaches to teaching aimed at improving the education of Latino students is dire. However, many educators (and the institutions of higher education that prepare them) have been slow to respond to what scholars have referred to as the "Latino education crisis" (Gándara and Contreras, 2009). In an attempt to partially fill this void, this book brings the voices of Latino youth into the conversation. *The Latinization of U.S. Schools: Successful Teaching and Learning in Shifting Cultural Contexts* forwards the perspectives of youth who were engaged in a multiyear participatory action research project examining the educational experiences and outcomes for Latino students. The project's goal was to better inform the practice of teachers, administrators, and other school personnel so that it is more culturally responsive to the needs of those students.

Although there is a growing body of research addressing the education of Latino students, most of it is written by scholars who have done research *on* Latinos. This book is unique in that it emerges from research conducted *by* Latino students with their teacher as a coresearcher. Although many Latino youth can communicate in multiple languages, their voices are often rendered silent by policies and practices in schools. Moreover, the perspectives of youth are rarely, if ever, included in discussions of school reform or teacher professional development efforts. Grounded in empirical data collected and analyzed by students, this text aims to be theoretically rigorous yet highly accessible, a practical book that provides concrete recommendations for teachers seeking to improve their practice, particularly in relation to Latino students. It also provides a resource for those invested in the education of teachers—both preservice and inservice—to address the educational achievement of the largest and fastest-growing group of minoritized students in K–12 schools.

YOUTH PARTICIPATORY ACTION RESEARCH: PROJECT FUERTE

I refer to the project from which this book emerges as Project FUERTE (Future Urban Educators conducting Research to transform Teacher Education). *Fuerte,* meaning "strong" in Spanish, is an ongoing, multiyear participatory action research project that engages Latino youth in urban schools in meaningful, co-constructed research while enhancing their academic skills. FUERTE was designed specifically to inform the personal and professional trajectories of Latino high school students by addressing issues related to the sociocultural and sociopolitical realities of their lives.

A primary goal of the project was to familiarize the students with the conventions of Youth Participatory Action Research (YPAR) as a means of exploring the educational experiences of Latino youth and other students who have been historically underserved by schools (Cammarota and Fine, 2008). Although a wealth of research explores urban teacher preparation, very little draws from the experiences of youth themselves or forwards their recommendations. Instead of being positioned as the "problem" within school improvement efforts, participants in Project FUERTE served as researchers of their own experiences within schools, developing and disseminating recommendations to improve the practice of teachers and other school personnel working with Latino students.

This collaborative action research project aims to improve the achievement of students as well as the professional development of teachers. Project FUERTE addresses the significant discrepancies in the academic achievement, experiences, and outcomes of Latinos by fostering the development of the critical thinking, literacy, numeracy, and analytical skills necessary to embark on higher education. Second, by engaging students in the study of urban education and how to improve it, Project FUERTE attempts to address the underrepresentation of teachers of color by attracting youth of color into the profession. Project FUERTE seeks to contribute to the preparation of teachers by generating scholarship that can be utilized in professional development efforts while also diversifying the teaching force by "home-growing" teachers of color for urban schools (see Irizarry, 2007). Finally, this project has the potential to help teachers and researchers better understand the educational needs of Latino youth.

Project FUERTE was embedded in a course titled "Action Research and Social Change" that I developed and offered at a local urban high school. In 2007–2008, the project's pilot phase, the course was offered at Metro High School, an interdistrict magnet school serving a large percentage of Latino students and other students of color from urban communities. From 2008 to 2010, the course was offered at a different, more traditional, comprehensive public high school where Latino youth represented approximately half of the student population. The class was open to any students at Rana High School (RHS) who self-identified as Latino or who articulated an interest in improving the quality of the education offered to Latino students. Twelve RHS students registered for the course, but after meeting with guidance counselors to review their schedules, several students were forced to drop the course in order to take other required courses necessary for graduation. The seven students who remained joined the Project FUERTE team as student-researchers, collaborating with me and two graduate students from the university where I teach.

The course was offered as an elective credit for students who met biweekly for two consecutive academic years, staying with it from eleventh grade through graduation. In addition, while preparing research presentations and working on the chapters included in this text, students regularly met with me and the graduate students on the research team during free periods, after school, and during their school vacations. During one of our presentations at a regional conference on educational research, one of the student-researchers calculated that we had spent more than 200 hours during our first year together working on the research project.

Theoretically, Project FUERTE builds on the pioneering work of Orlando Fals-Borda (1979, 1987), Julio Cammarota and Michelle Fine (2008), and Jeff Duncan-Andrade and Ernest Morrell (2008) and their approaches to YPAR. Consistent with the tenets of youth participatory action research (YPAR), Project FUERTE was organized around three principles:

1. *Youth are experts of their own lives.* In his monumental text, *Pedagogy of the Oppressed,* Paulo Freire (1970/2000) posed the questions: "Who better than the oppressed to understand the terrible significance of an oppressive society? Who can better understand the need for liberation?" Building on the work of Freire, youth participatory action research is grounded in the belief that actions taken to dismantle oppression require the knowledge and skills of those most directly affected by the problem (Fals-Borda, 1979). Project FUERTE assumes that Latino youth, as a group that has been historically marginalized and underserved by schools, have important insights they can bring to bear to address the issue of Latino underachievement in schools. The project rests on the belief that if school reform efforts are to be truly successful, creating quality learning opportunities for all students, then they must include the perspectives, needs, insights, and visions of the youth they aim to serve.

2. *The policies and practices that affect Latino youth are alterable.* A review of U.S. history, from the American Revolution to the civil rights movement and more recent examples (such as the organized student protests of Proposition 187, which threatened to deny public services, including education, to undocumented students, and students' responses to the proposed elimination of ethnic studies programs in Arizona in 2010), demonstrates the ability of groups of committed individuals to challenge and transform oppressive limit situations. These efforts and countless

others also bear witness to the power of youth to challenge oppressive structures and work for a more socially just society. Continuing the legacy of this activist tradition among youth in the Latino community, our work emphasized "that conditions of injustice are produced, not natural. They are designed to privilege and oppress, but are *ultimately challengeable and therefore changeable*" [emphasis added] (Cammarota and Fine, 2008, p. 2).

3. *YPAR is both an ideology and methodology.* YPAR provides not only a research methodology but also a new conceptualization of youth, particularly youth of color. Dominant discourses paint youth in one of two ways—as helpless and in need of constant protection or as rebellious and threatening to the social order (Ginwright, 2008). YPAR challenges these essentialist views of youth, including deficit perspectives, to create a new view of resistance as a process rather than an orientation (Cammarota and Fine, 2008; Duncan-Andrade and Morrell, 2008).

METHODS TO ADDRESS THE MADNESS

Stepping out of the comfortable confines of the ivory tower and into a high school classroom to meet students face to face as co-researchers proved as exhilarating as it was challenging. Although I have experienced firsthand the "savage inequalities" (Kozol, 1992) of urban education, both as a student and later as a teacher in New York City public schools, and have formally studied the education of urban youth of color through graduate coursework and an array of research projects, I was still profoundly disturbed by the low skill level of many of the students and the lack of rigor in their previous educational experiences. With the exception of the two student-authors who were members of the first cohort and attended a magnet high school, none of the student-researchers whose voices permeate this book had ever written a paper longer than two pages prior to this class and none had ever engaged in a process of systematically revising their writing. All the students articulated aspirations to attend college, yet more than half of the group had yet to take Algebra I and other prerequisite courses for college admission. Their writing, though replete with fascinating ideas and untapped potential, was void of many of the conventions of academic writing necessary to reach a wider audience.

Underscoring the importance of critical inquiry as part of a liberating education, one in which students and teachers critically reflect and act upon the world, and critiquing approaches to education that suppress inquiry, Paulo Freire (1970/2000, p. 85) asserted, "Any situation in which some men prevent others from engaging in the process of inquiry is one of violence; ... to alienate humans from their own decision making is to change them into objects." Penned before 1970, his words aptly describe the educational experiences of the Project FUERTE youth researchers more than forty years later. These young people have been victimized by an educational system that treated them as disposable, unworthy of investment, and incapable of original thought and higher-order thinking.[6] Schooling, for most, was a process whereby they were expected to memorize discrete sets of facts that were completely disconnected from the material conditions of their lives.

Beyond gaps in their skill level, there were also profound holes in their knowledge of history and relatively recent social movements, especially those connected to their cultural histories. None of the students in the group had ever even heard of Cesár Chávez or Dolores Huerta, the civil rights pioneers associated with the United Farm Workers of America and other labor struggles; the Young Lords or Brown Berets, groups of Latino youth activists who respectively organized to challenge social injustices in their communities; the Zapatista Army of National Liberation, a revolutionary movement beginning in 1994 aimed at calling attention to and disrupting the inequities that exist between the wealthy and the poor and advocating for the rights of indigenous peoples in Mexico; or Pedro Albizu Campos, the Harvard-educated lawyer, key figure in the Puerto Rican independence movement, and leader of the Puerto Rican Nationalist Party from the 1930s until his death in 1965. As they learned more about themselves, their histories, and the present sociopolitical contexts in which they were being educated, the students' voices grew, and they were anxious to share their newfound knowledge.

We did not begin our journey together with the goal of writing a book. Instead, the aim was to critically examine the educational experiences and outcomes of Latino students, use the research process to improve their academic skills, and employ the research data to create recommendations aimed at transforming the conditions that limit Latinos' access to quality educational opportunities. However, still looming large as we approached the end of the first year was the groups' negative appraisal of the academic ability of Latinos. After reading the work of a plethora of Latino scholars in the field of education, including, but not limited to Sonia Nieto, Angela Valenzuela, Luis Moll, Gloria Anzaldúa, Rosalie Rolón-Dow, Julio Cammarota, Jeff Duncan-Andrade, Louie Rodríguez, Ofelia García, Maria Torres-Guzmán, and René Antrop-González, they had softened their position. Now they believed that "there are smart Latinos out there," but the students held steadfast to the belief that they and other Latinos at their school were not intelligent, continuing to reference teachers' appraisal of their abilities and their placement into the lowest academic tracks in the school. After a practice session for an upcoming presentation of their research, I told the students that I thought they were brilliant and pointed out that they were demonstrating how smart they really were. Without a hesitation, Taína responded: "This is easy." "Really smart people," she argued, "write books and articles and stuff." At that moment, the idea for this book was born. Certainly there are "really smart people" who have not published their thoughts or received validation of their ideas through a process of peer review. And I vehemently reject the notion that the academy's approval is necessary to legitimize one's intellectual acumen. Nevertheless, it seemed like an immediate and tangible way to help the student-researchers reflect upon and, hopefully, disrupt their calcified perceptions of Latino youth as less than intelligent. Writing this book also offered an opportunity to amplify the subaltern, emic perspectives of a group of Latino youth navigating school as the cultural and linguistic landscape of the United States continues to shift, integrating new, often silenced perspectives into the discourse on school reform. On a more personal note, the book project became a way for me to balance life as an assistant professor on a tenure track with my commitment to use this platform to serve urban youth and communities. It represents my attempt at "humanizing research" (Paris, 2010, p. 1), "a methodological stance, which requires that our inquiries involve dialogic consciousness-raising and the building of relationships of dignity and care for both researchers and participants." It is a deliberate effort to challenge the draconian yet dominant mode of research in urban schools, in which ivory tower researchers collect data, publish their findings, and reap all of the resulting individual rewards—including tenure, promotion, speaking engagements, consulting jobs, and merit pay raises—without making any investment in those communities or assuming any responsibility for transforming the oppressive conditions and limiting situations that confront their research participants.

While the debate regarding poet and activist Audre Lorde's powerful metaphor "The master's tools will never dismantle the master's house" (1984) rages on, I thought we could use at least use those tools to subvert the master's grip over the narrative, tell our own story, and present an authentic counternarrative.

Writing an individually authored ten- to fifteen-page chapter for a book, when presented as an idea to the class the next day, was quickly rejected by the students. "You're buggin', Mister!" "No way!" students began to shout. Despite their reluctance to embark on writing a lengthy academic paper for publication, I was convinced that the students' stories needed to be told, not just to confirm their brilliance and raise their self-confidence but because educators, researchers, and policymakers needed to hear and be moved by them. At that point, I decided to try to work collaboratively with the students to record their perspectives on issues related to their schooling experiences by having them write and dictate their stories, through *testimonios*, a qualitative methodology emerging from the field of Latin American studies and gaining traction within Latino/a Critical Race Theory scholarship. Testimonios honor and affirm sources of knowledge that are often overlooked or delegitimized within academic research (Delgado Bernal, 1998) and "seek to disrupt the apartheid of knowledge in academia, moving toward educational research guided by racial and social justice for Communities of Color" (Huber, 2009, p. 640). Testimonios are narratives of life experiences that pay special attention to the injustices one has suffered and the ways in which the narrator has made meaning and responded to them.

There are four central characteristics that guided my use of testimonios as a methodology for data collection in this text, generated primarily from Latino/a Critical Race Theory research (Yúdice, 1991; Latina Feminist Group, 2001; Solórzano and Yosso, 2002; Haig-Brown, 2003; Burciaga and Tavares, 2006; Dyrness, 2008; Huber, 2009).

1. They document life experiences with special attention to instances of injustice.
2. Testimonios are narrated by members of oppressed groups.
3. They are transformative, aiming to dismantle oppressive structures and allow the individual narrator to positively shape his or her future trajectory.
4. Testimonios honor the knowledge produced by the narrator.

In this case, testimonios were used to foreground the perspectives of Latino youth, a group whose experiences in schools and educational needs have been largely overlooked and undervalued; they were narrated by the students themselves; and they aimed to transform practice and policy and to make a unique, valuable contribution to the emerging body of literature on Latino education and youth participatory action research. Contributing to this book was a chance for students to counter racism and other forms of structural oppression, including classism, linguicism, sexism, and nativism, as they are manifested in schools and society at large. The stories documented in the subsequent chapters are born out of their pain and rooted in their collective hope for the future.

Students selected topics they were passionate about, issues that related directly to their experiences in schools and connected to our larger collective action research project. As part of our work together, I worked with the student-researchers to develop collaborative chapters documenting their thoughts and perspectives. Each chapter, with the exception of the last, was coauthored by me and a different member of the research collaborative. Although they are coauthored, the chapters written with students are written from the students' perspectives. To develop the chapters that comprise this text, students engaged in multiple "free writes," responded to prompts I created to initiate their writing, and in many instances dictated their stories to me, and I tried to capture their thoughts in writing. At times students wrote or dictated their stories in English, at other times in Spanish, and often in a mixture of the two. Most often, students wrote the way they speak to friends, producing text using informal language and hybrid language practices, including slang and youth jargon, which might have been incomprehensible to many readers. Using their writing, I met multiple times with each contributor and engaged with them in a process to transform their writing into more traditional academic language to reach the widest audience possible, particularly educators, policymakers, and others committed to improving the education of Latino students. This process honored the forms of expression with which they were most comfortable and helped them cultivate the literacy skills they would need to successfully complete high school and prepare to embark on higher education.

In an effort to build on their stories, help them develop formal academic writing skills, and provide an important theoretical grounding for the topics covered in each chapter, students also conducted reviews of existing literature and included references to relevant studies in the chapters. Again, students were assisted in analyzing texts, synthesizing the research, and representing it in their stories. The chapters, then, represent a collaborative effort, with special attention given to keeping students at the forefront of all aspects of the process. I went through multiple drafts with each contributor to get the chapter ready for publication. I made every effort to honor the students' voices in this process, meeting with them to clarify certain points and working with them to rephrase parts of their work using their words. Certainly, I introduced students to specific bodies of literature and theorists, particularly Latino scholars and other scholars of color aligned with the critical tradition within educational research. The decisions I made regarding what literature to share and what directions to point them in relation to their study; my own history and perspectives as a Latino student, teacher, and researcher; and my active role in writing the text undoubtedly influenced the content, tone, and tenor of the chapters. The topics of study and ideas expressed in their chapters, however, are largely those of the students. Any shortcomings in the writing or preparing of this work for the academic press are mine alone.

OVERVIEW OF THE BOOK

This book critically analyzes what may seem to the uncritical eye like commonplace practices in urban schools, such as tracking or school suspension, and then documents how these structural impediments often serve to limit educational opportunities for Latino students. The chapters developed with the student-researchers provide an overview of the relevant literature on their topic and transition into their own findings, informed by both their personal experiences and more formal research emanating from the YPAR project. Each chapter concludes with three concrete recommendations for teachers and a discussion of the implications of the students' findings for teaching and teacher education. Seven of the chapters document the work and experiences of students from Rana High School who participated in the project between 2008–2010. Two of the chapters were constructed with students who participated in Project FUERTE during the 2007–2008 academic year; both attend the University of Connecticut and have remained connected with the project as undergraduate student coresearchers.

The voices of the student-researchers provide an informative analysis of the policies and practices that influence Latino student achievement and also serve as a powerful counternarrative to the well-entrenched myth of the apathetic, underachieving Latino student that dominates the educational landscape and popular media. Another unique feature of the book is that it includes a chapter written by a non-Latino, a white teacher and graduate student who, as a part of the collaborative, speaks to the potential of YPAR as an opportunity to positively shape the professional preparation and continued development of other non-Latino teachers.

Refranes *as a Repository for "Funds of Knowledge"*

The book is organized into four sections, reflecting key themes that that emerged in the participants' writing, and each section begins with a brief overview that provides useful background information and establishes a foundation for the topics addressed in the subsequent pages. In my efforts to make meaning of the themes that emerged from the data as well as to honor and value what Luis Moll and his colleagues (1992) referred to as the "funds of knowledge" present in Latino communities, I use *refranes,* or Spanish proverbs, to help shed light on and unpack these important aspects of Latino education.

As a young Puerto Rican child in New York City, my grandmother would often offer words of wisdom, typically after I had done something foolish, veiled in a *refran,* which would provide insight into my youthful dilemmas and occasional indiscretions. For example, "Mijo," she would say, "el vago trabaja dos veces" ("the lazy person works twice"), urging me not to cut corners in my schoolwork or household chores. On another occasion, I ignored her multiple warnings about playing baseball in our apartment. During one of my unauthorized practice sessions, I broke the glass coffee table in the living room. Simultaneously scolding me firmly while offering me food for thought, she asserted, "Él que no coge consejo, no llega a viejo" (loosely translated as "He who doesn't heed advice will never make it to old age"). Her words were simple, yet her message was profound. Through these short utterances, I learned life lessons that would guide me into adulthood, lessons that I am committed to passing on to my children.

In the context of this book, the refranes serve several, interrelated functions. First, they affirm the "funds of knowledge" and collective wisdom that exist in Latino communities. Next, the application of refranes in this text also serves a teaching function, connecting readers with a Latino tradition used to pass valuable information from one generation to the next. Finally, using these Spanish-language proverbs, which have a long history of application in Latino communities to illuminate complex concepts, provides a unique, Latinocentric framework for analyzing, understanding, and improving the educational experiences of Latino students in U.S. schools. Although relatively simple phrases, refranes can be insightful and replete with meaning. I hope the refranes used here are informative and help elucidate the complex issues addressed throughout this text, much like the *consejo* (advice) offered through refranes by my grandmother.

Chapter Overviews

Chapter 1 offers an overview of Latino education, ranging from historical perspectives on the schooling of Latinos in U.S. schools to data on the current state of Latino education. It provides a brief statistical portrait of Latino education, underscoring the need for increased attention to the preparation of teachers for working with Latino youth. It explores the challenges and opportunities presented by the Latinization of U.S. schools.

In Chapter 2, a Latina student-author responds to the racist characterizations of Latino students offered by some of the faculty at her high school. This chapter explores deficit perspectives regarding Latino youth and the ways in which these perspectives often dominate student-teacher relationships. It describes how high school students surveyed their teachers and were surprised to uncover the depths of anti-Latino sentiments held by many members of the faculty at their school. In addition, the chapter explicates a usually hidden perspective regarding how deficit perspectives influence teacher expectations and the quality of education they provide Latino students. The chapter concludes by exploring "critical care praxis" (Rolón-Dow, 2005) as a framework for promoting the educational and personal success of Latino students.

Chapter 3 argues that teaching is fundamentally rooted in relationships between teachers and students. It further asserts that teachers' inability to effectively educate Latino students—as demonstrated by dropout statistics, standardized test scores, and other indicators of student achievement—stems, at least in part, from the inability of many teachers to cross lines of cultural and linguistic difference.

Who are Latino students, and what makes someone Latino? These questions are at the heart of Chapter 4, where essentialized notions of identity are challenged and issues related to multiethnic/multiracial Latinos are unpacked. It calls for the affirmation of the identities of multiethnic and multiracial students, a growing yet often neglected group of students in U.S. public schools. This chapter suggests that as teachers seek to connect with Latino students and develop culturally responsive curricula, they must also consider the diversity that exists among those that are typically lumped together as simply "Latino."

Latino youth often come to school speaking a variety of languages and/or language forms, including English and Spanish, as well as Spanglish and African American languages. The use of Language other than Standard English is often frowned upon in schools, where teachers and other school agents may create rigid rules that force students to suppress important aspects of their identities. Chapter 5 draws from data collected as part of a "hallway ethnography" that explored how teachers subordinate student discourses, even in "nonsanctioned zones" such as hallways and the school cafeteria, as well as during free time. The student-author argues that students are alienated from school as a result of not having space to express themselves freely using the variety of linguistic and cultural codes at their disposal, resulting in higher dropout/push out rates among Latinos. The chapter concludes with specific recommendations for teachers and teacher-educators for increasing student engagement by supporting diverse language practices.

The research literature suggests that teachers frequently hold low expectations for Latino students. Their expectations for undocumented students are often even lower, in part because—particularly in states that do not have legislation such as the DREAM Act—access to college for so-called illegal students is even more difficult to attain. Chapter 6 draws from research regarding teachers' views of undocumented students and speaks back to negative portrayals of the undocumented that result in depressed expectations for this group. Student voices included throughout this chapter also call for teachers and others to support the DREAM Act and extend opportunities for higher education to undocumented students. The chapter concludes with recommendations for teachers seeking to support Latino students who may be undocumented.

Despite a plethora of research studies in the areas of language and literacy extolling the benefits of bilingualism, many teachers continue to believe that students for whom English is a second (or third or fourth, etc.) language are impeded from learning as a result of their native language. Consequently, as evidenced by the elimination of bilingual education programs in various states, there is a growing antibilingual, English-only sentiment in society that has been manifested in schools. For example, a recent Arizona policy has mandated that teachers with recognizable accents are not permitted to teach English courses (Jordan, 2010). In this chapter, a bilingual Latina student critiques rigid language policies in schools aimed at preventing the use of languages other than English. She implores teachers to create a climate that is conducive to students' growth as speakers of more than one language. She challenges the assumption that students from homes where languages other than English are the primary mode of communication are "at risk" or "deficient." Rather, the chapter challenges the prevalent deficit notions held by many teachers regarding language learning and replaces them with counternarratives emerging from Latino students themselves.

Chapter 8 tackles academic tracking as a practice for organizing education at the secondary level and pays special attention to the impact of tracking on Latinos. Although the general effects of tracking on educational opportunity have been well documented, less is known about the personal impact of tracking on individual students and on Latino students more specifically. This chapter draws from data collected by Latino students to critically examine the impact of tracking on student identities and offers suggestions for teachers and administrators for de-tracking education and promoting success among all students.

Research has shown that new teachers consistently identify classroom management as an area of weakness in their preparation. Particularly in urban schools serving poor students and students of color, teachers' management practices are often overly restrictive, disproportionately targeting African American and Latino males (Black, 2009; Drakeford, 2004). Chapter 9 draws from research and the student-author's personal experience to examine teachers' classroom management strategies and school discipline policies, with special attention given to how they often serve to alienate and further marginalize Latino students. The chapter includes a student's perspective of what recent scholarship has referred to as the school-to-prison pipeline and how the surveillance of Latino males in schools has fueled a significant rise in incarceration rates among this population. Chapter 9 concludes with recommendations aimed at reforming school discipline policies and practices.

Chapter 10 shares insights from an academically successful student who felt alienated throughout much of his schooling experience as a result of being singled out by teachers as "the one Latino who can make it." Throughout his interactions with teachers, the student-author was constantly told he was the exception because "Latino families don't typically value education." Reflecting on the incongruence between his teachers' perceptions and his experiences in the community, the student-author conducted interviews with community members to learn more about the aspirations Latino parents have for their children. His findings challenge widely held assumptions about Latino students and families. The second half of the chapter speaks to the personal transformation of the author as a result of engaging in participatory action research.

More than three-quarters of all teachers are white females; therefore, any efforts aimed at transforming teaching and teacher education must address the needs and experiences of this influential group. Chapter 11 is written by a white teacher and current doctoral student pursuing a career in teacher education who participated in the research collaborative. It describes the author's growth and development as a result of learning with and from Latino youth. The author documents how she negotiated power and positionality in this Latinocentric project and explores the construct of whiteness in the context of Latinization.

The book concludes with an epilogue reviewing the key findings shared in the previous chapters. The epilogue addresses the impact that this collective journey has had on the participants, with a special emphasis on the impact on the students' academic achievement and critical consciousness. It concludes with a discussion of how the YPAR approach might contribute to efforts to promote equity and excellence in education.

PA' QUE LO SEPAS

Finally, this book represents a collective journey. Several of the stories documenting the schooling experiences of Latino youth in the pages that follow might be shocking for some readers, challenging their understanding of what happens in schools and offering additional explanations for student underachievement. For other readers, particularly those who have endured the conditions described in this text or individuals who have worked closely with Latino students and families, these stories will confirm what they already know—many Latino students are being grossly underserved by schools. The impact of this structural violence—a subtle form of violence in which a given social structure or social institution harms people slowly by preventing them from meeting their basic needs (Galtung, 1969)—is evident in Taína's declaration of internalized oppression that opened the chapter and in the grim data regarding Latino student underachievement presented here.

Although they have been victimized, Latino youth and their communities are not victims. Despite facing omnipresent structural inequalities in schools and society at large, Latinos have continued to assert agency while maintaining their identities. Even though schools have done much to assimilate Latinos, particularly at the expense of preserving their ethnic, linguistic, and cultural identities, many Latinos continue to declare their presence in U.S. schools and call attention to their needs. This sense of pride in being Latino is evidenced by a call-and-response assertion that I heard often as a child, especially at events celebrating ethnic pride, like the Puerto Rican Day Parade in New York City. One group or individual would shout, "Yo soy Boricua" ("I am Puerto Rican"), and another would respond, "Pa' que tu lo sepas!" ("So that you know"), thus affirming one's presence and pride in one's identity. This text, too, is an affirmation. It affirms students' appraisal of and insights into their educational experiences. It affirms distinctly Latino perspectives on the education of Latino students. It affirms the knowledge, "community cultural wealth" (Yosso, 2006), and wisdom present in Latino communities and the potential to use these perspectives to inform school reform efforts. Lastly, it affirms that Taína and the Latino students whose voices permeate this book are indeed intelligent and that they have much they can teach us about teaching and learning in shifting cultural contexts.

PART I

CON UN DEDO NO SE TAPA EL SOL
AN OVERVIEW OF LATINO EDUCATION

꘡

The issues confronting schools serving an increasing number of Latino students are vast and complex. At times, the task of educating
students of any racial/ethnic or linguistic background in an era of
high-stakes testing and rigid accountability measures may seem daunt-
ing and overwhelming, even for the most seasoned, optimistic, and
ambitious educators. In their haste to respond to the persistent gaps
in achievement between students of color and white students, fostered
by an unequal opportunity structure, many schools have turned to
the latest "canned curricula" to create a script that, if adhered to,
"is guaranteed to increase" test scores, often at the expense of co-
constructing a quality, well-rounded education for students.

Often overlooked in these efforts to improve Latino student
achievement are larger forces at play that also affect the quality of
education students receive, including but not limited to racism, linguicism, nativism, and xenophobia, among others forms of oppression. In these difficult times, many teachers, students, and families
are struggling to fight back against what Ira Shor (1992) refers to
as the "conservative restoration," right-wing efforts to dismantle
the gains of the civil rights movement. Specifically targeted in these
"culture wars" are many of the progressive innovations in education,

including ethnic and women's studies, affirmative action, and multi-cultural and bilingual education.

The conditions under which students are educated are rarely addressed as part of the curriculum. In these difficult times, transformative educational practices are sorely needed but too often go overlooked. The marginalization and undereducation of Latinos and other students of color cannot be remedied by following the newest fad in pedagogical practices, making changes in policy without the resources to support their implementation, or focusing more on assessment. The chapters contained in this section explore the contexts influencing Latino education. They remind us that continuing to construct educational experiences that fail to address the sociocultural and sociopolitical realities of youth and their communities is a futile endeavor, like trying to cover the sun with your finger.

I

THE LATINIZATION OF U.S. SCHOOLS
CHALLENGES AND OPPORTUNITIES
with Susana Ulloa, Graduate Student

⤴

The increased Latino presence in the United States over the past twenty years is undeniable, and the influence Latinos have had on shaping the cultural tapestry of the country is profound. Latinos have been at the epicenter of elections for political office, targeted as a swing vote and credited with playing a key role in the elections of former president George Bush (Suro, Fry, and Passel, 2005) and the current president, Barack Obama (Lopez, 2008). The increased numbers of Latino voters have enticed many politicians to begin to speak to the needs of this burgeoning, diverse community. Population gains among Latinos have not been lost on those within corporate America, who have shifted marketing strategies to attract their piece of the approximately 1 trillion dollars in Latino yearly spending power (Bowker, 2009). The winds of change are blowing and will continue to blow across *Los Estados Unidos de América*.

The more than 47 million Latinos in the United States currently account for approximately 14 percent of the population, making Latinos the largest "minority" group in the United States. Because of the youthful average age of Latinos, as well as increases in immigration to the United States from Latin America and the Caribbean, the

Latino population is expected to soar to approximately 133 million by the year 2050 (U.S. Census Bureau, 2008a). Fueled largely by population growth among Latinos, in less than four decades people of color will outnumber whites in the United States. Although often referred to as "minorities," Latinos are an emerging majority, already surpassing the white population in many communities and constituting the majority of students in school districts across the country, from Los Angeles, California, to Hartford, Connecticut, to Miami, Florida.

Although often lumped together, Latinos are not a monolithic group. The majority of Latinos in the United States are of Mexican descent (62 percent), followed by Puerto Ricans (9 percent), Central and South Americans (9 percent and 7 percent, respectively), Cubans (5 percent), and those of other Latino backgrounds (8 percent) (U.S. Census Bureau, 2008a). The experiences of groups included under the umbrella term *Latino* are varied, reflecting different histories, (im)migration patterns, and experiences in the United States.[1] Although viewed largely as an "immigrant population" or "new arrivals," Latinos have a history in the United States that dates back centuries (MacDonald, 2004; Montero-Siebuth and Melendez, 2007). More recent growth in the Latino population has not been confined to states in the Southwest or Northeast, where Latinos have had a long-standing presence. The fastest-growing Latino populations are in the Northwest, South, and Midwest, in states like Tennessee, Utah, Minnesota, Washington, and Georgia (Center for Immigration Studies, 2003; Pew Research Center, 2005), where nascent Latino communities present new challenges for educators suddenly immersed in the "new Latino diaspora" (Wortham, Murillo, and Hamann, 2002). This chapter examines the Latinization of U.S. schools as well as the challenges and opportunities for educators presented by the changes to the racial/ethnic and linguistic texture of the United States.

MAPPING LATINIZATION

Although the surge in the Latino population and greater visibility of Latinos and Latino culture may be novel or even unfamiliar to some, Latinization is not a new phenomenon. The process of Latino self-definition and self-representation in the context of what is now commonly referred to as the United States can be traced back hundreds of years to the establishment of the first Latino communities in this country (Lao-Montes, 2001). Although the recent numeric increases among Latinos have resulted in increased attention—both positive and negative—given to the rapidly growing Latino population, we would be remiss to mark the inception of Latinization with the "Latin Explosion" (Cepeda, 2001; Farley, 1999) in music in the 1990s, when artists like Ricky Martin, Shakira, Jennifer Lopez, and Marc Anthony enjoyed mainstream success, selling millions of records and concert tickets to Latinos and non-Latinos alike, or with the monumental 2000 census, which provided empirical evidence for the oxymoronic title given to Latinos: "majority-minority." Rather, Latinization in the United States has been an ongoing process in which Latinos have attempted to assert and preserve their cultural identities in the face of constant pressures to assimilate, shed their cultural identities, and adopt Anglo cultural norms. Certainly, cultural identities don't develop in a vacuum. As Latinos have asserted their cultural identities, they have left an indelible mark on the cultural landscape of the United States and simultaneously been shaped by "outside" forces that influence the production of *latinidad,* or ways of being Latino.

Current manifestations of Latinization find their historical antecedents in the cultural collisions between Anglo and Latino culture dating as far back as the mid-nineteenth century. Much of the southwestern United States was once northern Mexico, annexed by the United States in 1848 after the Treaty of Guadalupe Hidalgo ended the Mexican-American War (Zinn, 1999). When more than half of Mexico was seized and incorporated into the United States, those Mexicans that remained did not immediately shed their cultural identities and blend into the melting pot that welcomed and absorbed many western European immigrants. In fact, Latinos in the Southwest, a region that many continue to refer to as "occupied America" or Aztlán, the cultural home of the indigenous Nahua peoples (Acuña, 2004), sought to preserve their language and culture by championing provisions in state constitutions and through other legal means that would acknowledge the cultural and linguistic sovereignty of Latinos in the newly colonized territory (Cockcroft, 1995; MacDonald, 2004, MacDonald and Monkman, 2005).

Sizable Latino communities were established on the East Coast in the early and mid-nineteenth century, in places like Ybor City, Florida, and New York City, as exiled Cubans and Puerto Ricans launched struggles for independence from Spanish colonial rule from the mainland United States (MacDonald, 2001; Lao-Montes, 2008).

Simply put, the Latinization of the United States began prior to the mass influx of western Europeans entering the country through Ellis Island and the ports of New York, referred to as the "Great Migration," and still continues today. Sole consideration of Latinos as "foreigners" and "newcomers" and the process of Latinization as a recent or short-lived phenomenon would be shortsighted and historically inaccurate.

Evidence of Latinization abounds; you can hear it, see it, and taste it. The sounds of Latinization are audible in the public sphere, where Spanish is spoken by more than 12 percent of the population of the United States; extolled through reggaeton, salsa, cumbia, Tejano, hip-hop, mariachi, and merengue rhythms emanating from radio stations and across television programs catering to Latino viewers; and in the popular press through periodicals and media outlets such as *People en Español* and *CNN en Español,* as well as Spanish-language newspapers such as *El Diario La Prensa, Nueva Opinión,* and *La Voz.*[2] The United States is the second-largest Spanish-speaking country in the world, with more than 42 million people reported to speak the language fluently (U.S. Census Bureau, 2008b). This number does not include the approximately 4 million Puerto Ricans who live on the island of Puerto Rico, a colonial possession, whose native-born residents are citizens of the United States. The population of *Hispanohablantes* in the United States is larger than the Spanish-speaking populations of Spain (41.5 million), Colombia, (40.7 million), and Argentina (38.8 million) and is second only to Mexico, which has more than 101 million residents who speak Spanish. The cultural milieu created by the interactions between Latinos and members of other cultural groups forces us to reconceptualize the cultural identity of the United States as a nation.

Latinization has clearly become more visible, particularly as "brown" folks become the largest identifiable minority. Again, the Latino presence has infiltrated the "mainstream" with popular television shows like *Ugly Betty,* which was originally a Spanish-language *telenovela* broadcast throughout Latin America as *Betty La Fea,* as well as *Dora the Explorer* and *Diego,* cartoons appealing to both Latino and non-Latino children. The process of Latinization is evident in marketing campaigns and the commodification of Latino culture. It is palpable in the proliferation of Latino restaurants and expansions of fast food chains offering Latin-inspired cuisine like Pollo Tropical and Taco Bell.

Latinization, however, is about more than music, television shows, marketing plans, and food; it is about Latinos constructing and enacting identities of *latinidad,* asserting agency, and announcing their presence to the world. Latinization and discourses of *latinidad* occur in a broader sociopolitical context that can be characterized by a climate of antipathy and suspicion toward Latinos, especially Latino immigrants. Recent publications have taken an alarmist tone, citing Latinos' retention of aspects of their cultural identities as detrimental to the future of the country:

> The persistent inflow of Hispanic immigrants threatens to divide the United States into two peoples, two cultures, and two languages. Unlike past immigrant groups, Mexicans and other Latinos have not assimilated into mainstream U.S. culture, forming instead their own political and linguistic enclaves—from Los Angeles to Miami—and rejecting the Anglo-Protestant values that built the American dream. The United States ignores this challenge at its peril. (Huntington, 2004, p. 30)

Comments like these are reflective of an anti-immigrant and, more specifically, anti-Latino immigrant climate. Hate crimes against Latinos increased by 40 percent between 2003 and 2007, augmented in large part by a rise in violence against immigrants (U.S. Department of Justice, FBI, 2008). Physical violence against Latinos has been rampant in states along the border between Mexico and the United States, as armed civilian militia groups target alleged so-called illegals. In the summer of 2009, the former executive director of the Minuteman American Defense, an anti-immigration vigilante group that purports to defend the U.S. border, and two of the group's members were charged with the murder of an Arizona man and his nine-year-old daughter and the attempted murder of the man's wife (Oppmann, 2009). Many other alleged border crossers have been killed by vigilante violence. The anti-Latino backlash can be felt in other regions of the country as well. One case receiving considerable attention occurred recently in Shenandoah, Pennsylvania, where two white men beat Luis Ramirez, a twenty-five-year old Mexican immigrant and father of two children, to death while shouting racial epithets. The two assailants were convicted of simple assault but cleared of the more serious charges. After a federal investigation, three police officers involved with the case have been indicted for their alleged role in a cover-up, which more than likely influenced the outcome of the case (Pitts, 2009). The potential police cover-up suggests that in communities like Shenandoah, Latinos don't have meaningful access to a system to redress their maltreatment.

Racist, anti-immigrant, and anti-Latino sentiment shapes the larger sociopolitical contexts in which Latino youth are educated. Schools, as sites where Latino identities are enacted, contested, and renegotiated, have not been exempt from nativist tendencies or a propensity for assimilationist approaches to the education of Latino students. As such, the tensions emerging between Americanization and Latinization agendas in schools require a closer examination.

THE LATINIZATION OF U.S. SCHOOLS

Because many communities are segregated by race/ethnicity as well as socioeconomic status, schools are often the first places where Latino youth encounter discrimination based on race, language, and/ or class. Most immigrant groups have experienced discrimination at some point in their history. However, Latinization in the context of the United States has been especially contentious because of Latinos' desire to hold on to important aspects of their cultural identities. For this reason, Latinos have been described as "unassimilable" (Glazer and Moynihan, 1963), opting for a model of integration based on cultural pluralism, where individuals can retain and have their identities affirmed, as opposed to one based on assimilation and Anglo conformity, where individuals shed their cultural identities in favor of adopting the cultural norms of the dominant group.

Latino struggles to preserve their cultural identities and receive equitable educational opportunities have been met with resistance throughout history. Take, for example, initiatives in the Southwest to exclude Latino children from schools serving white students, as evidenced in *Alvarez v. Lemon Grove School District* (1931), *Mendez v. Westminster* (1945), and other court cases. In both cases just mentioned, Latino families were victorious, securing access to schools for their children. Although these legal victories established a foundation and legal precedents for the Supreme Court's decision to declare *de jure,* or legal, segregation unconstitutional in 1954, Latinos were not officially recognized as covered under the *Brown v. Board of Education of Topeka, Kansas,* decision until 1973 (Cockcroft, 1995) and today remain one of the most segregated groups in U.S. schools.

More recent efforts to curb the tide of Latinization can be seen in the attack against bilingual education and the elimination of bilingual programs in California, Arizona, and Massachusetts, states that educate more than 10 million English learners (ELs), the overwhelming majority of whom are Latino Spanish speakers. Instead of treating Latino students for whom English is a second language as "emergent bilinguals" with the potential to communicate in multiple languages, as posited in the work of Ofelia García and her colleagues (García, Kleifgen, and Falchi, 2008), schools in these states and most others across the country have as their primary goal getting students to become fluent in English with little, if any, attention given to nurturing the development of the students' first language. Teaching content and academic skills in the students' primary language while they acquire English is a seen by many critics as "anti-American" (English First, 2009). Notably, the one-year sheltered immersion models that replaced bilingual education programs in California, Arizona, and Massachusetts are not based on widely accepted data on language acquisition, which unequivocally state that it takes, on average, five to seven years to gain academic proficiency in another language (Brisk, 2006; Crawford, 2000; Cummins, 1999; Garcia, 2005).

The elimination of bilingual education has been devastating for ELs (Gutiérrez et al., 2002). A case in point is Boston, Massachusetts, where a comprehensive evaluation of the impact of the policy change documented negative results. English learners in Boston Public Schools (BPS) had one of the lowest dropout rates in the city prior to 2002, the year the ballot initiative eliminating bilingual education was passed. More recent data regarding the achievement of ELs in BPS indicates that seven years later, they now have the highest dropout rate in the city (Tung et al., 2009).

Research has documented the success of bilingual education in simultaneously teaching students curriculum content in their native language while helping them acquire academic English (Freeman, 1998; Perez and Torres-Guzmán, 1996; Valdés, 2001). However, because of the controversies surrounding bilingual education, stemming, we argue, from efforts to curb Latinization, bilingual programs across many of the other forty-seven states have been truncated. In many schools, as described later in Chapter 7, teachers and administrators have implemented unofficial English-only policies that prevent students, even students who are biliterate and fluent in English, from communicating in Spanish. Some teachers may even think they have the best interests of the student in mind, contending that they are preparing "them for the real world and the real world operates in English," as one teacher shared at a professional development presentation we delivered with the students. The population of Spanish speakers in the United States, numbering more than 40 million, might argue otherwise. The real world is multilingual, although English undoubtedly remains a dominant mode of communication in the United States.

Beyond the curbing of multilingualism, one-way, assimilationist frameworks for educating Latino students are evident as well in recent attempts to eliminate ethnic studies programs at public institutions in Arizona. Under the guise of national unification—purporting to bring the country together through the use of only one language in schools and government institutions and targeting the ethnic studies program in the Tucson Unified School District—Tom Horne, superintendent of Arizona's public schools, has championed legislation that proposed to withhold 10 percent of the state funds allocated to the district each month from state high schools offering courses in ethnic studies. According to the proposal, funding would be restored once the course offerings were abolished. Ethnic studies have been described as "harmful and dysfunctional" by Horne, who also noted, "The job of the public schools is to develop the student's identity as Americans and as strong individuals. It is not the job of the schools to promote ethnic chauvinism" (Kossan, 2009). Interestingly, research regarding the effectiveness of the ethnic studies program has documented higher graduation, achievement, and college attendance rates among students in the program as compared to students with similar demographic characteristics not enrolled in ethnic studies courses (Cammarota and Romero, 2006). This example, specific to Arizona, finds resonance in school districts across the country. Schools serving Latino students, with some exceptions, have put the goal of assimilation ahead of education. To reiterate, although Latinos are a diverse group with varied experiences and goals, generally speaking, getting a good education and retaining one's cultural identity have been inextricably linked goals for Latinos (Nieto, 2000; Valenzuela, 1999).

The Latinization of the country and the growing Latino presence in U.S. schools present new challenges for a teaching force that is overwhelmingly white and monolingual. As we begin the second decade of the twenty-first century, we have a unique opportunity to educate the largest culturally and linguistically diverse school-age population this country has ever seen. The fact that approximately half of Latino students are not experiencing school success and graduating with the twenty-first-century skills necessary to survive and thrive in a knowledge-based economy suggests that current approaches are largely insufficient. A change in strategy is desperately needed.

THE CHALLENGES AND OPPORTUNITIES PRESENTED BY LATINIZATION

Multicultural education—an approach to teaching and learning that focuses on students' cultural and linguistic frames of reference, promotes social justice and equity, and affirms the cultural diversity of students and teachers—emerged as a byproduct of the civil rights movement and in response to the undereducation and marginalization of students of color and other groups who have been traditionally underserved by schools (Banks and Banks, 1989; Grant and Sleeter, 1994; Nieto and Bode, 2008). One can argue that the conditions for marginalized communities in school are as dire, or perhaps even more so, than at the inception of the multicultural education movement in the 1960s and 1970s. Although the research base for multicultural education is extensive, far too many teachers enter the field without the skills they need to implement a multicultural approach to teaching (Minaya-Rowe, 2002; Villegas and Lucas, 2002). Teacher education coursework and district-based professional development efforts typically fail to adequately prepare teachers to teach ethnically and linguistically diverse learners (Gort, Glenn, and Settlage, 2007; Milner, 2010; Villegas and Lucas, 2002). For example, a survey of more than 5,000 teachers found that less than one in every four teachers had any training to work with English learners and fewer than one in three had any professional development focused on learning to teach students from diverse cultural backgrounds (Parsad, Lewis, and Farris, 2001). Professional development focused on teaching students of diverse backgrounds has been lacking in most districts. Approximately 90 percent of teachers working with culturally and linguistically diverse students have fewer than eight hours of professional development in this area (U.S. Department of Education, NCES, 2006).

Because many teacher education programs prepare teachers "from a monocultural perspective that eschews the pervasive impact of race, class, linguistic background, culture, gender, and ability and emphasizes instead a universal knowledge base for teaching" (Cochran-Smith, Davis, and Fries, 2004, p. 933), many teachers are immersed in cultural contexts without being sufficiently prepared to respond appropriately. Enhanced professional preparation and continued support for educators are needed to help teachers work more effectively with Latino youth.

Many teachers work under difficult circumstances and are forced to operate in highly politicized contexts that can stifle creativity and innovation in a time when such approaches are desperately needed, presenting another significant challenge for educators. In earnest efforts to increase achievement, school and district administrators often mandate that teachers implement scripted curricula, which aim to improve student outcomes on standardized tests but rarely include content or approaches that students would find culturally relevant (Lipman, 2004; Valli and Buese, 2007). In response, students often disengage from school.

Both well-intentioned teachers and Latino students are caught in a vicious cycle of cultural collisions that often serve to reify each other's stereotypical perceptions. For instance, many Latino students internalize their invisibility in and omission from the curriculum, their position in low academic tracks that don't prepare them to pursue higher education, and policies regarding speaking languages other than English in school and conclude that the perceptions of culturally insensitive teachers and administrators are a reflection of who they really are. In keeping with the self-fulfilling prophecy (Merton, 1948), in which individuals perform to the level of expectation, and as a deliberate effort to resist the ways that they are positioned in schools, many of these students, understandably, don't put forth the effort that is necessary to overcome these barriers and succeed. Teachers, administrators, and other school agents can then point to students' lack of effort or resistant behaviors, such as not completing assignments or disrupting class, as evidence to support the belief, consistently identified by the student-researchers contributing to this book, that Latino youth are apathetic about education.

Conversely, when teachers tacitly operate within the confines of a system that is oppressive to students rather than working with students and families to change it, students can and often do conclude that teachers are not invested in their well-being. But that may not be the case either. Teachers, especially novice teachers, often feel powerless in decisions regarding what to teach and how to teach it (Irwin,

1996). Improving Latino education requires teachers to view teaching as Paulo Freire (1970/2000) envisioned, as an inherently political and potentially liberatory act. By working with students to challenge and transform the sociopolitical contexts in which they are educated, teachers will also liberate themselves from the shackles of oppressive policies and approaches that lead to the de-intellectualization of the profession and undereducation of Latino students.

The final challenge we explore in this chapter addresses the shift in thinking necessary for many educators to become more effective teachers within the context of Latinization. The majority of educators come from families who have, over the course of several generations, assimilated and gained entry into mainstream American culture. The effectiveness of the melting pot model for many ethnic groups, particularly those of white, western European descent, can lead some teachers to believe that it is the only or most effective way to deal with diversity. As noted earlier, at the core of Latinization are expressions of *latinidad*. Assimilationist paradigms that require students to discard or suppress elements of their cultural identities for an opportunity to achieve academic success, therefore, are largely inappropriate and ineffective when working with Latino youth. Before working with Latinos or other students from culturally and linguistically diverse backgrounds, educators need to recognize and reflect upon their own assumptions regarding cultural difference and the role of education in shaping the cultural landscape of the United States.

Latinization also presents a host of opportunities for schools and the country at large. Under the current system, workers in the United States support elderly and disabled citizens by contributing tax revenue that funds Social Security and other entitlement programs. The future of the country, in a very real sense, depends on creating a workforce that will contribute significantly to the sustenance of the system. Employment prospects for many Latinos underserved by schools are bleak, because quality job opportunities for undereducated individuals in a knowledge-based economy are becoming increasingly scarce. The education of Latinos thus cannot be disconnected from the well-being of all Americans.

The "browning of America" has not been accompanied by similar shifts in the demographics of the teaching force or among policymakers. Approximately 85 percent of teachers in U.S. schools are white European Americans—mostly monolingual, middle-class women. The growing diversity of the U.S. population offers the opportunity to fill segments of society where Latinos have not traditionally been well represented with diverse and potentially multilingual individuals. Even though Latinos account for 22 percent of student enrollment in public schools, only 6 percent of teachers in public schools identify themselves as Latino (U.S. Department of Education, NCES, 2006). Approximately one-quarter of all teachers are within ten years of retirement age (Podgursky and Ehlert, 2007), and more than one-third of teachers of color have been in the profession for more than twenty years (U.S. Department of Education, NCES, 2006). Improving the educational outcomes of the emerging Latino minority can lead to a more diverse teaching force in the future, replacing retiring baby boomers with Latino teachers who are multilingual and familiar with the sociocultural realities of Latino communities (see also Quiocho and Rios, 2000; Sheets, 2004).

Certainly there are non-Latino teachers who have been able to work effectively with Latino youth. Many of these teachers have actively sought opportunities to connect with this community and have worked diligently to develop the knowledge, skills, and dispositions necessary to be a quality teacher of Latino students (Raible and Irizarry, 2007; Irizarry and Raible, forthcoming). Nevertheless, increasing the representation of Latino teachers is an important goal for a plethora of reasons. Most notably, research suggests that Latino teachers are more likely to understand and affirm Latino students' languages and cultures, which has been shown to be important in fostering school success (Villegas and Lucas, 2002; Garcia-Nevarez, Stafford, and Arias, 2005; Achinstein and Aguirre, 2008). Diversifying the teaching force also provides opportunities for non-Latino teachers to learn from their Latino colleagues.

In this time of radical demographic shifts, schools are confronted with the responsibility of preparing millions of culturally and linguistically diverse students for an ever-changing world in a context that is not always conducive to quality teaching and learning—a herculean task, to be sure. Methods with empirically based evidence to support their effectiveness, such as bilingual education, are abandoned in favor of approaches that conflate learning English with learning *in* English. Latino students are being pushed out of school in droves, compromising their futures as well as that of the entire country. Generally speaking, approaches to educating Latino students have sought to curtail the rise of Latinization and use education as a vehicle for socializing Latino students into narrowly conceived notions of "American." Embracing Latino students requires embracing Latinization, which represents a departure from previous models of integrating immigrants and addressing issues of diversity within the United States. Schools cannot do it all, but they can certainly do more to improve the education of Latino youth. Our collective futures depend on it.

LIVING AND LEARNING IN THE BORDERLANDS

Geographic borders serve to define and distinguish spaces from one another. The borders separating the United States of America from its neighbors to the south (and north) are well defined on maps and in the consciousness. Yet, as the result of colonization and conquest undertaken under the banner of Manifest Destiny, the borders between the United States and Mexico, the ancestral homeland for more than half of all Latinos in the United States, and between the U.S. mainland and the island of Puerto Rico, *la tierra maternal* for the second-largest group of U.S. Latinos, are conceptually and culturally more porous, allowing for a flow of people, ideas, and culture in both directions—from Latin America to the United States and vice versa. Having connections to the United States and Latino countries of origin (defined both physically and culturally, for example, through travel back and forth or through more abstract cultural connections) can result in living life on a metaphorical psychological and social border, in the space between multiple worldviews, social worlds, and positionalities.

Chicana feminist theorist Gloria Anzaldúa, who grew up in Texas on the border between Mexico and the United States, describes this dual consciousness as follows:

> The psychological borderlands, the sexual borderlands, and spiritual borderlands are not particular to the Southwest. In fact the Borderlands are physically present wherever two or more cultures edge each other, where people of different races occupy the same territory, where under, lower, middle and upper classes touch, where the space between two individuals shrinks with intimacy (Anzaldúa, 1999, p. 20).

Anzaldúa's expanded notion of borders, both literal and figurative, is a helpful heuristic for understanding the experiences and social consciousness of many U.S. Latinos living in these amalgamated and amorphous spaces. As a U.S.-born Latino and a Latina immigrant, we are intimately familiar with the psychological space described so eloquently by Anzaldúa. Navigating life as a Latina/o in the United States requires one to become familiar with the Anglo side of the proverbial border, and we cross in and out of this territory daily as we negotiate life and work. For those whose cultures are reflected and affirmed in the mainstream, there is little pressure to cross cultural and linguistic boundaries and learn how to navigate new, potentially unfamiliar terrain. Conversely, for Latinos and other people of color, our success, survival, and emotional well-being are predicated on skillfully navigating between what often feel like dichotomous social worlds and negotiating the in-between spaces in which our lives unfold.

Schools, based on the definition forwarded by Anzaldúa (1999), can be considered borderlands, where two (and often more) cultures embodied by people from different histories, social positions, and levels of privilege come together. As spaces that are often *in* Latino communities but not *of* Latino communities, schools sometimes establish their own rigid borders, "othering" or alienating those who seek to have the institutions mandated to serve them reflect their identities and appropriately address their educational needs. Because of the pervasiveness of residential and educational segregation, schools become one of the first places, and sometimes the only place, teachers get to meaningfully interact with Latino youth and families. The interactions among individuals of different cultural backgrounds do not have to be jarring, intimidating, or something to be feared, although encountering new forms of diversity and inhabiting or co-inhabiting unfamiliar spaces can be uncomfortable at times. However, the educational success of Latinos is predicated on teachers meeting students "where they are." It is our earnest hope that educators seize the opportunity to join their students in the borderlands created by the Latinization of U.S. schools.

PART 2

OJOS QUE NO VEN, CORAZON QUE NO SIENTE
LATINO STUDENT IDENTITIES

⤝

In contrast to the colorblind approach to ignoring difference, the student-contributors to this section call upon teachers to center their cultures in the teaching and learning process. However, the students in the project describe their cultural identities in more complex ways than traditionally conceived by teachers and researchers. For instance, Cassandra, who identifies herself as a multiracial Latina, passionately writes, "I am Latina and white. There doesn't seem to be a box for that. I am both and at times I don't feel like either." Caridad, who describes herself as Afro-Latina to reflect her African and Latin roots, doesn't understand or speak Spanish but rather prefers to communicate in class and with friends using African American Language (AAL). She cites the use of AAL by teachers as culturally responsive pedagogy.

Several students in the project have immigrated or migrated from Puerto Rico or Mexico, while others identify as Mexican or Puerto Rican but have never even visited their ancestral homelands. Some are bilingual, speaking English and Spanish, but others are monolingual English speakers. A wide range of diversity exists among those individuals described collectively as Latinos. The voices of the student-researchers suggest that culturally responsive approaches to teaching must be more broadly conceptualized to address the cultural identities of students who have complex identities because of their experiences with diverse peers, those whose urban roots have resulted in hybrid identities, and those who are multiethnic/multiracial.

As the chapters in this section demonstrate, the first step in working with students is learning about and affirming their cultural identities. If teachers don't allow themselves to see their students in the ways they want to be seen, or if they choose to see things only from one perspective, they are prevented from empathizing with students, feeling their pain, and, standing in solidarity with them. Thus, teachers who don't allow their eyes to see and their hearts to feel, as the refran in the part title suggests, are less likely to co-construct teaching practices that center students' cultures and value the ways in which they make meaning of the world.

2

DON'T BELIEVE THE HYPE
CHALLENGING DEFICIT PERSPECTIVES
FROM THE INSIDE
with Carmen Ortiz, High School Student

⟿

For me, like many students today, growing up has been really hard because my family has had to struggle with issues of poverty. Being born into poverty doesn't mean that I was born without the ability to learn and do great things in life. One of the most difficult things I have had to deal with has been teachers' low expectations of me, and students like me, as a result of their perceptions of what it is like to grow up poor and Latina. I decided to collaborate on this chapter to share some of the data that I collected that demonstrate how many teachers hold deficit or negative perceptions about us, to compare those perceptions to our realities, and to explore how deficit perspectives limit opportunities for Latino youth.

Deficit perspectives, according to Nilda Flores-González, "argue that low achievers, including underachievers and dropouts, lack the characteristics that lead to school success." Teachers who hold deficit views of Latino students "place the cause of the problem on the individual, family, or culture" (Flores-González 2002, 5). If teachers believe you lack the characteristics needed to succeed academically, they often lower the expectations and "dumb down" what they teach you. Students, including myself, do in fact struggle with issues outside of school, but that does not mean that we cannot achieve at the highest levels. In this chapter, I demonstrate that deficit perspectives are not accurate, explain the negative impact they have on Latino (and other) youth, and show how they limit our chances at a quality education that prepares us for college and beyond.

THE STRUGGLES OF LATINO STUDENTS

As part of my work in Project FUERTE, I learned about the Latino struggle for equal rights in the United States. Even though my school is almost half Latino, I have never learned anything about Latinos in my classes—not even as a part of U.S. history. After reading parts of James Cockcroft's books, *Latinos in the Making of the United States* (1995) and *Latinos in the Struggle for Equal Education* (1995), and watching videos about César Chávez, Dolores Huerta, Pedro Albizu Campos, and the Young Lords, I see that my social science teachers (as well as teachers in other subjects) have completely excluded aspects of U.S. history that involve Latinos. As a result of this class, I now know that Latinos have been struggling to fight an oppressive system for a long time. Even though we have definitely made some progress as a result of the work of Latino activists, many of us still attend schools that don't teach us well and don't prepare us for college.

I agree with Jay MacLeod's conclusions in *Ain't No Makin' It: Aspirations and Attainment in a Low-Income Neighborhood* (2005). MacLeod argues that the educational system is actually set up to track kids into different positions in life. Schools often modify the quality of education offered to students based largely on their economic and racial/ethnic backgrounds. Rich kids, the majority of whom are white, most often attend schools that have more money and prepare them to be the future leaders of the world. Schools for poor kids, who are disproportionately people of color, usually have less money and prepare students, for the most part, to work *for* the rich kids in the future. MacLeod referred to this deliberate differentiation of educational opportunities as *social reproduction* (MacLeod, 2005). Instead of looking at how the system affects what we do in school and how we perform, many teachers, administrators, and staff view students as the problem. Many of the kids start to believe this hype, based on false stereotypes, as well, thinking that they are not smart when they really are. As documented in the introduction, they start to internalize the negative perceptions about themselves (Padilla, 2001). In reality, middle- and upper-class white kids often have more opportunities than we do, largely as a result of social reproduction. If you don't closely examine the conditions that affect us as we try to get a good education, or if you just look at standardized test scores out of context, you could conclude that Latinos and other students of color are not as smart as white students (see Herrnstein and Murray's *The Bell Curve,* 1994).

This is not a conspiracy theory or some crazy idea I came up with. If our society really cared about the education of poor students and Latino students, they would, at the very least, fund schools equally. Right now, schools are funded primarily through property taxes (Kozol, 1992; Ladson-Billings and Tate, 1995). Therefore, districts with more wealthy people and elevated property values have more money for their schools. Students like me, who live in districts with lower home values or where most of us rent apartments or live in public housing, have less money funneling into our schools, even though you can easily make the case that we need more.

Poverty shouldn't limit students' access to a good education. Being born poor isn't the same as being born unable to think or do good work. However, there is definitely a relationship between poverty and outcomes in school. My home state has the largest so-called achievement gap in the country (Coalition for Achievement Now, 2009). That means that the difference between the standardized test scores of students of color and white students is the greatest here. We also have a huge income gap. The state can be aptly categorized as having two types of residents—those with significant financial resources and those without them. Often, when teachers and administrators try to explain the achievement gap, they first blame us, our economic situation, or our cultures for the differences in performance on tests. They rarely, if ever, consider how increased attention given the achievement gap masks the differential historical legacies of white students and students of color, where opportunities are structured based on race and class (Kirkland, 2010), or they ignore the role they personally play in social reproduction.

There are many research studies that support my observations. Jean Anyon (1981) found that in schools that serve low-income students, teachers are more likely to give the kids worksheets and require them to complete low-level work. According to her findings, teachers working in schools serving students from low socioeconomic strata schools rarely engage students in higher-level work and critical thinking (Anyon, 1981). There is a relationship between poverty and race/ethnicity: many schools that serve poor students also have high populations of students of color (Howard, 2003). A study by Patricia Gándara and Frances Contreras found that in schools with the highest concentrations of minoritized students, 80 percent of teachers scored in the bottom quartile for quality. By contrast, schools with the lowest percentage of minoritized students had only 11 percent of teachers score in the bottom quartile of the teacher quality index (Gándara and Contreras, 2009). In other words, students of color in majority-minority schools are far more likely to have less qualified and less skillful teachers than white, middle-class students. Teacher quality has an significant impact on student performance (Darling-Hammond, 2000).

As Latino students, we have multiple struggles. First, it is a struggle to do well in schools that don't support you and are not set up to help you achieve your goals. Second, because we are stuck in a system that doesn't necessarily see us as future presidents, businesspeople, teachers, or other professionals, we have to work to change the system. Teachers have the potential to teach us the academic content we need to know while simultaneously engaging us in transforming the educational system so that it works in our best interest and not to our detriment. However, it is difficult to think about teachers joining in the struggle to change schools when many view Latino students through deficit lenses that completely blame students for their poor performance in a system that is set up to impede, if not prevent, our success.

DEFICIT PERSPECTIVES

I have often talked to my friends about how teachers treat Latino students. There are many good teachers out there, but there are also many that don't think highly of Latinos. I have had too many experiences with bad teachers. So, it goes without saying that I have encountered deficit perspectives of Latino youth during my time in schools. Before working on this participatory action research project, I never really had the vocabulary to talk about it or classify those actions as deficit thinking. To learn more about teachers' perceptions of Latino youth, the students in Project FUERTE administered a survey to a group of eighty-seven teachers, administrators, and staff at our school. There were twenty-five survey items that used a Likert Scale, and there was one open-ended question that asked, "Why do you think that so many Latino students fail to graduate from high school in four years?" We coded all the responses to the open-ended questions, as well as the comments some teachers wrote in the margins of the survey, using inductive and deductive coding (Patton, 1990). Inductive coding means we developed original categories to group the faculty responses; deductive coding means we grouped other responses into categories that we appropriated from some of the research studies we read. Seventy-seven of the eighty-seven responses given by teachers located the "problem" only with students and their families, reflecting what Flores-González (2002) defines as deficit perspectives. These responses completely ignored the role that schools play in shaping the experiences of students. Only a small percentage of those surveyed said that teachers need to find better methods to help their Latino students, and even fewer said that the school and the system need to change to better help Latino youth and others who continue to be underserved by schools.

Many of the responses offered by the educators at my school were hurtful. One teacher wrote, "They [Latinos] look for handouts," a response that is really offensive. I don't want a handout; I just want a chance to learn and an opportunity to go to college and make something of myself. Another teacher said, "it is hard to teach students who are rude and disrespectful." This is a stereotype that they are applying to all Latinos. Sure, there are some students who act poorly in school, but they often do so as a response to teachers treating them badly. More than one-third of the responses suggested that our families don't care about education. These responses included: "Education is not a primary focus from birth"; "It seems that education is not a top priority in this culture"; and "Latino parents say education is important because that is what they think researchers want to hear." These responses, which are direct quotes from teachers documented on the surveys, are grounded in the premise that Latinos don't care about education, a belief that has been challenged and debunked in various research studies (see Fry, 2008; Irizarry and Antróp-González, 2007; Moll et al., 1992; Montero-Seiburth, 2005; Valenzuela, 1999).

Teachers and other school personnel completing the survey also believe our parents are liars who just want to please researchers. My family doesn't need to lie to researchers to make a point. If teachers have these negative perceptions about us, they can't possibly be good teachers of Latino students. In fact, I don't know how the teachers who said these things are allowed to be teachers. Teachers' perspectives—both positive and negative—influence me every day. Even if they don't say it, I can feel it when teachers have a less than positive appraisal of my potential as a student and as a person. When many of my teachers look at me, I don't think they see a young poet and writer with college aspirations. At worst, they see me as a walking set of stereotypes. At best, they ignore me and treat me as if I am invisible, looking through me, over to the closest white student, whom they actually care about and think has a chance to succeed.

Sonia Nieto also provides a helpful definition that describes many of the teachers' responses. She wrote:

> There is ample evidence that some educators believe that bicultural students have few experiential or cultural strengths that can benefit their education. Teachers consider them to be "walking sets of deficiencies" or "culturally deprived" just because they speak a language other than English, or because they have just one parent, or because of their social class, race, gender, or ethnicity. (Nieto 1999, 85)

We knew that there were teachers who didn't like us, but we had no idea that the overwhelming majority of teachers, judging from the survey, held deficit perspectives. When we invited the school staff to support our project by completing the survey, we spoke confidently and used our new research vocabulary to describe our research interests and this particular line of inquiry. They knew that we had developed the survey and that we were going to analyze the data. Still, they all sat there and wrote these cruel, harsh comments, reflecting their deep-seated animosity toward Latinos.

What was just as troubling as the teachers' responses was the teachers' behavior during our data collection at their faculty meeting. Most of our teachers yell at us if we are late to class. The rule in our school is that if you are late for class, you get a detention. After three detentions you get written up. Since we were going to be the first presenters at the faculty meeting, we arrived ten minutes early and watched as the teachers arrived. Surprisingly, about half of the teachers showed up late to their own faculty meeting. We are constantly encouraged by teachers to sit in the front of the room and be active listeners. Teachers should take their own advice. As our teachers entered the library where the meeting was held, they took the seats closest to the back of the room and the exit. The front row remained virtually empty. Furthermore, cell phones are prohibited in our school. Faculty and staff don't want students calling and texting each other, and cell phones can be disruptive when used during class. When we introduced our work and the survey to the teachers, many of them were texting on their cell phones and not paying attention to us. They criticize and punish us for doing some of the same exact things they do! Why is it that they hold deficit perspectives about us yet still see themselves as professionals?

Personal Experiences with Deficit Perspectives

Beyond the data collection for the survey, I have also had many experiences with people within educational settings who hold deficit perspectives of Latinos. When I was in elementary school, my best friend was white; we had been friends since our preschool days in Head Start. In third grade her parents learned that I wasn't white, and they made her stop talking to me. When I confronted her and asked her why she had cut me out of her life so abruptly, she had one of her friends tell me the whole story, and I was extremely hurt. Even though she wasn't looking at me, I knew she was listening when I told her I'd always love her no matter what color she was because she was my best friend. She started crying and gave me a huge hug. Then she told her parents how much she hated not being my friend and that my race shouldn't matter. She said they understood, but I have my doubts. I never told my parents about the incident because I didn't know how they would have reacted. A person's color, race, ethnicity, language, and so on are not a problem by themselves. The problem comes from the meaning that people assign to these categories. The meaning they ascribe to white, middle-class or upper-class, and English-speaking categories is positive. The meaning many in society give to black, brown, Spanish-speaking, and poor categories is almost always negative. When my friend's parents thought I was white, they liked me, or at least the idea of me. When they learned I am an Afro-Latina, a Latina of African descent, they didn't want their daughter to be friends with me. I didn't change, but in their minds my identity did, and they consequently thought negatively about me. I have continuously been confronted by deficit perspectives throughout my life, especially in school.

One time during my freshman year, I was talking with a friend about my aspirations of becoming a veterinarian, and my science teacher told me, "You are never going to be anything in life." I believed she was saying this because I am Latina, and many teachers think all we are going to do in life is have babies and be unemployed. I want a family, but I also want to have a career and know that I can do both. That is a horrible thing to say to any student, no matter what the circumstances are. Think about how you might feel if a teacher told you this. Would you continue attending school? How would you feel about taking science, or any other subject, with this teacher? That negative comment also says something about the way that the teacher thinks about his job. If I don't graduate from high school, attend college, and embark on a successful career, it is my fault as well as the fault of those that are paid to educate me. Yes, it is my responsibility to learn, but it is teachers' responsibility to teach me. That is their job. We both have to take responsibility for what we do. The big difference is that if I don't do my part, I fail and maybe even drop out. My life chances are severely compromised. If the teachers don't do their part, they still get paid. In my school, more than half of the Latino students don't graduate in four years. Some of the blame should go to students, but much of it should fall on the shoulders of the educators that are compensated to teach us. The failure of the majority of Latino students to move from ninth grade to graduation has been a trend for years, yet rarely are there real consequences for ineffective educators and administrators. Occasionally, some teachers leave and go to another school, but their lives are not negatively affected by teaching and treating us poorly. We suffer the consequences of their deficit thinking and subsequent actions.

In another, more recent example, I encountered a group of teachers mocking our research in the hallway in full view of students who were changing classes. After our findings were presented at a faculty meeting, teachers became angry that their perceptions of Latino students were exposed and categorized by us as deficit thinking. Instead of reflecting on their perceptions of Latino students and families, they tried to discredit our work. They began by criticizing the survey we developed, saying we manipulated the survey to make them look bad. Although our survey wasn't perfect—we are still high school students, after all—there isn't any situation that should cause a group of educators to say some of the horrible things they said. Overall, they were acting like kids do when they get mad at a teacher. This was personal for me because I was part of the group that made the survey, analyzed the data, and constructed the presentation. When they criticized our research, they were criticizing me and my coresearchers. Teachers like those mocking our work in the hallway contribute to creating a negative climate for Latino students. Although my spirit hasn't been broken as a result of their insensitivity, I have cried many times as a consequence of my interactions with insensitive teachers and administrators.

One example of deficit thinking can be seen in some of the cruel comments made by teachers that I have shared in this section. Another example can been found in what is *not* said. That is, teachers don't often put information about Latinos in the curriculum because they do not think it is as important as other things. In May 2010, the Texas School Board pushed an agenda to "whitewash" history textbooks, choosing to emphasize "capitalism, the military, Christianity, and modern Republican figures" (Brick, 2010). Because Texas has such a large population, textbook decisions made there often have widespread influence across the nation. This is an issue of great concern to me and my fellow student-researchers. When students don't see themselves reflected in the curriculum, they can start to think that their group (Latinos, for example), is not that important or that they have not done anything worth noting. It can make some kids feel inferior to others whose cultural histories and frames of reference are represented positively in schools. Latinos' absence from the curriculum also has an impact on teachers. Since most teachers did not learn much about Latinos and other groups of people who have been historically marginalized within the United States in school or college, they can conclude there is nothing worth including. Our history and culture are not viewed as worthy of inclusion in the curriculum, which also underscores the persistence of deficit perspectives throughout the schooling experiences of Latinos. The dearth of Latino teachers means that there are few teachers who bring emic perspectives and knowledge about Latinos into the spaces where decisions about curricula are made. Not only do some students develop feelings of inferiority because they never see themselves reflected in what they learn, but also teachers may feel a sense of superiority because their culture receives more attention in the curriculum and so they conclude that their culture is better or more valuable.

The inclusion of white history and perspectives and the exclusion of Latino history and perspectives might explain the negative appraisal of Latino students reflected in teachers' comments on the survey and shared by various teachers outside the research context.

However, much of what I found in my research also seems to come from stereotypes that teachers have developed about us. Based on what they see in the media or get from other sources, many teachers develop stereotypical ideas about Latinos and their capabilities. Research on preservice teachers done by Christine Sleeter (2001) suggests that white teachers often enter teacher education programs with stereotypes and inaccurate information about students of color, including Latinos. She argues that when teachers work with students of color, they often look for data to support what they already think, thus reinforcing their stereotypes. Not all teachers are bad, and not all teachers hold stereotypes about Latinos. Nevertheless, I have heard more than my share of negative things from teachers. Many of these teachers may not even realize how hurtful they are. Teachers need to rethink what they think they know about Latino students. They need to become familiar with what Jeffrey Duncan-Andrade and Ernest Morrell (2008) refer to as counternarratives, stories that go against, challenge, and disrupt these stereotypes.

Challenging Deficit Perspectives with Counternarratives

It is important for teachers to see that most of us don't fit their stereotypes. If more teachers saw Latino students in different settings—contexts that promote our success, such as church groups or community organizations—maybe they would think more positively about us. In other words, they need to become familiar with counternarratives that help them see their deficit thinking is flawed and potentially hurtful to students. If teachers got to know me, they would see some of the ways that I fight against their stereotypes about Latino students. First, I am an award-winning, published poet. Most teachers treat us like we are dumb and don't bring any valuable skills with us to school. I love poetry and love to read, but teachers either don't know this about me or don't think it is important. I rarely, if ever, get assignments that allow me to connect my love of poetry to school work, not even in my English classes. I am a Puerto Rican born on the mainland United States, not on the island, and had never heard of NuyoRican poetry until I read several poems by Tato Laviera, Pedro Pietri, and Sandra Maria Esteves as part of my work in Project FUERTE. I think about how much more I would have connected with my classes, and with school in general, if I had had the chance to read and get excited about poetry written by poets

I share a cultural identity with, written in a style and language that I could identify with. I am in my senior year of high school and for the first time I am beginning to really enjoy learning. I attribute this increase in my passion for education to having an opportunity to learn about things that interest me. I now see how I can take those skills that I have developed as a result of participating in this research project, reading and writing about things of interest, and transfer them to other assignments.

Another example of a counternarrative is our work in Project FUERTE. Many teachers think that because we are poor, come from homes that may not have "traditional" family structures (whatever that may mean), and speak Spanish as our first language that we are not capable of doing high-level work and going to college. That is why so many Latinos in my school, and, as I have learned, in schools across the country are stuck in fundamentals level, non–college prep courses. Do teachers think less of us because we are in the low-level courses, or are we in the low-level courses because they think less of us? Both, maybe? Either way, Latino students get hurt by teachers' low expectations. Despite what some teachers may think about us, we are capable of completing high-level work. We are all high school students, but in the Action Research and Social Change class, we do college-level work. Before taking this class, the longest paper I had ever written was two pages, hand-written, and I was never asked or encouraged to revise a paper. Contributing to this chapter demonstrates that with support, I can accomplish great things. Also, as part of the course, we had to develop a presentation that shared our understanding of the research literature relative to our topic, the methods we employed to collect and analyze the data, findings emerging from our analysis, and our subsequent recommendations for teachers. We delivered the presentation several times to schoolteachers, preservice teachers, professors, researchers, policymakers, and others. They were all amazed that a group of Latino high school students could inform their perspectives on the types of reforms that are needed in schools. We actively participated in professional conversations with them, and many of the audience members left our presentations thinking more positively about youth in general and Latino students more specifically. The presentations gave us a platform to assert identities as intelligent young people with much to offer the world, identities that are ironically suppressed in school settings.

Chapter 2

IF I WERE A TEACHER EDUCATOR ...

If I were consulted by a dean of a school of education regarding my thoughts on the preparation of teachers, I would articulate a vision for the preparation of teachers that is grounded in community. If I were charged with preparing teachers to teach in schools that served Latinos, I would take my class of preservice teachers into the community to experience Latino culture. I would bring them to cultural sites and museums. I would love to take them to the Nuyorican Poet's Café in New York City, so that they could see Latino participation in the arts. I would take them to colleges to experience Latino cultural centers, such as the Puerto Rican and Latin American Cultural Center (PRLACC) at the University of Connecticut and Brandeis's Multicultural Center (AHORA), two places we visited to deliver presentations. I would have them read research about Latino students and other students who have not been served well or embraced by schools, as well as a bunch of studies about Latinos from authors that I have recently read, such as Julio Cammarota and Augustine Romero (2006); Luis Moll, Cathy Amanti, Deborah Neff, and Norma González (1992); Sonia Nieto (2000); Rosalie Rolón-Dow (2005); René Antróp-González, William Vélez, and Tomás Garrett (2005); Louie Rodríguez (2008); and Tara Yosso (2005). These powerful and insightful studies really challenged me and shaped my perspectives on the education of Latino youth. The majority of my teachers have never heard of any of these scholars and are not familiar with their research findings.

Because I also love literature and poetry, I would integrate ethnic literature into the teacher education curriculum. There is much you can learn from reading literature, especially stories authored by Latinos. Also, after visiting the University of Connecticut and Brandeis for this project, I realized there are not a lot of Latinos or other people of color at many universities. You learn most about people when you interact with them, but because people of color are underrepresented in most colleges and universities, many white future teachers have few chances to learn from people of color. In addition to creating a curriculum aimed at improving the multicultural awareness of teachers, teacher education programs have to simultaneously commit to recruiting more people of color into the profession.

I am not just saying this because I am a part of this project, but I believe that I would utilize youth participatory action research (YPAR) with students and have them present their work to teachers. Because we are experiencing school every day, we have unique insights that can inform the work of teachers. As part of their internships and field placements, preservice teachers work in my school doing a variety of jobs, but they, like the teachers that supervise them, are disconnected from us. They just come here and maintain the status quo. YPAR is about changing the system, so I think teacher educators need to connect with schools and youth to change the system so it works for kids like me. If teachers build relationships with students and connect with us, more of us would consider going into teaching, and that would change things too. When I first began this class I wanted to be a veterinarian, but now I am planning to be an English teacher, specifically because of my work on this project.

If I were a teacher, I would practice *critical care praxis,* which is

> grounded in a historical understanding of students' lives; translates race-conscious ideological and political orientations into pedagogical approaches that benefit Latino/a students; uses caring counternarratives to provide more intimate, caring connections between teachers and the Latino communities where they work; and pays attention to caring at both the individual and institutional levels. (Rolón-Dow, 2005, p. 77)

In other words, since teachers who practice critical care praxis care about you, they also feel an obligation to work with you to change the system. These teachers are not colorblind or cultureblind. As a student you can be yourself in their classroom, and they will love you for that. They want you to do well as an individual student, but they also want your community to do well and improve. Teachers who use critical care praxis listen to what students have to say because they believe students have valuable insights and their voices should be heard. Lots of people think that students are too young and too inexperienced to co-construct a class, but through this research we proved that even high school students can do high-quality, important research to stimulate change.

As an English teacher, I would give my students meaningful work in which they have time to invest their talents and passions. I would offer my students diverse opportunities, such as field trips and experiences in the community, to learn in a real world context, and assign texts and tasks that connect to their cultures rather than relying just on "classic" texts. Most of my teachers focus on the so-called classics. Although these texts may be important and can teach us a lot, we can also learn from more recent works closer to our experiences. I am not saying we need to get rid of Shakespeare, but I am saying that we need to add Latino authors and books with Latino protagonists to the curriculum. If you look at all the novels on the assigned reading list for grades nine through twelve in my district's curriculum frameworks, there is only one written by a Latino author! The almost complete lack of representation is unacceptable.

My classroom would be colorful, and the curriculum and the space would reflect the cultures of the students. Having a classroom that is culturally responsive would help the students feel at home and comfortable in their learning space. Right now most of the walls in my schools have pictures and posters of white kids. There are few, if any, signs that Latinos or other students of color go to school here. In one English classroom, there are only posters of dead, white male authors and a map of Europe. Not all the classes in this room focus exclusively on European literature, and white men don't accurately reflect the entire range of European authors. As I traveled through the school examining how Latinos were represented, I found either classrooms and hallways featuring almost exclusively pictures of white kids and a glorification of European history or empty, sterile walls that made the space uninviting. It makes sense to me that half of my Latino colleagues leave school before graduation, given the marginalization we experience throughout all facets of life in schools.

Because I think student histories and experiences are so important and should be valued, I would start my class by having students write autobiographical essays. Doing so would help me get to know them and give them a chance to learn about each other. I would have a day where they could bring in their cultural belongings and share parts of their biographies. I think these activities would create a good sense of community in my classroom and help other people, especially those who hadn't been exposed to certain cultures before, learn about these cultures. This exercise would also put students in the position of teacher. Based on my work in this project, I really have come to see the importance of giving students a chance to demonstrate what they know in meaningful ways. We are not just empty minds waiting for teachers to fill us up with what they think we need to know. If you work with us, we can do great things, and we have a lot to offer.

When I become a teacher, I will not view students from deficit perspectives. In contrast, I will take a positive approach that doesn't define kids by what they don't have but instead focuses on the wonderful things they do have. For example, many of the kids in my community are poor and come from homes that may be dealing with some tough issues. Sometimes when they come to school, learning may not be first on their minds. However, things are not all bad in our communities. There are a lot of wonderful things that I see every day. For example, I think that when people struggle here, neighbors and others try to help you. If you have an issue and need information, people who have experience with the issue can and do offer assistance. Luis Moll and his colleagues (1992) referred to these social networks and the information that exists in these communities as "funds of knowledge." Instead of defining us by some of the negative experiences we have to endure, teachers should acknowledge and appreciate the positive things that we do and the resources we do have.

I want to teach in an urban school that serves students of color and to live in the community where I teach. I would try to live close to my students so that I could be there for them if they needed help in any area, even those outside the academic realm. I would want them to see me as accessible and as a potential role model. Living close by could also allow me to support their academic growth outside school. Ideally, I would like to teach at the high school I currently attend to provide a better experience for future students than I have had. Although my experience in school has been largely negative, I still feel strongly about giving back to the school and to the community. By becoming a teacher and returning to work in my home district, I can serve as a counternarrative to teachers on the staff who hold deficit perspectives of Latino youth. Currently, I don't really like my school, but I feel that through my efforts I could improve the culture here and influence students and teachers to improve the school environment. I would also like to teach somewhere where I could be close to my friends and family, and I have lived here for a long time. I have strong roots in this community, and I want to keep them. Those roots are key to who I am and could inform my future work as a teacher.

Most teachers have strict rules about socializing with students outside school. Some of the most powerful learning experiences for me in my Action Research and Social Change class and Project FUERTE have happened outside school, in the community and at research presentations. Unfortunately, I don't have any teachers that live in my community. That contributes to the disconnect that exists between many teachers and students. They only get to know us in one setting—school. School rules force us to act a certain way and hide or suppress certain parts of our identities. There is a lot more to us than what teachers see in school. If more teachers got to know us beyond the walls of the school, then maybe they would not have deficit perspectives.

RECOMMENDATIONS FOR TEACHERS AND TEACHER EDUCATORS

Based on my research, I have come up with three recommendations for teachers and teacher educators to help make them more effective instructors of Latino students. Even though these recommendations are specifically designed to help them teach Latino students, I think they can apply to other students as well. First, I would suggest that teachers stop blaming student characteristics that they can't control (i.e., socioeconomic status, family structure, home language) for student failure. Teachers should think positively about students and what they bring to the classroom and do the best they can to teach them. They should teach Latino students as well as they want teachers to teach their children. It is worth mentioning that there are approximately seventy-five full-time faculty members and professional staff working in my school. Many of them have children, yet only a small minority sends their kids to schools in the district. Many teachers don't think schools in this district are good enough for their kids. Teachers should help change these schools so they are as good as the schools they send their kids to. Instead of blaming students and families for student failure, teachers need to do more to identify the ways in which schools harm kids and work with students to fix these problems. That is how we are really going to learn, not by memorizing some random facts for a test. Judging from the survey data, almost all my teachers believe that students' families and culture are the only reasons for Latino students dropping out. It isn't until they look in the mirror and see their role in social reproduction that we can really change schools and make them desirable learning spaces for all students.

Second, I would tell teachers to employ critical care praxis (Rolón-Dow, 2005). As I mentioned earlier, good teachers, according to this theory, care about students as individuals and critically look at the institutional structures that affect them. Many teachers who think they are good teachers focus only on their classrooms. They don't see their work as playing a role in changing schools and the larger system of our society so that kids have a real chance to learn and make something of themselves. So although I might have a great fifty-four-minute period with a good teacher, I am stuck for the other five periods (or close to five hours) in classrooms and spaces within the school that are hurtful and oppressive. If teachers enact critical care praxis, they would work with us to change the system so that we can have good days, weeks, and months instead of just the occasional good class period. Our entire school experience should be positive. I see students, particularly Latino students, being treated badly almost every day. If I see it, I know teachers see it. You can just look at the in-school suspension room to see how students of color in this school (and others) are disciplined at higher rates. (For more discussion on school discipline policies, see Chapter 9). Teachers have power within schools. They should feel obligated and empowered to challenge these injustices, but often they ignore them. Sometimes they even contribute to them. When teachers see an event that might be unfair to students, they should ask themselves, Would I say or do something if that was my child? If the answer is yes, they should act. If teachers did more to improve the school climate, students would think more positively about them, allowing for relationship development and the fostering of student success.

Finally, teachers need to raise expectations for students and provide support for students to meet these standards. It may not be what teachers want to hear, but I think teachers need to do more to support students. When students feel supported, they do better in school. I know that teachers are busy, but they have to think about their work outside the traditional school day of 7:30 to 2:30. When kids feel supported, they want to do more work. For example, in this project, in addition to our regularly scheduled classes we stay after school at least once a week. We have also met on Saturdays and during school vacations. For the most part, none of the members of Project FUERTE love school so much that they always want to be engaged in schoolwork. Still, we all put in a lot of extra time into this class, which demonstrates our commitment to our education and to promoting educational equity and social change.

In terms of support, teachers need to engage us outside the traditional classroom so we can show them more of what we are capable of accomplishing. For us to be successful, we need forms of support—such as access to technology after school and teachers who will advocate with and for us—that are not common in schools serving large percentages of Latino youth. According to the deficit perspectives teachers have shared with us, many teachers think we are lazy. They couldn't imagine how hard my colleagues and I have worked for this project and other endeavors in which we are invested. The key was we had the support we needed to meet the high expectations. If more teachers provided support for students and created situations in which students could support each other, I think Latinos and other students would do better in school.

DON'T BELIEVE THE HYPE

It is easy for teachers to think that students' cultures, family situations, and language are the reasons almost half of all Latinos don't graduate from high school. (That is a national rate for Latinos; the rate for my school is actually higher.) Poor students and families are an easy target. I wish teachers could get beyond the hype, or exaggerated stereotypes of students, and connect with Latino students and families to support real learning. So many of us are not being educated well because many of our teachers, whether they are aware of it or not, hold deficit perspectives. I hope this chapter will convince current and future teachers of how harmful these perspectives can be. I also hope that as a result of reading this chapter, teachers will be motivated to improve their practice. I know that teachers are already underappreciated and underpaid. I am not trying to criticize all teachers or say that all teachers hold deficit perspectives. However, given the data we collected and analyzed, it seems to be a bigger problem than you might think. My goal is to inspire teachers to look beyond simple explanations for student failure. To that end, I forward a vision of teaching in which teachers connect with students' cultures and practice critical care praxis. From the bottom of my heart I believe that if teachers worked differently with students in the ways that I have described in this chapter, Latino students would do much better in school.

3

HOW CAN YOU TEACH US
IF YOU DON'T REALLY KNOW US?
RETHINKING RESISTANCE IN THE CLASSROOM
with Jasmine Medina, High School Student

⊕

May identity as a high school student is only one of many I have. I am a daughter, a sister, a friend, and so many other things. Sometimes when I am at school, I feel like teachers don't expect me to be all of who I am, only a student. I am sure that teachers have more complex identities than they share with students in school, and they seem to want us to be as one-dimensional as they seem to be. Many of my teachers want to put labels on me and fit me into nice, neat categories that allow them not to think too much about who I am and what I can be, just where I belong—or where they think I belong. In this chapter, I talk about the labels that are used to describe students in schools. I know teachers are definitely not the only ones who put labels on people; we students do it to each other too. But I think the effect of teachers, principals, and other school officials labeling students can be more devastating. Sure, we have all been called names before, and it hurts, but eventually we get over it and move on. When schools label kids, they often make decisions about what they can and cannot do, and these decisions have effects that are more far-reaching, limiting the life chances of students labeled negatively.

Even though I am in the special education program, it does not mean that I am not smart or capable. Everyone is unique, and we all learn in different ways. I know from experience that it is disheartening to have people judging you because of the label attached to you. On top of all of this, I am Latina. There are lots of places where I feel that my Latina identity is honored and celebrated. At home and in my community, I can be my Latina self. The culture and climate of my school aren't affirming of my diverse identities.

In my experience, Latino students are seen through rigid lenses informed largely by stereotypes. Students who are given labels like "English learners" or "special ed students," are sometimes constructed as "problems," and stereotypes about these groups shape how many teachers think about us and the approaches they use to teach us. Since there are few positive images of Latinos out there, particularly of young Latinos like us (Leadbetter and Way, 1996; Reyes and Ríos, 2003), many teachers think we are all drug dealers or gang members. Unfortunately, that means a lot of teachers just don't trust us. Once, a teacher let one of my classmates, a white girl, leave to use the restroom during class. The teacher signed her pass and let her take her belongings with her. A couple of minutes later the student came back, and then I asked if I could use the restroom. The teacher said yes, and he signed my pass. On my way out I had grabbed my bag, just like the first student, and was about to walk out the door when the teacher stood in front of me and told me the only way for me to go to the bathroom was for me to leave my stuff on the desk. He said, "I don't believe that you are going to come back, so put your stuff down and then you can go." I then told him that I didn't feel comfortable leaving my belongings in the classroom while I wasn't there and mentioned that he had let the other girl take her bag. His response was, "I don't care what she did. I just want to know what you are doing. She is different." I got very frustrated and left the room. I constantly feel as if teachers think the worst about me, even though few of them know me on a personal level. Most teachers don't see how they treat Latino students differently from white students. Or worse, maybe they do see it and still discriminate against us.

When incidents like this happen, and unfortunately they happen often at our school and are not uncommon at other schools like ours, many students will react by swearing at the teacher or acting out. They are upset so they lash out in response and do something that makes them look bad or gets them in trouble. Teachers often focus on the response and not the actions that provoked it. Consequently, we get a bad reputation and reinforce the stereotypes many teachers have of us. Isolating student behavior from the larger context in which it occurs allows teachers' practices to remain unexamined and reinforces the decontextualization of students' behavior, resulting in more data to support the negative labels thrusted upon many Latino students.

In our class, we have been learning about different ways to challenge, speak back to, and make meaning of incidents like this. My classmates, the ones who swear or respond disrespectfully to teachers, are demonstrating what Daniel Solórzano and Dolores Delgado Bernal (2001) refer to as "self-defeating resistance." Basically, it means that they are resisting the way that the teachers are treating them in a fashion that is going to do them more harm than good in the long run—land them in suspension, keep them from attending a class trip or event, or something like that. Even worse than those consequences, the conflicts between teachers and students can serve to reinforce the stereotypes that cause some teachers to treat us badly in the first place, creating a vicious, never-ending cycle. Who can blame Latino students for getting mad at our teachers when they treat us poorly? Why wouldn't we stand up for ourselves? Some of the things that my classmates and I have to endure are completely unfair, and there are no consequences for the teachers because the way most schools are set up, they are the ones with all the power. Because we are viewed as the source of the problem, we often have no other recourse to redress our grievances. So what can we do? One method for addressing this quandary is to engage in transformational resistance (Solórzano and Delgado Bernal, 2001). Transformational resistance is a way to stand up for ourselves in a fashion that helps us, and in the long run will help dismantle and transform this system, which is oppressive for many Latino students. Telling our stories and sharing our perspectives is an example of transformational resistance. Through youth participatory action research (YPAR), one manifestation of transformational resistance, we are proving that Latino students are not a walking set of deficiencies but rather young people with unlimited potential.

THE CURRICULUM AS A SITE OF RESISTANCE

Even though it is hard sometimes, my Project FUERTE coresearchers and I are doing our best to choose transformational resistance over self-defeating resistance. But we can't transform the system without the support of critical allies. If we are really going to change schools so that they operate in the best interests of students, then teachers need to choose transformational resistance too. For example, if you are currently a teacher or enrolled in a teacher preparation program, you probably know that schools have a set curriculum that teachers are expected to follow. Have you ever noticed that Latinos hardly ever appear in the curriculum? As a student, I have never learned about Puerto Rican or Mexican history. Before Project FUERTE, I just figured that Latinos hadn't really done anything worth teaching about. If they had, our teachers would tell us, right? Because all the books we are introduced to in school are written by non-Latino authors, I doubted the existence of Latino writers and scholars. In our Action Research and Social Change class, we talked about a variety of other books penned by Latinos, including fascinating pieces of young adult literature, that should be used in our classes but aren't. As part of our research, we had to read articles documenting studies that could inform our work. I appreciate "the classics," as the books we are required to read are often called, but I argue that more Latino students would get into reading if our lives were better reflected in the books we were assigned. This is not just the case at our school. Most schools still have a monocultural curriculum that focuses on white, European American (and male) values, traditions, and contributions (Gay, 2000; Nieto and Bode, 2008; Sleeter, 2006).

My schooling can best be described as Eurocentric. The curriculum at my school (and many others serving Latino youth) typically focuses on European contributions with little, and sometimes no, attention paid to the contributions of others. Given the sizable Latino population in this country, why, then, is everything we learn so Eurocentric? Latinos have played a seminal role in the development of the United States, yet are largely omitted from what is taught in schools. In my U.S. history class, it is almost the end of the school year, and the only thing that we have been talking about is white people and how they have contributed to the formation of the United States of America. We have hardly touched on the subject of how Latinos came to this country (or how this country "came to" Latinos) and how we have affected it.

The labels imposed on us prevent teachers from really getting to know us on a more personal level. The absence of that relationship disrupts the flow of information between the student and teacher and prevents the modification of the curriculum and the inclusion of our cultural histories and lived experiences. We need more teachers who are willing to stand up for what is right for students and be brave enough to make changes to the curriculum, despite the fact that school districts are narrowing the scope of what we need to know in order to focus on the content we need to master to perform well on the state test. We need teachers who are willing to join with students in transformational resistance on behalf of Latinos and other groups who never see themselves in the curriculum and are discriminated against in schools.

Most teachers, I believe, would do more to change the curriculum if they had a more profound knowledge and understanding of Latinos and our participation in the struggle for civil rights and other initiatives that have shaped this country. I bet many teachers or soon-to-be teachers have never heard of Pedro Albizu Campos, Dolores Huerta, or the Young Lords. If you think about it, the curriculum probably has not changed much since they went to high school, so they read the same Eurocentric history books and "classic" novels that we are reading. Actually, it is exactly the same in some cases. This year I found my aunt's name in one of my textbooks for the English class I am currently taking. She went to my high school in the 1980s, and I am currently using the same book she did in one of my classes! As part of our study of Latino education, my colleagues and I analyzed the curriculum at our school. We each brought in some of the books we were assigned as part of our classes to examine how Latinos were represented, if at all. We found very little, aside from our textbooks for Spanish classes. In the book I am using for my literature class, the one my aunt used more than twenty years ago, there is nothing about Latinos and only one short paragraph about African Americans. That is it! I had always wondered in the back of my mind why Latinos and other people of color were never talked about, but once we started exploring our exclusion from the curriculum in class—and more specifically, how this contributes to so-called achievement gaps and teacher perceptions' of Latino students as nonacademic and not cut out for school—it made me really angry. Again, it goes back to teachers and other people only wanting to put one label on us instead of seeing that we are more complex and interesting. Latinos are a people with a vibrant history and a rich present. I understand that my teachers have lots of identities too. They are not always in "teacher mode." Why don't they understand this about Latino students?

I think part of the issue is that most teachers who aren't Latino don't know much about Latinos. Since they don't know much about Latinos, they too, may not think that there is anything related to Latino history, literature, and so on worth teaching. So, they teach the same content they learned and don't try to tailor the curriculum to meet the specific needs of marginalized groups. If they were to learn more about us, they would realize that the curriculum should not be so Eurocentric. Were they to sit down and talk to us and ask us things like, "What don't you like about school?" or "What can I do as a teacher to help you in school?" or "What would you change about our class?" they would get a better perspective on how we learn in school and gain insights into how to promote our academic and social success. If the curriculum was more Latinocentric or more balanced, I am certain Latino students would be more engaged in their classes and teachers would be prompted to develop more positive labels for us. I'm not saying that there aren't any Latinos who do well in school the way it is set up now. There are Latino students out there who do well in school and get good grades (Antróp-González, 2005; Conchas, 2006). I assert that sometimes these students have to put aside their Latino identities to do this, and that isn't fair. If schools were to change the curriculum to include the stories of Latinos and other people of color, their actions would signal to students that they value these groups—that they are worthy of being taught. With significant changes to the curriculum, including more diverse perspectives and models of resistance, schools would slowly become places where Latinos would feel accepted, cared for, and loved. Instead of trying to suppress our resistance, teachers should try to identify the underlying stimuli to which we are responding. At times we disconnect from school because we feel completely alienated from the content we are forced to learn. I would encourage teachers to resist the ways they are often positioned in schools—as robots forced to complete a task and restricted from creatively applying their craft—and stand in solidarity with us to co-construct curricula and create transformative spaces within schools.

TEACHER TRAINING AS A SITE OF RESISTANCE

It is important to look at the issue of Latino underachievement from a "big picture" lens, in the larger sociopolitical context. It is not fair to say that insensitive teachers and a Eurocentric curriculum are solely responsible for the plight of Latino youth. Similarly, placing the entire burden of Latino achievement on kids is equally short-sighted and problematic. Like many young people, I never really thought about my educational experiences as being influenced by factors largely outside of my control. Examining the ways in which educational opportunities are structured and how schools contribute to the problem of academic underachievement opened my eyes and gave me a better understanding of the issue. Another way to improve achievement among Latinos is to improve the preparation of teachers and diversifying the teaching force. Just as it would be great to see images of ourselves in textbooks and novels, it would be great to see people who look and sound like us standing up in front of our classrooms teaching. Unfortunately, Latinos are underrepresented in the teaching force and in preservice teacher education programs. There is an acute need for colleges, schools, and departments of education to recruit Latino students into their teacher preparation programs. Increasing the pool of Latino teachers is predicated on more Latinos completing high school and gaining access to higher education. With more Latino teachers, Latino students are likely to do better in school (Dee, 2005). There are no Latino teachers that teach core subject classes in my school. The Latino teachers we do have teach either Spanish or English as a Second Language (ESL) classes, and it is possible that many students in my school, including Latino students, can complete four years of high school without ever having a Latino teacher.

To reiterate, I don't think that I need to have all Latino teachers in order to do well in school or to make a connection with a teacher. There are some white teachers, even a few at my school, who have reached out to Latino students and have made strong connections that inform their work. I'm not really sure why some teachers have done this and some haven't. My colleagues and I developed a line of research around this question. As part of the survey, we asked teachers questions about their preparation to work with Latino students. Some teachers said they did not feel well prepared by their colleges or by professional development experiences, and others said they did feel well prepared because students' race or ethnicity was not important and they treated all students "the same." When reading these responses, we were surprised by the teachers who reported feeling well prepared, particularly given our collective experiences with school-based marginalization and discrimination. My interactions with culturally insensitive teachers prompted me to ask: What do people who are studying to be teachers learn in college about Latino students, if anything? If they don't get taught about Latinos while attending K–12 schools or college, where, then, do they learn how to teach us?

To answer these questions, I interviewed preservice teachers who assisted with Project FUERTE. After talking with some of them and mining the body of research related to the preparation of teachers, my colleagues and I realized that many teacher education programs limit learning about Latinos to one course, and often that class isn't about Latinos specifically. It is usually in the form of one "diversity" or "multicultural" class that covers all differences—not just race or ethnicity (Dilworth, 1992; Vavrus, 2002). Instead of taking these courses throughout their programs, teacher education students get it all at once. To me, it sounds like studying for a test. You may study really hard right up until you take the test, and then you take it and it's over. Usually after that, I don't really think about whatever I was studying that much, if at all. I remember things better and think about them more if I am talking about them in more than just one place and with different people. For example, in our class we learned how to conduct research and make our findings accessible to wider audiences because we practiced almost every day in real-life situations. We attended conferences and spoke with different constituencies about our work, and sometimes they told us about theirs. We knew the importance of our research based on the time we spent on it and its practical use in the present. The same goes for this book. We knew our work was important because we worked on our contributions to the chapter, through interviews and some writing as well as by engaging in a process of collaboration for revisions that continued, for months, during class, in one-on-one sessions after school, and during study halls. The more we worked on it, the more we took ownership of it and wanted to do our best work for ourselves and the collective good of the group. I wonder if that can happen for teacher education students who are only learning about Latino students and other students of color in one class. Admirably, some teachers pursue learning about Latinos on their own, but given what is at stake, I would make it a more permanent, systematic part of the preparation of teachers. Another point of comparison can be found in the value placed on language classes in high school. We have to take four years of English to graduate, but not as many years of a language class. Basically, the message is that schools want you to be well versed in the English language and literature but don't really care as much about students being fluent in a second language or knowledgeable about another culture. If colleges aren't providing their future teachers with opportunities to learn about other cultures, the likelihood of teachers being prepared to work across lines of cultural difference is left to chance, and the preparation of teachers to work with Latino youth shouldn't be based on luck.

Discrete, stand-alone "diversity" courses offered to preservice teachers are often peripheral to the rest of the teacher education curriculum. By not addressing issues of power and cultural difference sufficiently during their coursework, teacher education programs may be inadvertently teaching future teachers that a colorblind view of students is acceptable or even preferred. Colorblind approaches, widely popular among teachers, provide the illusion of equity while making students like me, who want people to acknowledge their cultural identities, feel invisible and unwanted in the classroom. Society at large, not just teachers, seems to find value in the colorblind philosophy (see Irvine, 2003; Milner, 2006; Sleeter, 2001). The problem with this perspective is that if you are a person striving to be colorblind (assuming the state of metaphorical colorblindness is even possible to achieve), then you probably see no point in learning about people different from you. If differences "don't matter," then why learn about them? My Project FUERTE colleagues and I disagree. Racial/ethnic differences do matter, and teachers make many decisions, often ones that aren't in our best interest, based on the value they ascribe to these identity categories. It is important for teachers to think about how they see difference and also to learn more about the cultures represented in their classrooms. In the title of his book, Gary Howard (1999) made an important admission, "We can't teach what we don't know," in relation to white teachers trying to teach students of color. In a similar vein, I build on his important assertion and ask educators, "How can you teach us if you don't know us?"

TEACHING AS A SITE OF RESISTANCE

There are certainly great teachers of Latino students out there working in schools (Irizarry and Antróp-González, 2007; Irizarry and Raible, 2011). Even in the most oppressive schools, you can usually find exceptional teachers who promote achievement and have earned the respect of students and families. Often those teachers practice *culturally responsive teaching*. This approach to teaching, forwarded in the work of Geneva Gay (2000) and other scholars, recognizes the knowledge, experiences, learning styles, languages, and strengths of students in order to instruct more effectively. Teachers may have to leave their comfort zones in order to engage students like me in their classes. There have been many examples of successful culturally responsive teaching. Research conducted by Ernest Morrell and Jeff Duncan-Andrade (2002) describes how a group of urban students engaged in English class when their teacher began incorporating elements of hip-hop culture. The students were able to make connections between their cultural frames of reference and works from the literary canon and apply the critical perspectives found throughout hip-hop to analyze literature. Sometimes culturally responsive teaching involves even more than making the content of the class more interesting or relatable to students. The findings from a study of exemplary teachers of Latino students (Irizarry and Raible, 2011) demonstrates that teachers, regardless of racial/ethnic background, can practice culturally responsive pedagogy if they allow their practice to be informed by the funds of knowledge (Moll et al., 1992) found in our communities. Culturally responsive pedagogy as described in these studie, requires that teachers get to know their students, value the knowledge and skills students bring to school, and build on these strengths to provide learning opportunities that prepare them to be critical citizens in a multicultural democracy.

RECOMMENDATIONS FOR EDUCATORS

The problems facing Latino students are vast, and they cannot be eliminated everywhere overnight. However, there are still ways for teachers and teacher educators to improve the educational experiences and outcomes for Latino students in the present. Teachers can commit to learning more about their Latino students. They can come to our communities, not as tourists taking pictures but as people who really want to learn about us and with us. The overwhelming majority of educators at my school don't live in my community. If they were immersed in this setting, they would naturally come to realize that the negative perceptions they have are not accurate. The knowledge teachers gain from forging these bonds with the community can inform their efforts to transform curriculum and their teaching practices. I am not suggesting that teachers replace Eurocentricism with Latinocentricism. Rather, I am advocating for a multicultural approach that affirms all our identities (see Nieto and Bode, 2008). I just want to feel cared for in school and valued enough to be taught well by adults in the building. The data regarding Latino student achievement highlights the immediate need to transform schools to more effectively teach this group.

One of the main frameworks that we have been exploring as a means to improve the education of Latinos is *praxis* (Freire, 1970/2000). Praxis is reflection and action on the world in order to change it. Teachers can use the following five-step praxis plan to forge relationships with students around a shared goal and teach them valuable content that will serve them well in school and beyond.

- *Identify the problem.* Teachers can work with us to identify problems in our schools and communities that we want to address and use these explorations to improve their understanding of the barriers that impede academic success for many Latinos.
- *Research the problem.* After becoming familiar with our areas of interest, teachers can collaboratively research the issues with us, thereby increasing their knowledge base and demonstrating solidarity with students.
- *Develop an action plan.* Teachers can work with students and the community to develop a plan to address the problem. Taking action to address issues of import to Latino youth reflects a heightened level of commitment to ensuring they receive a quality education.
- *Evaluate the action.* Once the plan is implemented, teachers can work with students to determine the effectiveness of the initiative.
- *Revise the plan and act again.* Of course, some things will work and others won't. Depending on the outcome, teachers and students can continue to address the initial issue, or they can collaborate to address another barrier of concern to Latino youth. The process of revision and a sustained commitment to action are reflective of a long-term commitment to students and their education.

Collaborating with students and using praxis as a framework to guide co-constructed learning experiences provide perhaps the most valuable, most authentic professional development experiences teachers will ever have. Having a more profound understanding of the issues facing Latino students and working with them to overcome them will inspire the reconceptualizaton of resistance in this context. When people are oppressed, they should resist their oppression. The argument can easily be made that teachers are oppressed by constant attacks in the popular media and policies that force them to teach to the test and stifle their creativity as professionals. The chapters thus far have documented how some teachers, in turn, oppress students and how their actions affect students. If we join together in collaborative acts of resistance, we can create learning environments that work for all of us.

4

WHO COUNTS AS LATINO/A?
PERSPECTIVES FROM A MULTIRACIAL/ MULTIETHNIC LATINA
with Tamara Rodriguez, High School Student

⟿

This chapter explores the diversity among those of us grouped together under the umbrella terms *Latino or Hispanic*. My goal is to get teachers to think more broadly about the complexities associated with identity and the implications this more nuanced understanding presents for teaching and learning. As a multiracial/multiethnic Latina—I am black, white, and Puerto Rican—I rarely feel like teachers or my fellow students appreciate my diversity. Although I want to be accepted by all people, my multiracial/multiethnic identity, or what I refer to as my "multiracialness," is often not acknowledged by friends, teachers, and others in my school. It seems as if teachers and my fellow students want everyone to fit neatly into an identity box. I am not sure if anybody fits perfectly into these identity categories, but I know that I definitely do not.

One might think schools would be sensitive and supportive of multiracial/multiethnic students, given the fact that being multiracial and/or multiethnic is not a new phenomenon. There have been students like me attending schools for a long time, but educators have been slow to respond to our needs. I reflect back on my experiences in schools and find myself asking these questions: what history month do I celebrate? Can I really be Latina if I don't speak Spanish? How do others perceive me? I don't know if I will ever have the answers to these questions, but I wish that more teachers cared to know that these issues are important to me. I find that teachers are often so caught up with other things, such as teaching us to pass tests or trying to control student behavior, that they fail to realize what teaching should be about—the students! In addition to all the academic content that I need to learn, I am also concurrently trying to figure out who I am as a person, a key feature of adolescent development. This journey to understand my identity is connected to my years attending middle and high school. Because of pressure put on them by the district and state to get us to pass the statewide standardized tests, most of the teachers I have encountered over the years have focused almost exclusively on teaching content without recognizing all the other important developmental issues that I am dealing with, specifically my ethnic/racial identity. If schools would do more to make me feel included, I am sure that I (and most students) would do much better academically.

I often wonder if teachers don't care about these issues or if they just don't know about them. As documented in the previous chapter, the curriculum at my school is almost completely Eurocentric, focusing almost exclusively on the experiences and perspectives of white people. At times, I feel connected to the curriculum and identify with many of the teachers because I share some aspects of my racial and cultural identities with teachers and many of those figures addressed in the curriculum. Simultaneously, I long to learn more about Latinos and African Americans and am upset that I don't know more about these aspects of my identity. Given the important contributions African Americans and Latinos have made to the development of this country, to literature, and to other areas of life in the United States, we should learn more about them in school. Based on my experiences, I believe that multiracial/multiethnic students are positioned in unique, sometimes precarious ways that remain largely obscure yet have a lasting impact on our identity development and academic achievement.

MY MULTIRACIALNESS

Teachers respond to me as a multiracial/multiethnic student in different ways, depending on the context. The way teachers respond to students of certain cultures doesn't affect me the way it does some of my colleagues whose stories are included in this text. For example, as contradictory as it may sound, I am both appreciated and discriminated against at the same time in school. The curriculum in my school is more focused on white "students," and whiteness is praised and valued. As a student with a white parent and white family members, I can often connect with aspects of the curriculum and at times feel affirmed for aspects of my racial identity. This bifurcation really confuses and conflicts me at times. I was raised by my mother, who is white, so I sometimes feel more white than anything. Part of that also comes from internalizing the culture of schooling. If you "act white" or are seen as white, teachers treat you better. I benefit from white privilege (McIntosh, 1989), yet I am still Latina and black as well. Privilege, as I learned during the course of this project, is an unearned resource. For example, I didn't do anything to earn the benefits that come with being perceived as white and having the curriculum and my teachers speak to that aspect of my identity. Similarly, people of color have little say about how they are perceived. Youth of color are often perceived negatively and blamed for many of the problems in schools and society. As a multiracial/multiethnic Latina, I have personally experienced life as both a white person and a person of color, depending on the situation or context.

When I play sports or spend time with my white friends, it is easy not to see discrimination. The coaches, teachers, and administrators all think positively of white students. In fact, I would go so far as to say that the school is set up for these students. Most of the books we use are written by white people and feature their perspectives. Most of the teachers are white. Most of the posters and pictures in my school depict white people. Because of my light skin and white identity, I often "blend in" and "pass" as white. However, when I spend time with Puerto Ricans in my school and enact a more Puerto Rican identity, I see how teachers are insensitive to and dismissive of Latino students. Experiencing blatant, racialized discrimination hurts. I have noticed that teachers treat me differently, depending on the group of students I happen to be spending time with. If I am in a group of white students and we are in the hallway during class time, we never get asked by teachers or security to show a hallway pass. When I am with my Latino friends in the hallway, though, we always get asked for a pass and questioned about what we are doing. The irony is that my white friends and I are sometimes in the hallway to socialize or avoid class, and teachers and administrators leave us alone. I could be working on a school-related project with my Latino friends or we might be on our way to class or doing something positive, and almost without exception teachers and administrators will question us.

My racial/ethnic identity doesn't change during the day, yet I am perceived and treated differently by adults at my school solely based on the group that I am with at that moment. This double standard is a constant presence in my school, making it hard for Latinos to connect with the school and the adults that cohabit the space. Then teachers act mystified and completely absolve themselves from any responsibility when Latino students fail to complete high school. It isn't rocket science. If you feel adults in the school don't like you or don't think highly of you, then you probably won't want to do well in that class. For this research project, we have read a plethora of journal articles and book chapters about how to improve the achievement of Latino students. Many of the theories in the research literature shed light on the plight of Latino youth and offer unique insights. I think the remedy for Latino underachievement is rooted in a simple, yet elusive concept: you have to care about your students—in and out of the classroom. You have to think positively about them and support them. As a result of my multiracialness, I have seen firsthand the differential treatment and disproportionate applications of care offered by teachers, based largely on the students' racial/ethnic identity. These contradictions, which are obvious to me and other youth of color, remain hidden to many white teachers.

FORCED TO CONFRONT MY *LATINIDAD*

While I often blend in with white students because of my light skin, as a result of my research I came face to face with teachers' negative perceptions of Latinos, and I, as you can imagine, took it personally. Examining survey data collected from teachers, administrators, and professional staff working with Latino students served as a wake-up call that more work needs to be done to create a teaching force that is well prepared and dedicated to working with Latino youth. The questions on the survey were designed to get teachers to share their thoughts on policies and practices at our school and their impact on Latinos. Even though they knew we would see the data when we analyzed the surveys, teachers nevertheless said some horrible things about Latino youth and families. One teacher wrote that Latino students fail more often than white students because they have "no fathers"! It seems as if teachers use stereotypes and decontextualized demographic data to absolve them from the responsibilities of teaching us well. I have not grown up with my father. However, that does not mean I am not going to graduate or that teachers should teach me less. I also have a very supportive extended family, including wonderful grandparents who are active in my life. Many of my white friends also live in single-parent households, but teachers don't think negatively about them or assume that half of them won't graduate because their fathers don't live at home with them. Teachers need to reevaluate their notions of "traditional" family structures. A recent report suggests that 40 percent of children born in the United States in 2007 were born to an unmarried mother (Hamilton, Martin, and Ventura, 2009). Therefore, it is not necessarily the norm anymore to have a two-parent household. Students' family structure should not result in a predetermined academic fate.

There were so many negative responses on the survey that I can't include them all here. Suffice it to say that many of the teachers were cruel and insensitive, and some were outright racist. These negative perceptions of Latino students at my school, the majority of whom are Puerto Rican, undoubtedly influence teachers' interactions with us and affects the quality of education we are offered. Conversely, because they are white and have positive assumptions about their own group, they consciously or unconsciously create supportive environments for them. In her seminal work on the second-largest group of Latinos in the United States, Sonia Nieto (2000) noted that where Puerto Rican students have been attending U.S. schools in large numbers, they have been labeled as "problems," "losers," and "at risk." The education of Puerto Rican students, she asserted, has been characterized by linguicism, or discrimination based on language. Drawing from our collective research, I argue that the struggles of Latino students to succeed in school stem, at least partially, from teachers' depressed expectations that are generated largely from stereotypes.

Being a multiracial/multiethnic Latina isn't completely negative. I have rich histories and cultures with which I identify and that are a source of great pride. I only wish that teachers would see my cultural identities as strengths and not as weaknesses or deficiencies. Being a teenager and figuring out who you are and what you want to be is hard enough. Oversimplified notions of identity and racial discrimination don't make my road to adulthood any easier.

LATINOS AS A MULTIRACIAL PEOPLE

I have spent much of this chapter addressing my multiracial/multiethnic identity. For the most part, this chapter has been very personal, but it is also important to explore the multiracial/multiethnic histories of Latinos as a group. As a Puerto Rican, I can trace my roots back to Africans, the Spanish, and indigenous peoples. The island of Puerto Rico was originally inhabited by the Taínos, who are believed to be related to the Arawak peoples of pre-Columbian South America. The Spaniards then colonized the island, beginning in 1493. Eventually they brought enslaved Africans to Puerto Rico, building a culture founded on mixed-race identities (González, 1993). Being multiracial is not new to Latinos. Historically, words like *mestizo* have been used to describe the multiracialness of this community. Latinos are diverse, with all different types of skin tones, facial features, and hair textures, not only across Latino groups (such as Mexicans and Puerto Ricans) but within groups and even within our own families. However, being multiracial in the U.S. mainland context is not as common or at least not treated in the same ways.

In addition, we all have different experiences that shape our identities. As I noted earlier, I get treated differently based on how people identify my physical appearance (specifically my skin color) and based on the perceptions of the group I am spending time with at that moment. Identity is difficult to describe at times, but one thing that teachers need to know is that my identity is not a problem or a defect. I can be and am more than one thing. This concept, although accepted throughout much of Latin America and among many in Latino communities in the United States, is not highly regarded in my school or in U.S. society at large.

I have my own ideas about multiracialness stemming largely from my experiences, but it is important to compare my emic perspectives with others' descriptions of what it means to be multiracial. The research literature and popular media are replete with negative portrayals of multiracial youth and families. A study published by the Center for the Study of Biracial Children (2006) challenges the pervasive myth of biracial children or foster/adopted children as victims who suffer identity confusion because they want to fit into one category. Similar myths, such as the claim that biologically mixing races produces children who are mentally and physically weak, are hurtful and inaccurate. To me, these myths sound ridiculous and archaic; however, many people operate from these popular assumptions. For example, in 2009, Louisiana justice of the peace Keith Bardwell refused to marry interracial couples, claiming, "I don't do interracial marriages because I don't want to put children in a situation they didn't bring on themselves. In my heart, I feel the children will later suffer" (Misra, 2009).

Those that agree with the position that multiracial/multiethnic kids are doomed are basically suggesting that kids like me are destined to live in a state of confusion. These overly deterministic myths are hurtful and false. In reality, biological "hybrids" are often stronger than a single race or single species. Hybridity is valued in scientific circles, but I don't think it is beyond that. All children should be loved and supported, regardless of what racial/cultural group or groups they belong to.

If you look at popular media like television, you could conclude that multiracial people don't exist or are a really small percentage of the population. There are only a handful of television shows that focus on characters or people who are mixed race. Most shows have all-white, all-Hispanic, or all-black casts, particularly if the show revolves around one family. The real world is not as homogeneous as the popular media portrays it. Many families are multiracial, multiethnic, and multilingual. Rarely will you see such families depicted on television or in the media in general. Ironically, I can think of more shows that *used* to be on television that centered on multiracial families than are on the air presently. Although they were not perfect depictions and were controversial in their own right, shows like *I Love Lucy* and *The Jeffersons* portrayed interracial couples and families. Through informal interviews I conducted for this project, I learned about shows from the 1980s like *Diff'rent Strokes,* which focused on a single-parent family with adoptive children of a different race than the parent. Today, I can only think of maybe one show that focuses on a multiracial couple or family. That doesn't make sense to me because the shows that I just discussed were all on before I was born! I know there were interracial couples and multiracial kids back then, but statistically there are more of us out there now. Yet multiracial people continue to be seriously underrepresented in the popular media, and counternarratives in the media debunking the myths that haunt multiracial youth are even more rare. For example, when movies depict multiracial people, the plot is always about the couple or family being interracial. Rarely do you see an American movie featuring a mixed-race couple or family with a plot about something else. Given the demographics of the United States, this underrepresentation is perplexing.

Being multiracial means not having to choose one identity or another. It means being a part of different groups but also being something special and unique. Unfortunately, as I have noted throughout this chapter, schools don't really operate this way. It seems like teachers and school personnel are more comfortable with establishing discrete categories for every student. And it's not just teachers; even some standardized tests we take and college applications we have completed require students to "check a box" to identify their race and/or ethnicity. Some college applications allow you to check more than one initially, but then you still have to choose one to tell them how you would like to be identified in their records. Whenever I have to fill in information about myself, I see the five or six boxes that say white, Hispanic, black/African American, Native American, and so on, and I want to check almost all of them because all of those descriptions make up who I am. However, because I don't want to pick one ethnicity over the other, I always choose the "Other" box. Having to choose "Other" makes me mad because I should be able to choose more than one. I know I'm not the only person who identifies with more than one race or ethnicity. There have been people like me forever. It is 2010, and I still can't list all of my identities on a test or on school forms. I don't think that schools, tests, or job applications, should require me to change or suppress parts of my identity.

A MULTIRACIAL/MULTIETHNIC LATINA ADOLESCENT STRUGGLES TO FIT IN: WHAT YOU NEED TO KNOW

In what follows, I continue my discussion of identity and how it is hard for students like me to "fit in." I also try to use vivid examples that can help teachers understand what kids like me deal with everyday and what they can do to support us. People who are multiracial may have trouble fitting in because of rigid and narrow identity categories created by schools and often implemented by teachers and sometimes by students. For me, it is like I am multiracial/multiethnic and at the same time don't have a racial/ethnic identity. I consider myself Latina but I don't speak Spanish, which makes it hard to connect with some Latinos who may see me as "less Latino" because I do not speak Spanish fluently. I am proud of my Latina identity, but I sometimes am ashamed that I don't speak Spanish. As part of my work with Project FUERTE, we presented at several conferences. I was responsible for presenting the literature review slides, sharing data we culled from the research literature we read and analyzed. I was scared to refer to some of the authors because I thought that I didn't sound right articulating names like Cammarota, Nieto, Valenzuela, and Flores-González. I had to work hard at pronouncing them in Spanish and not Anglicizing them.

Through my work on the research project, I feel that all of my identities are affirmed and I don't have to hide being Puerto Rican, black, and white. In my other classes, I tend to connect more with my white identity. And why wouldn't I? Most of my teachers are white, we learn about white people, and although not explicitly said, white is understood as "the norm." To assert an identity as a Latina would, in a very practical sense, be inviting teachers to view me through deficit perspectives. In this project, I feel like I can connect more with my Latina self and also my African American self, because we focus on the historical and current contributions and struggles of people of color. Race and identity are typically topics that people try to avoid talking about, especially white people, who often view themselves as raceless or colorless (Pollock, 2003). This project also created a space for me to openly discuss issues of race and ethnicity and the ways in which these variables shape students' access to education. Participating in these discussions was liberating; I felt a sense of freedom that I had never experienced in school. We spent a significant amount of time exploring our own ethnic/racial and other identities, supporting each other as we each uniquely developed a stronger, more confident sense of self. During one of our first class meetings for the research project, we spent the entire time talking about the array of identities students perform over the course of one day. We were given five pieces of paper, each a different color. On each paper we wrote down different aspects of our identity, such as name, gender, ethnicity, religion, and anything else we wanted the other people to know about us. As the activity progressed, we had to discard the sheets of paper one at a time and metaphorically relinquish that aspect of our identity. It was really difficult, to pick and choose which identities we would shed, and at times I wanted to quit participating in the activity. As we processed the exercise as a group, I realized that the activity mirrored what Latino students, and others whose identities are marginalized, must endure every day when they come to school. We are literally forced to suppress important parts of ourselves to conform to the culture of the institution established largely by adults. The identity characteristics most valued in my school are those that are most congruent with the cultural identities of the majority of teachers and administrators.

Language is an important part of identity, yet students, especially students of color, who enjoy communicating using a variety of languages and language forms, are often forced to choose between communicating solely using Standard English, remaining silent, or being targeted for communicating in another language. Generally, school policies do not support multilingualism (see Chapter 7). This is especially true for Latino students who speak Spanish. Studies show that students who come to school speaking German or Chinese do not seem to be targeted by teachers in the same ways Latino Spanish speakers are (Zentella, 1997). It is as if those languages—and consequently, those identities—are more accepted by schools than Spanish. Ana Zentella's (1997) assertions regarding the disparate treatment of linguistic communities are visible in my school. We have some German exchange students attending our school this year. I have observed that when they start speaking German in class, teachers will enthusiastically support their language practices, saying, "Oh, that is so cool!" or "How would you say this in German?" For some reason, many of my teachers don't think bilingualism is cool when Latino students speak Spanish. I think the differential treatment of German- and Spanish-speaking students has a lot to do with race, with Germans being predominantly white and most Spanish speakers being identified as people of color.

Schools that aren't used to having many students who speak multiple languages ask, "What do we do with these kids?" I feel like this question is also asked about me sometimes because I don't neatly fit into the typical "white student mold" either. Even though I am a monolingual English speaker, I still have other identities that show through in different contexts. In this way, I can understand how my bilingual friends and colleagues feel when they are forced to be monolingual at school. It is similar to me feeling pressured by teachers to choose one identity over another.

Life experience shapes personal identities as well. For example, two people who have the same identity will have different experiences throughout life that influence them in unique ways. No two people are exactly the same, even if they share an ethnic identity. If children do not live with a parent of a particular race, they might not be exposed to that culture at home every day, but they may still feel connected to it. I think good teachers value who you are and the different identities you bring to class. Many teachers seem to understand diversity among white students but don't extend this framework to students of color. If you were to say to teachers, "Aren't all white kids the same?" they would probably laugh at you. They would tell you about how white students come from different types of families with different traditions and values and how there is great individuality and variety among them. They would say that some white students are Italian, Irish, French-Canadian, or Polish, and many are a mix of all or some of those different ethnic groups. Based on our data, we found that the dominant perception of Latino students is rigid, negative, and narrow—that they are disrespectful kids who are apathetic about education. That is ridiculous! Of course, Latinos, just like white students and teachers, come from many different ethnicities. Latinos can be Puerto Rican, Mexican, Dominican, Cuban, Central American, and so on, and, of course, several of them at once. The same goes for black students. They can be African American but also Haitian, Bahamian, Jamaican, West Indian, or any combination of these (and other) identities. But many teachers see all of them as African American and assume that they are all the same with similar histories and cultural practices. Many white teachers I have encountered are somehow able to understand that they themselves can be many things at once and still be individuals, but they are often unable to see the individual differences and diversity among and between Latino and African American students. Furthermore, Latino and African American students are often lumped together, which further blurs the individualities and unique characteristics we have.

Teachers' shortsighted conceptions of identity are challenged and complicated by multiracial students like me. I identify with three different racial/ethnic groups, and within each of those identities lie several cultures and blends of cultures. Many teachers have preconceived images of students' potential, based largely on the racial identities ascribed to them. Generally speaking, white students are perceived by teachers as rule-followers, as polite, good students who are college-bound. The perception is that black and Latino students, in contrast, skip classes and talk back. In response to the open-ended question on the survey, one of my teachers commented that Latino students "are very rude and disrespectful." If their perceptions of each group are so rigid, how do I get positioned in this racialized framework? If I get good grades, does that make me a white student? If I skip a class, does that make me a Latina? If I talk back to a teacher, does it mean that I am black that day? Teachers often claim that they don't "see color" when it comes to their students (Irvine, 2003; Sleeter, 2001; Howard, 1999), but clearly that is not the case.

The majority of teachers, like the majority of students, grow up in and live in segregated communities and attend segregated schools (Orfield, 2001; Kozol, 2005). Therefore, they may have limited exposure to people of color, including multiracial people. Because of a lack of experience with culturally diverse communities, teachers sometimes make assumptions when they hear Spanish accents or see a student who "looks Latino" (as if all Latinos look the same). Similarly, someone could look at me and say, "She doesn't look or sound Latina" and deny me the right to claim certain identities. It should be my decision to identify in ways that feel authentic and comfortable to me.

MULTIRACIAL STUDENTS AND THE CURRICULUM

Multiracial students are also ignored in the curriculum. Teachers rarely select books that aren't prescribed by the district frameworks, so we don't get assigned literature from multiracial authors or that has multiracial protagonists as part of our schooling experience. We are all created equal, or so the Constitution says, but being created equal doesn't translate into equal or even proportionate representation in the curriculum. When students of color see themselves represented in the curriculum, it is often tokenistic. We have Black History Month in February and Hispanic Heritage Month from September 15 to October 15. Despite the fact that 50 percent of the students at my school are Latino, nothing significant is done to celebrate or even acknowledge this month. The mere fact that learning about black or

Hispanic history is restricted to certain months clearly demonstrates that schools do not value diversity in the curriculum. Furthermore, these events have the potential to further alienate biracial or multiracial students because they single out certain groups and don't support an in-depth conversation about diverse groups and how individuals might identify with multiple cultural communities. The single-month focus on ethnic studies, while valuable for providing minimal exposure to culture and cultural differences, also excludes and marginalizes multiracial people. Without question, the most famous biracial person in the world right now is President Barack Obama. Clearly he has made and will continue to make significant contributions to the United States and the world during his administration and after he finishes his time in office. The fact that we have a biracial president will open the door for more teachers and school staff as well as textbook authors and publishers to think more critically about the multiracial individuals and groups that have been previously omitted from the dominant narrative of U.S. history. Although he is most often raced as a black man, President Obama not only reminds the public about the existence of multiracial people in the world but shows that we can be and do anything. Having a multiracial president has been co-opted by some who suggest that his rising to the highest political office in the country signals the end of racism and the emergence of a postracial society in the United States. Despite the potential benefits a multiracial president may have for race relations, racism is still alive and well in the country and manifested daily in schools.

RECOMMENDATIONS FOR TEACHERS

If teachers, principals, or other school staff members want to better serve multiracial/multiethnic Latino students, they need to first recognize these students and try to learn more about them. Each person is unique, and the only way to really learn more about students is to be open to learning from them. We are the experts on our lives. Educators need to take every opportunity to connect with students of diverse backgrounds and develop relationships with youth that allow teachers to learn from their expertise. In addition to increasing exposure to and knowledge of Latinos and other students of color, teachers need to reflect on their own biases regarding multiracial/ multiethnic individuals. When race and racism remain unexamined by teachers, they will undoubtedly bring their prejudices into their classrooms. With all that teachers are asked to do, this may seem like a difficult task. Nonetheless, understanding the pervasiveness of racism and how it shapes their lives and those of their students is crucial for teachers.

Multiracial students often speak a variety of languages and language forms. Language, as noted in several chapters of this book, is part of identity. My second recommendation to teachers and future teachers is to learn to speak and/or support the use of languages other than Standard English. Teachers need to be able to connect with kids, and verbal communication is a central aspect of teaching. Teachers talk to us all the time, but the communication is usually one-way. Students need to communicate with teachers too, and for the most part we do this in the language or language form that is most comfortable for them. We should have space to communicate in languages that feel comfortable to us too, whatever they may be.

The goal of becoming lifelong learners, a mantra extolled to students throughout their schooling experiences, should also be applied to our teachers. Teachers should not only learn about the subjects they teach but also about us as people. Assignments like developing case studies of Latino students would be helpful for students learning to be teachers because it would help them learn more about their future students and allow teachers to connect with students more easily. Colleges should prepare teachers to better differentiate their teaching style to more effectively serve students with all different types of learning styles. Teachers should also be prepared to work individually with students in order to support their success. These recommendations have the potential to inform the practice of educators, making schools more culturally responsive for students who have historically been marginalized there.

FINAL THOUGHTS

Overall, this chapter is meant to help teachers better understand multiracial students. I never thought I had any knowledge from which teachers could benefit. I have come to realize that because examples of white teachers connecting with students of color on a genuine level are not abundant, it is imperative that teachers learn from students like us to inform their work in schools. More teachers need to come to understand the meaning we ascribe to our identities and how they position us as we strive to reach our academic and personal goals. My coresearchers and I assert that our identities are more fluid than teachers often perceive and are manifested in a variety of ways, depending on the context. I cannot separate my identities and just be white, Latina, or black at school. I can't be just one race. I am all those things and all at the same time, all the time. Teachers need to see the world, and their students more specifically, from this inclusive, multicultural perspective. They need to resist the temptation to put students into a rigid single category or ignore their identities altogether. They also need to resist the temptation to "dumb down" the curriculum (Cammarota and Romero, 2006) for students who may not share their racial/ethnic or socioeconomic backgrounds. Being a multiracial/multiethnic Latina has given me a unique perspective on the world. I have experienced the range of discrimination and affirmation and the cold shoulder of isolation. While the majority of the nation has embraced the concept of a multiracial president, kids like me are waiting for that spirit of approval to trickle down into our classrooms.

PART 3

QUIEN SIEMBRA VIENTOS, RECOGE TEMPESTADES

POLICIES AND PRACTICES AFFECTING LATINO EDUCATION

⤸

The contributions to Part 3 address several of the policies and practices affecting Latino education. Judging by most educational indicators, including standardized test scores, high school completion, and college attendance rates, Latino students are not being served well by schools. Given the shifting cultural contexts in which teachers work, new strategies are necessary to improve the educational experiences and outcomes for Latino youth. If, as educators, we continue to do the same things that are already not working in the best interests of students, then we should continue to expect negative outcomes. To follow the same road and expect to arrive at a different destination is unrealistic and potentially dangerous.

As demonstrated by the chapters included in Part 3, students face structural inequality in schools that manifests itself in a variety of ways, including the racialized aspects of academic tracking, bias in the application of school discipline policies, and restrictive language policies that stifle students' voices and limit their linguistic expression. The student-researchers suggest that these policies, not depressed aspirations, are responsible for elevated dropout/pushout rates among Latinos. They suggest, paraphrasing the refran included in the title of this section, that if educators continue to sow the wind, they will reap whirlwinds.

THE "LANGUAGE POLICE"
TEACHERS' RESPONSES TO DIVERSE LANGUAGE PRACTICES
with Kristina Nieves, Undergraduate Student

As a Latina high school senior, I rank in the top ten of my class based on my grades and have above-average SAT scores.[1] Many would assume that I have it made, that school has been this wonderful place that was good for my development as a student and a person. In some ways it was. I encountered many positive teachers and other school officials throughout my education, especially in middle and high school. However, it was always difficult for me to feel completely whole as a student in school. I grew up in a house where we spoke Spanish most often, although my parents, my brother, and I are all fluent English speakers as well. Living in a community with a large Latino population, I got used to hearing Spanish in the streets, in church, at the *bodega,* and echoing out of the speakers of cars that drive down the street. It is the language of my home, the language of my community.

As with any language, Spanish takes on a different form depending on who is speaking it, to whom, and for what purpose. Young people have been shaping language throughout history and engaging highly contextualized language practices. For the most part, young people don't walk around sounding like William Shakespeare when interacting with friends. Rather, they mold the language to suit their needs. People put their own stamp on language. I think this is evident in the development and practice of African American Language (AAL), where members of the African American community and others who are connected with that culture have reshaped and reconstituted English, creating their own language with its own rules and structure (Paris, 2009). Similarly for Spanish speakers and speakers of other languages, we speak varying forms of the "mother tongue." Schools have been slow to respond to our linguistic needs as multilingual students. Instead of supporting our various uses of language, most teachers do all they can, at least in my experience and research, to silence us or make us conform to the language standards that they have established. To be absolutely clear, I think that students should learn and be fluent in Standard English. Whether we agree or not, it is the language that dominates in the United States and is an important mode of communication. You need a solid command of Standard English to do well in school, pass standardized tests, and be able to successfully interview for most jobs. However, I don't think that students should have to operate *in* Standard English—or formal Spanish for that matter—100 percent of their time in school. This chapter draws from research regarding the intersections of language and identity, including my own original research conducted as a student-researcher in Project FUERTE, to demonstrate how teachers, who think they are doing students a favor by constantly correcting them, are actually marginalizing us and alienating us from them and from school in general.

HERE COME THE "LANGUAGE POLICE"

Whether students realize it or not, during their time in school they are forced to present certain identities and attitudes deemed acceptable in classroom settings. The norms dictating what is acceptable are created almost completely without student input, reflecting the values of teachers, the majority of whom are monolingual speakers of English. Although exploring which language practices are affirmed in classrooms is an important issue to study, I will concede that students need to present certain "school kid" (Antrop-González, Vélez, and Garrett, 2005; Flores-González, 2002) identities when in the classroom. We are socialized to see knowledge as coming from teachers, which gives them a certain position of power. They control what will and will not be acceptable within their walls for the amount of time that you spend there. Rarely are these norms co-constructed by teachers and students. Performing identities that conform to teachers' standards, with no space to use other languages and language forms with which you identify, can be exhausting. I have observed that many urban youth of color, including myself, enact different identities in the hallways and what I refer to as "non-sanctioned" spaces of the school. In these spaces people's identities change. They are no longer just students. They are friends, neighbors, teammates, or partners. Students play a variety of roles and choose to make visible certain identities depending on the situation and the people that surround them. This notion of identity can be applied to teachers and others as well. I would argue that educators' identity performances in school are often closer to their identities outside this setting, whereas a young person from a multilingual urban community makes a more drastic shift between her identity performance in her home or neighborhood and that in her school. I have found that students cannot truly speak the way they normally would in the community, even in nonsanctioned zones like the cafeteria or the hallway, because of imbalances in power that exist in most schools, especially those serving large percentages of students of color and poor students.

On the one hand, the rules are pretty clear in the classroom; for better or for worse, teachers make the rules regarding how the class is going to function. They decide which languages and language forms are most acceptable in that space. On the other hand, the rules governing spaces within the school but outside the classroom are more opaque. In these spaces young people come together and want some freedom from the constraints of the classroom. We spend most of our day within the walls of the school. There we start to develop as individuals in a controlled setting under constant surveillance by adults who are largely unfamiliar with the linguistic preferences and cultural norms of communities of color. What I am advocating for is a way for students to be able to express themselves in whichever languages they wish without having to constantly look over their shoulders and monitor what they say. I am not saying we should be able to act crazy, but I am saying that students, and especially multilingual students (broadly defined), should have spaces in the school where they can express themselves in ways that feel normal and authentic to them. Most high schools require students to study a world language as a requirement for graduation. Although many schools appreciate the value of world language classes, the lessons learned within those spaces are often left at the door. Students are allowed to learn and practice a language other than English, but only within the walls of that certain classroom and within acceptable parameters established by teachers. In fact, most world language teachers prefer that English not be spoken during class time, as a way to immerse the students in the language of study. Once we cross the threshold out into the hallway, we are no longer allowed to use the knowledge we have just gained because teachers who are not affiliated with the world language program and who may not be bilingual fear what they do not understand. What might schools look like if teachers were willing give up some of their power in the classroom and allow students to inform the development and implementation of the rules that shape which languages get spoken and when? We are a long way from the egalitarian classrooms I envision; however, in the present the hallways and cafeteria of the school, as nonsanctioned zones, have the potential to offer students some breathing room, space to perform their identities in ways that make sense to them, even if teachers may not fully understand them.

I undertook this project as a way of exploring the shifts in language and identity that I see happen every day in the nonsanctioned zones of my school and the roles that teachers can and do play in governing these spaces. Through my twelve years of schooling and my research over these past few years as an undergraduate student, I have come to the conclusion that school is like a game. It has certain rules that regulate how you play, and there is an expectation that students will play by the rules. If you don't like the game of school, however, you can't just put it in the closet like a game you purchased at a store. You are forced to play if you want to have a real chance at a good career. In addition, in most games the players police themselves. In other words, we enforce the rules or, in some cases, agree to change them if they don't work for us. In schools, the classroom teacher, who is most often a monolingual speaker of standard English, sets the rules that govern the classroom, and if we choose not to play by the rules, there are serious consequences that can have an adverse impact on our futures. I am writing this chapter to "call out" the "language police," those teachers that create rigid rules around language, determining what counts as valuable linguistic expression and enforcing their rules at any expense, including pushing multilingual students out of school. Being multilingual and having the ability to communicate with variety of people using their preferred modes of communication are skills that should be nurtured, not demonized. I hope that after reading this chapter, teachers will have a more positive view of multilingualism in all its forms and work with students to transform schools into places where students can be whole, where we can learn the conventions of Standard English and still speak using the language conventions of our home communities.

A HIGH SCHOOL STUDENT EXPLORES LANGUAGE AND LITERACY

The way people talk to their parents differs from the way that they communicate with their best friends. I know that I have to use a particular type of language when on the phone with a potential employer or when I meet a college admissions counselor. As you can imagine, your behavior would be different when you are at a fast food restaurant with friends than it would be if you were dining at a fancy restaurant for an awards ceremony. An individual's entire demeanor changes depending on the setting, and one of the ways that this shift in behavior is made visible is through language. For example, I am Puerto Rican, born and raised in the northeastern United States, and when I am speaking with my family, I most often communicate in a language form known as Spanglish, a blending of the two languages, Spanish and English. When I am speaking with my friends I use English, but not what is accepted as proper by "school agents," people who hold a position of power in schools. When I am talking to my teachers the type of discourse—a term I learned after reading the work of James Gee (2005)—I use is completely different. During interactions with teachers, I verbally enact the role of student as they have defined it, using the linguistic codes that are valued in that particular setting. In short, the language(s) people use are based largely on context.

What a teacher sees as unacceptable language can be perfectly appropriate and commonplace to the people who are actually having the conversation. Again, I think that African American Language (Paris, 2009) provides another clear example. Speakers of AAL, rarely, if ever, use the possessive form of the noun. So, instead of saying, "We are going to my brother's house," they may say, "We goin' to my brother house." That doesn't mean they don't know how to use the possessive form. They are following the rules of the language they are speaking. They just aren't speaking Standard English. Teachers go crazy when they hear these things because they are unfamiliar with and/or don't value the conventions of AAL, and I am certain that race and racism play a large role in that appraisal. In my experience, teachers absolutely flip out on students who speak AAL, going as far as to say they sound "ignorant." Similar, yet not as well researched, are teachers' reactions to Spanglish and other hybrid forms of Spanish. Although Spanglish is often frowned upon by teachers, a growing body of research touts its potential benefits. The work of Ramón Martínez, for example, highlights the potential of Spanglish to serve as a pedagogical resource to assist students in identifying, building upon, and extending the linguistic skills that they utilize every day as they develop and refine their academic literacy (Martínez, 2010).

When school agents ignore the value of our language practices and critique these discourses, they make us feel marginalized and pushed to the periphery. They make school a harsh place where we are constantly reminded that who we are and how we express ourselves are not valued. I would go so far as to say that most teachers want us to be like them; they want us to act and sound white. Education for many Latinos in U.S. schools can be viewed as an extension of colonialism (Irizarry and Antrop-González, 2007) in which students are pressured to shed aspects of their cultural identity in favor of those of the dominant group. As a result, many students refuse to play that game (or they play reluctantly) and are alienated or pushed out of school. I don't think most teachers understand the impact of their actions. I have a positive view of teachers and believe that most probably want the best for their students. The problem is that they think their language and their identities are the best, and they subsequently view assimilation and the shedding of Latino identities, as the gold standard. Of course, I want to do well in life, and I know I need to learn things from teachers to be successful and achieve my professional goals. But teachers need to realize that many of us take great pride in our cultural and linguistic identities and shouldn't be forced to choose between maintaining a healthy sense of self and success in school. If teachers really want multilingual students of color to succeed, they cannot continue to make us feel like some of the languages we speak are "wrong" or pathological.

Language, as I have demonstrated through the examples above, is inextricably linked to our identities as people. It offers a glimpse into the mind and soul of another individual. When teachers constantly remind you that your language is wrong and not valued, they are basically saying that your culture and identity are worthless outside of your home. These messages, sometimes subtle but often overt, also clearly convey to students that the identities teachers model through their language use are, conversely, more valuable. I believe that most students of color in urban schools, including Latino students, are multilingual, speaking different languages and language forms depending on the context. Despite what many teachers may believe, most Latino youth and other students of color are skilled at "code-switching" (Sankoff and Poplack, 1981); we make deliberate decisions about language use and are aware of the language forms called for in particular contexts. I understand that issues of power in schools are difficult to negotiate, but we are imploring teachers to value the cultural and linguistic identities of students of color. If teachers continue to suppress the languages of youth, they will continue to push many of us out of school.

THE CREATION OF A "HALLWAY ETHNOGRAPHY"

I have always been interested in issues of language. As far back as I can remember, I have loved to hear different languages spoken around me. As I walked the streets of my community as a child, I heard a variety of languages, and I always tried to figure out what people were saying by listening for roots of words that I understood. My love of language has even pushed me to consider becoming a world language teacher. When I began school, however, I learned quickly not to display my love for language and language forms by speaking them in front of teachers. First, I have experienced an anti-Spanish feeling from teachers and other school agents in many classrooms. I am not sure exactly where it comes from—perhaps it is a vestige of colonialism—but it is clear that Spanish is not valued as much as English in this country, even though the United States has the second-largest Spanish-speaking population in the world. Students come from other countries or are born into families in the United States in which Spanish is the primary language, and when they get to school, the school does everything it can to get them to learn English as quickly as possible, rarely offering support for the maintenance and continued development of their native language. The sad part is that schools spend money on trying to teach students a world language—most often Spanish—once they get to high school, yet they overlook the linguistic richness that already exists among Latinos and fail to help students develop into balanced bilinguals.

When I entered high school I was asked to select a language in addition to English to study. My options were Spanish, French, and Chinese. I chose Spanish because, even though I was already fluent in the language, I wanted to strengthen my skills in reading and writing so that I could really call myself bilingual. Once I had made my decision, the head of the foreign language department in my high school came to talk to me and asked me to pick a different language. When I asked why, he said it was because I was already proficient in the language. It took two meetings with my parents, the principal of my high school, and the high school Spanish teachers to finally come to a reasonable conclusion. I was allowed to study Spanish to meet the school's foreign language requirement as long as I skipped ahead a year in the program. So as a freshman I was taking a more advanced Spanish course with sophomores. When students speak a language other than English as their primary language, schools try to erase that language from kids' linguistic repertoires, most often refusing to provide support for the continued development of that language.

I realize that because I am a Latina who speaks English without an accent, teachers treat me differently, in fact better, than they treat many of my Spanish-speaking friends. In this sense, I am kind of like a chameleon. I can change my "color," or how I appear to others, depending on the setting. Although it definitely hurts at times, I can play the game and present myself using the languages and subsequent identities that teachers value. Many of my friends either cannot (because of accents or a limited, yet burgeoning proficiency in English) or choose not to relinquish or hide these important parts of their identities. For many of them, it hurts too much to always present themselves in school in ways that make the teachers and staff members feel comfortable but create discomfort for themselves. These understandings about language and context, which came from my personal experiences and those of my friends, were confirmed by reading the work of language researchers like Geneva Smitherman (1977), Bertha Peréz (1998), and Django Paris (2009). Exploring the intersections of my life and the research of these scholars motivated me to create a study of how teachers police the language practices of students in nonsanctioned zones so that I could explore the impact of these constant racial microaggressions (Solórzano, 2001) on students. The questions that guided my study were: in what ways do school agents suppress the different identities of students by limiting the discourses they are involved in outside the classroom? And what is the impact of teachers' suppression of language on student engagement in schools? The low graduation rates for Latino students and other students of color suggest that schools must address these questions if they are serious about "leaving no child behind."

Methods

To be able to answer these research questions, I observed the inter-actions of teachers and students in various nonsanctioned spaces and conducted follow-up interviews with the targeted students to learn more about how students felt after their interactions with teachers playing the role of the language police. Using the qualitative research skills I learned in the Action Research and Social Change class, I developed what I call a "hallway ethnography," a study of student-teacher interactions during passing times between classes and during lunch periods. I became a participant-observer (Creswell, 1998) in that I was a student in the hallway or lunch room like any other student, interacting with friends and just moving from one place to another. But I was also systematically researching interactions in these settings. Any time I noticed an interaction between a teacher and student in which the teacher corrected a student's language, I recorded the observation in my notebook and made arrangements to interview the student shortly thereafter to learn more about the inci-dent and their perceptions of the interaction. Some of my follow-up interviews with students occurred in school, but most were conducted outside the walls of the institution, away from teachers. There were several reasons for continuing the conversation after school that day or before school the following day. The most significant reason was that during our conversations we would be using whatever language forms we felt most comfortable using, and I didn't want teachers who might hear us to critique us. In addition, I wanted to protect the students' privacy and allow them to speak freely, without hav-ing to worry about the content of our conversation getting back to teachers.

I spent approximately six months actively collecting data, although I never really stopped thinking about the project. I filled almost an entire notebook with my field notes, documenting my observations and data recorded during interviews. During my months of observation, I noticed a constant pressure exerted upon students by school agents—including teachers, school aides, administration, and even security guards—to change their language practices in the hallways and nonsanctioned zones of the school. Students were corrected for speaking Spanish in front of teachers who thought that students might be talking about them and should, therefore, speak only in English so the teacher could understand; they were also punished for cursing or using inappropriate language. I couldn't examine all these interactions, so I only focused on occasions where students were corrected for speaking languages other than Standard English. The cases in which students used foul language were, in my opinion, appropriate for teachers to target. My hallway ethnography shed light on how teachers place Standard English on a pedestal and put down the use of other languages in school. Because this was the first time I conducted formal research, I never felt 100 percent confident with the process, although my teacher, Dr. Irizarry, thought my idea and research design were "brilliant." So the whole time I was observing teacher-student interactions and conducting follow-up interviews, I tried to read anything I could that related to my study or that could help me better understand the language subordination I was observing.

WHO GETS TO SAY WHAT AND WHERE?

As I mentioned earlier in the chapter, I identify with several different language groups and feel comfortable using a variety of different languages and language forms, including English, Spanish, Spanglish, and AAL. In this project I was interested in learning more about how students use language and teachers' reactions to their diverse forms of communication. One study that shaped how I think about the intersections of language and power was conducted by Wendy Luttrell and Janie Ward (2004). In the article stemming from their research, Luttrell and Ward examine teachers' role in policing students in and out of the classroom, focusing on students' use of the N-word in school. Understandably, people have strong feelings about the N-word. I hear it used often by African American and Latino peers alike. The negative origins of the word are clear. It was (and still can be) a terrible word used to put down black people and other people of color. The N-word has historically been used by white people as a derogatory remark used to describe and position African-Americans as "subservient" or "subhuman." If you look at how several high-profile white people have used it recently, it is easy to argue that the N-word is still used as a derogatory term to reestablish the master-servant mentality and to maintain a racial hierarchy with whites at the top. Both Michael Edwards, the actor who played the character Kramer on the hit television show *Seinfeld,* and Duane "Dog" Chapman, the star of the reality show *Dog the Bounty Hunter,* went on racist rants using the N-word that were made public. More recently, Dr. Laura Schlessinger appeared to try to reclaim white people's right to use the N-word, yelling it multiple times over the airwaves of her national radio broadcast and justifying her use of the term by citing its use by some members of the African American community. These three vitriolic attacks underscore that language, and specifically the N-word, are powerful forces in reifying racialized power relations and supporting racism.

Many youth of color currently, conversely, use the N-word as a greeting and term of endearment. For some it is a marker of shared oppression based on race. Youth of color, I argue, have a common bond and have both experienced racialized discrimination in schools and society at large, so there is no position of power related to race to be held by any one of them over the other. I believe the word loses its entire derogatory connotation when used in this context. From a sociocultural perspective, words in and of themselves do not have meaning; they have the meaning we ascribe to them. I believe that youth of color have assigned a meaning to the term that is fundamentally different from that given to it by those who originally introduced the term. Whatever side of the "er" versus "a" debate you fall on, it is clear that many youth of color are using the term differently than it has been used in the past. Teachers hear it, and many feel that they have to do something. But how they respond can depend on where they hear it—the classroom or in what I call nonsanctioned zones. The most interesting finding from Luttrell and Ward's (2004) study was this: "Both teacher and students acknowledged a difference between classroom culture, which is regulated more actively by teacher and their values, and hallway culture, which they saw as influenced more by students" (Lutrell and Ward 2004, p. 4).

When urban youth of color use the N-word, or any other words for that matter, they are doing it to perform a certain identity. In this case, students of color may use the word to feel power over white people because, no matter what form of the word you refer to, the majority of youth of color agree that white people should not use the term at all. Limiting white people's use of the term represents an assertion of power among youth of color. In this example, youth of color have created a rule to police the language use of white people, whereas, in almost every other aspect of life in the United States, white people are policing the behavior of people of color. Either way, as young people, we are trying to figure out who we are, who we want to be, and how we are going to navigate that journey. As we figure it out, we use language to let people know something about us, to let them know who we project ourselves to be at that time. As James Gee states, "When 'little d' discourse (language-in-use) is melded integrally with non-language stuff to enact specific identities and activities then I say that 'big D' Discourses are involved" (Gee 2005, 7). "Little d" discourse, according to Gee, refers to the language that you are using at that particular moment in time. Discourse with a capital D takes linguistic context into account. Big D Discourse involves your body language, the way you dress, the language you use, the language you don't use, your surroundings, and many other things. In school, students enact different identities in different spaces through Discourse (Gee, 2005).

Communication is a very fragile and contextual thing. The messages individuals wish to convey through language may not necessarily equate with the meaning that others assign to their words. Take the game called "telephone," for example. A game we all played as children, it requires that participants stand in either a line or a circle and one person whispers a message into the ear of a person next to them. That person passes on the message to the following individual in line. By the time the message is relayed back to the original sender, it is very rarely exactly the same. This game demonstrates the fragility of communication. So when two students are having a conversation, a third party (i.e., a teacher) could misinterpret the entire situation and take action based on faulty data, or they might hear the conversation correctly but assign the words a meaning different than that which the speakers intended. Indeed, schools need to create rules to protect students and staff. However, the rules that govern language use are most often created by adults who are unfamiliar with the diverse Discourses of youth of color.

In addition, teachers and other school agents have not recognized how students have created mixed languages or speak languages not typically associated with their racial/ethnic group as a way to show solidarity and shared identity. A study by Django Paris (2009), which looks at the use of AAL by diverse youth groups, supports my point. In his study of the language practices of youth in multiethnic settings, he found that students of different backgrounds often speak using the linguistic features of African American Language, even if they are not African American. Paris's research highlights the potential of this cultural and linguistic sharing for improving interethnic relationships.

I have had my share of personal encounters with the power of the language police. Some teachers have such a narrow-minded view of language that they cannot accept any type of Discourse that does not fit their established schema. As I noted earlier, I took Spanish courses to fulfill my school's world language requirement. At the end of my junior year, I took the Advanced Placement test for Spanish and received a score of five, the highest grade possible. I know how to speak formal Spanish, but in more relaxed settings I tend not to. On one such occasion I was talking to a friend in the hallway of my school after Spanish class, and the teacher overheard me use the term "Estado Unido," as opposed to the more formal pronunciation of the Spanish term for the United States "Los Estados Unidos," referencing the way that I have heard it used in my community my entire life. Instead of appreciating my command for different types of Spanish or different pronunciations based on regional or cultural differences, the teacher used it as an opportunity to mock me, commenting in front of the other students, "Puerto Ricans are never hungry because they always eat the letter s," referring to how many Puerto Ricans don't pronounce the letter "s" at the end of words when speaking with other Puerto Ricans (see Zentella, 1997; García, Morín, and Rivera, 2001). Obviously, I know what the standard pronunciation is, and I know how to spell the term correctly. It was an off-handed comment by the teacher, but it was enough to get me thinking. In my estimation, the teacher did not value the personal expression of my identity as a Puerto Rican from an urban community on the mainland United States as manifested in my pronunciation of the phrase. Had this comment been made within the walls of the Spanish world language classroom, I might have been less upset about the entire situation. The teacher ignorantly chastised me and made a hurtful joke at my expense in a space where I thought I would be able to express myself a bit more freely. I was deliberately using language to enact my identity as a Puerto Rican by speaking as my family and many other Puerto Ricans speak. Having a teacher correct that constantly is a problem, and it makes students not want to connect with the course content because they believe they have to change in order to adapt to the more powerful forces (i.e., school agents and standards) in the system.

RECOMMENDATIONS FOR TEACHERS

Based on my research, I have developed a few recommendations for teachers and others who work in schools. Teachers do not realize that they are often stifling a student's methods of expressing themselves when they consistently monitor and correct their language use. An off-handed comment made to a student by a teacher in the hallway can profoundly affect the way that a student acts and performs in school. The student may feel that you are attacking a part of who they are. From my personal perspective, if you value who I am and the cultural assets I bring to the table, I am going to be more likely to want to learn what you have to teach me. Many teachers have developed such tunnel vision on "standard" types of language, whether English or Spanish, that it is difficult for them to modify their thinking to appreciate kids'· creativity or the cultural practices of students' different language communities.

Teachers need to be very careful about the way they talk to students in the hallway, just as much as students need to be careful about the way that they talk to teachers in the classroom. The findings from my hallway ethnography lead me to believe that most teachers always want to be in control. I understand that it must be difficult to be responsible for a group of twenty-five or more students at a time. Nevertheless, teachers need to create spaces that are conducive to students' holistic development. Especially when it comes to language, teachers need to be more sensitive. Language is a primary form of self-expression. The hallways, cafeteria, and other nonsanctioned zones should be more relaxed spaces that provide students with a short break between classes to reconnect with their friends and breathe again after a hard class. Instead of trying to control us by controlling our language practices and continuing the legacy of linguistic colonialism against Latino communities, teachers need to balance giving Latino students and other linguistically diverse students the space to express ourselves with keeping us safe.

In addition to sharing power with students and giving students space to express themselves, teachers need to develop an appreciation for different forms of language. Instead of viewing Standard English or formal Spanish as the only acceptable forms of language, teachers should allow students to use different types of language for different purposes. Because teachers stay in one role most of the day, they don't appreciate the need for us to shift identities. In school, we're expected to act in one way; it feels like they want us to internalize and imitate middle-class white norms. We are different, but "different" is not synonymous with "deficient." With the constant pressure to assimilate and be "less Latino," there are times in school where my heart aches to be Puerto Rican again. In other words, I want to feel good about myself, and it helps when I can connect with my friends using the languages that feel most comfortable to me.

Through my lengthy research on this subject, I have found that changes in teacher behavior can lead to improvements in academic engagement and achievement. If a teacher "gets off your back," you will be less likely to get defensive when they offer you feedback or share their opinions. Instead of getting upset at students for something they said, teachers should try to speak with students and understand how and why they are using language. Solely chastising students without understanding their intentions will do little to forge the relationships that are integral to fostering school success. Whenever possible, teachers should learn additional languages. People who speak multiple languages, in my opinion, are more comfortable and supportive of people using diverse languages around them.

Finally, teachers need to support diverse language use and diversity in general. What teachers must understand about language is that it varies within and across communities. These shifts or nuances should not be considered a "butchering of the language," as I heard one teacher chastise a student, but rather a form of self-expression and a connection to others who speak that language or language form. For example, Puerto Rican Spanish has a lot of American words mixed in because of the fact that the island is a U.S. territory and Puerto Ricans have had a long-standing presence in the United States. Does this mean that the Spanish spoken by people from other countries in Latin America or in Spain is any better or any worse than the Spanish spoken by Puerto Ricans? Members of my core group of friends are of Jamaican, Nigerian, and Irish descent. Our differences in culture also unite us. The United States of America is a country with a long history of linguistic diversity, and a multilingual present. As the racial/ethnic and linguistic texture of the country continues to deepen, we should celebrate cultural and linguistic diversity instead of trying to stifle it. The metaphors that describe the United States as a melting pot or tossed salad fall short. In a melting pot, everything comes out the same. Salads are typically covered in dressing, homogenizing the taste of the dish. The most appropriate metaphor to describe the United States is that of a mosaic where every person is encouraged to contribute his or her own unique piece to the larger picture. Language diversity is an essential characteristic of the fabric of this country and as such should be embraced in schools.

Schools have consistently served as a vehicle for assimilation. Teachers, administrators, and other school personnel have established a climate that often stifles cultural expression through language. Because many teachers were taught under these harsh conditions, they often teach how they were taught and reinforce the cycle of linguistic and cultural oppression. Introspection and dialogue are needed to break these habits that are so well entrenched in our educational system. If students had the space and freedom (see Torres-Guzmán, 2010) to use all the linguistic and cultural resources at their disposal, they would feel better about themselves and school and perform better academically.

Current reform efforts seem misguided. When students don't do well on standardized tests, teachers and principals look for quick fixes that fail to address relationships between teachers and students. I spent most of my time in elementary school filling out worksheets and completing writing prompts to prepare for the state exam. I never had a science or social studies class until I got to middle school. The only subjects we covered were math and language arts, which, not coincidentally, were the only two subjects on which we were tested by the state. One reason many urban youth, including Latinos, don't do well in school is because they are not allowed to speak the languages with which they feel most comfortable. Instead of narrowing the focus of the curriculum, schools need to expand it and expand approaches to teaching that engage students in conversation around important issues, building on our diverse linguistic and cultural repertoires. Speaking other languages and language forms didn't prevent me from doing well in school. Since I originally coauthored this essay, I have graduated at the top of my class, earned a scholarship to the University of Connecticut, and am off to a great start in my college career. Right now I am planning to be a high school guidance counselor, and I know that I will do all I can to create spaces for students to express themselves in school, spaces that didn't exist for me and most of my friends. When I return to my home school district to work as a counselor, I will work to create an environment that affirms students cultural and linguistic richness. I hope you will do the same in the settings in which you work as well.

6

MAKING DREAMS REALITY FOR UNDOCUMENTED LATINO STUDENTS

with Alberto Juarez, High School Student

⤲

Immigration has been a hot topic in the media and was a key issue in the 2008 presidential election. The discussion regarding immigration seems to be focused on stopping or limiting immigration from Latin America because of the alleged negative impact immigrants have on the economy. This issue is important to me for a variety of reasons. I immigrated to this country from Mexico with my family when I was seven years old. As an immigrant myself, I have strong feelings about immigration and would like to shed some light on the experiences of immigrant students in schools. This chapter is written to offer teachers emic perspectives on immigration and education that can result in a better understanding of the experiences of immigrant youth in schools. As of right now, many people (including many teachers) are against immigration and think that students like me should not be here in the United States. Certainly, teachers are entitled to believe whatever they want, but their feelings are manifested in the ways that they treat and teach immigrant students. The problem is even more severe for immigrant students who are undocumented, meaning that they do not have U.S. citizenship or the necessary documentation to live in this country legally.

As a student in a school that has a large Latino population, I have many friends who are undocumented. They do not have citizenship in this country even though they may have lived here for many years. Undocumented students are often made to feel invisible, meaning that they are not allowed to speak about their experiences in public for fear of being detained and/or deported. Drawing from some of my research as well as my personal experiences, this chapter explores the experiences of undocumented students and addresses teachers' expectations for this group.

A GLIMPSE INTO THE LIFE OF YOLANDA

To help frame the issue of immigrant education and, more specifically, the education of undocumented students, I begin with a story about Yolanda (a pseudonym), a friend of mine from school. Yolanda came to the United States with her family from Mexico when she was in the second grade. As you can imagine, when she arrived in the United States she spoke only Spanish and didn't know any English. Her family came here to look for work. In that way, her family's story is similar to the histories of millions of people in the United States who are the descendents of immigrants. It was hard for Yolanda to adjust to living and attending school in a new country, and she worked extremely hard to learn English as a second language. Sometimes when she was in school she didn't feel comfortable because she didn't know what the teacher was saying. She was often scared, not knowing if someone would be able to help her if something happened because she couldn't speak English. As an immigrant myself, I can relate to that feeling of uncertainty, not knowing if someone will care for you or help you if you need it. I am intimately familiar with the frustration that comes with trying to express yourself in a language that most of the adults in school don't understand. Yolanda is currently a junior in my high school, and she wants to go to college. However, because her family doesn't have a lot of money and she is undocumented, there are huge obstacles that impede her pathway into higher education.

There are a couple of aspects to Yolanda's story that I would like to point out to current and future teachers. First, Yolanda has a valuable skill that should be nurtured and lauded. She is bilingual, speaking both English and Spanish fluently. While she was in the process of learning English, she was often made to feel as if speaking Spanish was a punishable offense. "English here," her teachers would yell at her, positioning Spanish, as one of her teachers commented, as "the language of the streets." Despite attempts to strip her of her native language, Yolanda is bilingual and is an asset to her community. She is often called upon to help her neighbors by translating for them when they go to the doctor or to court. The community really appreciates her ability to speak multiple languages and willingness to be of service. Yolanda wants to be a teacher or an official court translator when she graduates from high school, but it will be hard for her because she is undocumented. There are so few bilingual teachers, and the need for people who can speak more than one language fluently is high. Yolanda could be helping more people and making a meaningful contribution to society by working as a teacher, but her opportunities are limited because of her immigration status. I think that is unfair, especially since the current composition of this country is largely due to immigration.

Second, it is important to mention that Yolanda did not make the choice to come to the United States. Like many immigrant children, she came here with her parents, who were looking for opportunities to improve their lives and support their family. It is not Yolanda's fault that she is here without the appropriate documents, but still she suffers the consequences. Since this country has a history of immigration (both sanctioned and unsanctioned), you would think that people would be more sensitive to the issue. Yolanda, in my opinion, is being treated unfairly. She just wants what everyone wants—a chance at the American Dream: an opportunity to go to college, learn, work, and be a productive person in this country.

Third, Yolanda has lived in this country for most of her life, yet she still doesn't have the rights of other people here. There should be pathways for someone like Yolanda, who has worked hard and is a good person, to become a citizen. Although she wasn't born here, she is, in many ways, American. She has lived here and has gone to school here for ten years. She should have the opportunity to better herself beyond high school. In this country, you need to attend college to have a chance of obtaining a good job and pursuing a career. Unfortunately, no matter how hard she works, her immigration status creates a serious impediment for her transition into higher education.

I know that some people will say she is here illegally and should not get any services or special help. My response is that whether you like it or not, she is here and she isn't planning on going back to Mexico. So how does the country benefit more—from someone who goes to college, gets a good education, has a good career providing a much-needed service, and pays taxes, or from a high school graduate with limited options for work? People have really short memories. Many of my teachers have parents, grandparents, or great grandparents who were immigrants, yet they ostracize students like Yolanda and take unyielding stances concerning immigration from Latin America. It is important to think more critically about how teachers might teach and treat undocumented students when they know that there are limited higher education and quality job opportunities for undocumented immigrant youth. Most of the time, people's feelings about immigration are derived from misinformation that they receive through propaganda. In the next section, I try to separate the fact from fiction by sharing interesting information about immigrants in the United States.

FACTS ABOUT UNDOCUMENTED IMMIGRANTS

The issue of undocumented students is important to me for several reasons. Because of the shifting demographics in this country and in my community more specifically, many of my friends are undocumented. In addition, many of the undocumented people in this country are Mexican, like me, and I want to try to do all I can to help them. Finally, I think it is imperative that we all have a more accurate understanding of issues confronting immigrant youth because of the impact immigrants will continue to have in shaping the future of this country. I am too young to vote, but writing this chapter offers me the opportunity to insert my voice into the conversation about this important and timely topic.

Critics of immigration to the United States cite an array of reasons to support their desire to deport undocumented immigrants and have the government effectively shut the border between the United States and Mexico. The dominant narrative trope suggests that undocumented immigrants are using the resources of U.S. citizens (such as welfare, Medicaid, and Temporary Assistance for Needy Families programs). The reality is that "most non-citizens are not even eligible for the majority of welfare programs unless they are legal permanent residents and have resided in the United States legally for at least five years" (Immigrant's Rights Project,

2008). Even though most undocumented immigrants work and put money back into the economy, they are not eligible for the benefits that most working citizens receive. In fact, "on average, immigrants generate public revenue that exceeds their public costs over time, approximately $80,000 more in taxes than they receive in state, federal and local benefits over their lifetimes" (Immigrant's Rights Project, 2008). The data suggest that undocumented immigrants are actually putting more into the system than they are extracting. Steeped in xenophobia and racism, the "money argument" against undocumented immigration is weak.

Another oft-cited myth is that undocumented immigrants don't actually want to become citizens. In order to become a citizen, a person must have been living in the U.S. for five years, have been in good moral standing, have a good knowledge of U.S. history and civics, learn to speak and write English, and pay a fee for naturalization. However, this long, costly process makes it hard for many lower-income undocumented residents to apply for citizenship. The fee to become a citizen increased by 69 percent in 2007, from $400 to $675 (Immigrant's Rights Project, 2008). Most undocumented people I know would love to become citizens of the United States and shed the stigma and exploitation that comes with being undocumented, but there is an anti-immigrant fervor that discourages people like Yolanda from sharing her status with others and beginning the process of becoming a citizen. In addition, for many people I know the cost associated with applying for citizenship is prohibitive.

There has been a significant increase in anti-immigrant violence carried out by individuals and independent so-called border patrol groups like the Minutemen (Yoxall, 2006). The anti-Latino immigrant backlash is also evident in the recently passed State Bill 1070 in Arizona, which allows police officers to question anyone they "suspect" of being illegal to prove their citizenship status. How can someone discern between a Mexican (or other Latino) here legally and another here "illegally?" Practically speaking, people who look like me will be unfairly targeted as police go on a witch hunt for so-called illegals. Racial profiling, a significant feature of this bill, will do more to fuel anti-Latino sentiment than it will to curb the tide of undocumented immigrants entering the country. A wiser approach would be to target the U.S. businessmen and -women whose desire to maximize profits leads them to hire and exploit undocumented workers. Although far from Arizona and other border states, Yolanda and her family continue to be targeted and forced to live in the shadows of society.

THE DREAM ACT

The Development, Relief, and Education for Alien Minors Act (DREAM Act) would make college more accessible for undocumented students. Every year approximately 65,000 immigrant students who came to the United States as children graduate from U.S. high schools (College Board, 2009a; Watteau and Medina, 2009). Many of these students are undocumented, so they have few options for higher education. According to these statistics, immigrants and undocumented students are academically capable of graduating from high school and going to college, but many don't get the opportunity to pursue higher education because of their citizenship status. The DREAM Act would allow undocumented students who graduate from high school, are determined to have "good moral character," and who came to the United Sates as children to earn citizenship. Under this proposed piece of legislation, undocumented students could receive conditional permanent residency, and if they completed a college degree or served two years in the military, they could become citizens. If they failed to earn a degree or serve in the military, they would lose their residency status and could be deported. An important part of the DREAM Act is that it would allow undocumented students to pay in-state tuition rates for public colleges and universities. Undocumented students do not qualify for federal or state financial aid, so they would have to pay full tuition, which is still extremely difficult. In addition, those people that make use of the DREAM Act to become citizens are only going to be hardworking people with college degrees, individuals that should be welcomed into the fabric of the country with open arms. The life trajectories of undocumented youth would be positively transformed if this bill were to pass.

Different versions of the DREAM Act have been introduced in Congress but have all failed. In 2007, Senator Richard Durbin from Illinois introduced the bill, but it only received fifty-two of the sixty votes necessary to get past the filibuster (in which legislators just talk to waste time before voting) and bring it to an official vote. I am surprised that the bill didn't have more support because it wouldn't allow undocumented students to get financial aid from the state or federal government, so there is no extra cost to taxpayers. It seems like a win-win situation for undocumented youth and the country at large. Most recently, in December of 2010 the bill passed in the House of Representatives, offering a glimmer of hope. Unfortunately, there were not enough votes of support in the Senate to break the Republican filibuster and move to a vote, thus continuing to obstruct pathways to citizenship for undocumented youth.

Making the case for the adoption of the DREAM Act, the National Council of La Raza (NCLR), a consistent proponent of the bill, argues, "The United States is deprived when hard-working immigrant youth are unable to pursue a college education and contribute to the economy" (Watteau and Medina, 2009). In fact, the nonpartisan Congressional Budget Office estimates that passing the Dream Act and creating a pathway to citizenship for undocumented youth would cut the national deficit by U.S.$1.4 over the next ten years (Congressional Budget Office, 2010). The idea that undocumented immigrants can work so hard and accomplish so much and yet still be limited in their pursuit of a college education because of a lack of funds or paperwork is troubling and seems to contradict the principles upon which this country was founded. If undocumented immigrants do not get the chance to go to college, they will most likely end up working low-wage, dead-end jobs with no room for advancement (Cammarota, 2008). By denying undocumented youth access to higher education, the world will miss out on all the great things talented, educated people can accomplish.

UNDOCUMENTED STUDENTS

Many undocumented students I have spoken with as part of my research live in constant fear of being exposed and separated from their families. In addition, job prospects for undocumented youth after graduating from high school are bleak, often diminishing the value of school. At times, many of my friends who are undocumented talk about dropping out, saying it really doesn't matter what they do in high school because they are going to work in the local tobacco fields and farms anyway. They work hard and want a better life for themselves and their families, but their outlook on life can become tainted because there are few choices for them. Can you imagine how scared undocumented families can be or the pressure they live under, constantly worrying that La Migra (the immigration police) will come and get them, detain them, and send them back to Mexico?

Undocumented workers in the United States are taken advantage of all the time. Because they need work but can't apply for most jobs, they often have to work "off the books," which means working for someone who doesn't require that they have a social security number. The workers get paid in cash, so the employers don't have to let the government know whom they are employing. Undocumented people work really hard for little money doing backbreaking jobs. Like many Americans, they just want a chance at a good life, and they are willing to work hard for it. What bothers me the most is the way that the media and other people describe undocumented workers, Mexicans especially, as lazy (Reyna, 2000; Schmidt, 1997). If you go to Main Street in my neighborhood at 6:00 in the morning, you will see a bunch of undocumented workers waiting for someone to offer them a chance to work for the day. They are doing the same amount of work, if not more, than American citizens, but are getting paid less because of their status as undocumented immigrants.

Undocumented immigrants frequently get treated like animals. Even legal immigrants can get treated poorly because of their immigration status, often relegated to the "back of the house" positions (Erickson and Pierce, 2005; Zamudio, 2002). A friend of mine who immigrated legally to the United States from Mexico was working at a nightclub in my city, and they made him do the most menial tasks because of his status as an immigrant. He had to work in the back washing dishes, cleaning inside and outside the club, and moving furniture, while the other workers, who were white, got to be waitresses or waiters, bartenders, greeters, and so on. This happens not only in my community but across the country.

Attending K–12 schools as an undocumented student has its own challenges as well. Many of my friends' parents are scared to come to the school and participate in school functions because they fear that someone in the school will report them to La Migra. Another issue is that so few of the faculty and staff at my school speak Spanish. Although many immigrants are in the process of learning English, they may struggle with it. Many people would prefer to talk about important things like the education of their children in the language they know best, and for many of these families that is Spanish. In my opinion, there is definitely discrimination against undocumented people in both work and school. In the next section I share some of the findings from my research regarding teachers' perspectives of Latino students in general and undocumented Latinos in particular.

Teachers' Treatment of Undocumented Students

Generally speaking, there is an anti-Latino sentiment in the United States. Many people believe Latinos are un-American and the cause of many of the problems in this country. These negative perceptions in society also find their way into schools. Many teachers see students they believe to be undocumented (engaging in profiling similar to that endorsed by Arizona State Bill 1070) and conclude that these kids do not want to succeed in school. They think school is wasted on undocumented students who, by virtue of their status, shouldn't be in the country. I really want my friends, like Yolanda, to be successful in schools and pursue careers that are of interest to them. She is a wonderful, hard-working person and deserves a chance to pursue her dreams. Teachers take a "don't ask, don't tell" approach to working with undocumented students. This is similar to taking a colorblind approach (Bonilla-Silva, 2006; Irvine, 2003) to working with Latino students and other students of color. If you want to teach me or students like Yolanda, you have to acknowledge who we are, and being immigrants is a part of our identities. We love it here in the United States, but we are also proud of being from Mexico. Teachers often speak poorly about Mexico and Mexican immigrants. Sometimes they will overtly discriminate against immigrant students in school. For example, I observed a teacher tell one of my friends, who also immigrated to the United States from Mexico, that he was "never going to get anywhere" because he wasn't learning English as fast as they believed he should. This negative interaction with his teacher will undoubtedly affect him because it will lower his confidence and self-efficacy with regard to learning English. If teachers keep telling him he is too slow and isn't learning, it will most likely make him perform worse. The stakes are high, and if he gets disconnected from the people that are supposed to help him become proficient in English, it will become more difficult for him to learn. It is the responsibility of the school and its staff to help students not only to learn English but to feel good about themselves in the process. The only people who help undocumented students in my school are the small group of Latino teachers and one white counselor who speaks Spanish, because they are the only ones that really understand what people experience when they come to a new country and try to learn new languages and customs.

Some teachers are helpful, but many teachers discriminate against Latino students. As a Latino immigrant and bilingual student, I have been discriminated against a bunch of times in school. As a personal example, one day I was in the school gym to get some paperwork signed in order to lift weights after school. The physical education teacher was there talking to some white students. One girl he was speaking to said out loud, "I don't want to talk about it in front of them," pointing to me and my friend. The teacher replied, "Don't worry. They probably don't even speak English!" And they both started laughing at us. I just walked out and didn't even get the paperwork signed because I was really hurt and infuriated by the incident. These types of remarks from teachers are not uncommon in my experience. Such comments create an anti-Latino school culture that affects the ways teachers interact with us and how we feel when we are in school. Negative appraisals of Latino students' cultural identities can really hinder students' progress and suppress their aspirations.

Undocumented Students and the Curriculum

I often reflect on all the trivial stuff I learned in social studies classes over the years, and I realize that I never really learned anything about how Latinos came to what is now commonly referred to as the United States (or, in some cases, how the United States came to us). I learned about Ellis Island and immigration from western Europe, but what about us? This country has a long history of immigration and waves of people coming here in search of opportunities to make a better life for themselves. The same is true today. Because of the historical relevance and present realities of immigration, it would seem logical that this content would be covered with some depth in the school curriculum. I would be more interested in learning about Ellis Island and immigration from Europe if teachers were able to connect it to my experiences. Earlier waves of immigrants dealt with discrimination; current immigrants deal with discrimination. There are many similarities between the immigrant experiences of Europeans 100 years ago and Latinos today. Comparing and contrasting the journeys, reception in the United States, and employment opportunities for immigrants during these two distinct waves would help all of us develop a more profound understanding of the current sociopolitical context surrounding immigration in which Yolanda, myself, and millions of other immigrant youth find ourselves embedded. It might even help people of European descent to have a little more sympathy for newer immigrants, since their ancestors often encountered similar hostility.

Understanding the experiences of non-Latino immigrants today might also be helpful to teachers. The work of Gerald Campano (2007) focused on a group of diverse immigrants in Houston, Texas. As a teacher-researcher, Campano created a classroom context in which his middle school students were able to craft and share narratives documenting their own immigration and/or refugee experiences. These stories, all unique but sharing common threads of silencing, perseverance, survival, and intergenerational knowledge, shaped the students' identities. Campano (2007) points out the necessity of creating space in the curriculum for these stories, so that teachers can get to know their students in a more holistic sense, which helps them to understand and teach their classes more effectively. However, he also warns against simply adding in or assigning these narratives, emphasizing that teachers need to truly listen to them, something that they may need to *learn* to do:

> The students' narratives, and my own process of reflecting on them, have enabled me to better "imagine" individual children in their full "weight and solidity." In the process, I became more mindful of their presence under teaching and learning conditions that could be described, in all fairness, as daunting and at times dehumanizing. (Campano 2007, 70)

In addition to working from the "inside out"—in other words, using students' own stories to drive the development of curricula and learning experiences—history and social studies classes can be enhanced by bringing the "outside in." Given the prevalance of calls for immigration reform and the current backlash against immigrants in the United States, it should follow that teachers would address this topic with their students, but when it comes to issues of Latino immigration and the DREAM Act, they often don't.

Research by Alejandro Portes and Rubén Rumbaut (2006) takes a broad sociological perspective, highlighting immigrant experiences in several contexts—institutional, linguistic, religious, economic, and political, among others. They remind their readers that immigrant experiences are extremely diverse; to try to lump all immigrants together and assume that they have had the same experiences makes for incomplete stories. I think that some teachers, who may not have read Portes and Rumbaut and other research on immigration, fall into this trap. They often adopt the "grand narrative" of immigrants, clinging to tired, oversimplified, false, and sometimes contradictory assumptions echoed in phrases I hear regularly about immigrants, including: "They are here to take our jobs"; "Mexicans are lazy"; and "If they like Mexico so much, they should go back there."

It upsets me that I had never even heard about the DREAM Act before my research in Project FUERTE. In fact, when I was doing research for this chapter, I asked a social studies teacher about his thoughts on the DREAM Act, and he did not even know what it was. How can a social studies teacher working in a school with a large immigrant population not be familiar with this proposed legislation? This is a prime example of teachers being uninformed and unsupportive of undocumented students. In addition, in a survey we administered to faculty and staff, less than one-third of the teachers and professional staff surveyed reported they would support the DREAM Act, meaning that two-thirds were either against it or didn't have an opinion on this important issue.

Beyond the DREAM Act, teachers don't acknowledge how all immigrants, particularly those of us from Mexico and other countries in Latin America, are lumped together and considered "illegals." When people discriminate and make hurtful comments, they don't typically ask the person they are talking about if they are in the country legally. Anti-immigrant discrimination affects more than just the undocumented, and this too should also be discussed in the classroom. For example, in New Haven, Connecticut, in September 2008, the city flew a Mexican flag next to the American flag in honor of Mexico's Independence Day. There was a huge backlash from people who were upset that the mayor allowed the Mexican flag to be displayed, even though the city flies the Italian and Irish (among other) flags during special holidays in those cultures (Shelton, 2008). Protesters shouted anti-immigrant slurs, and their march was covered on evening news and in local print media. This event could and should have been discussed in a variety of classes. The connection to social studies is perhaps most obvious. We could have also written letters to the editors of local papers to share our thoughts as part of

English class, or we could have used data regarding immigration in our state and country to learn important math concepts. Teachers in my school missed a huge opportunity to connect with us and extend our learning through engaging in a discussion around a topic that many of us care about.

Another potential topic related to immigrant students that could have been included in the curriculum was the raids that have been happening in my community and across the country. A year prior to the dispute over the flying of the Mexican flag at the statehouse, the New Haven City Council approved the creation of identification cards that would allow anyone, including undocumented individuals, to open bank accounts and do other things that in many states require a driver's license, which you can't get if you do not have the appropriate citizenship papers. Two days after the passage of the legislation, the U.S. Immigration and Customs Enforcement (ICE) conducted a raid and arrested twenty-nine people they planned to deport to their home countries (Zapana, 2008). That day ICE also raided several homes in nearby Fair Haven, where they thought so-called illegal immigrants were living. The timing of the raids could have been coincidental, but I doubt it. Current events in communities we are familiar with are especially relevant to our education and should find their way into the curriculum.

HIGHER EDUCATION ASPIRATIONS

Although undocumented students may have gone to school in Connecticut, for example, for twelve years, they are not eligible to pay the in-state tuition rate at a state university. Because of their citizenship status, they are required to pay the out-of-state rate and do not have the option of receiving state or federal aid to assist with the costs of college. For a normal four-year degree, an in-state student would pay approximately U.S.$64,000; conversely, an out-of-state student would pay approximately U.S.$140,000 for four years of college (College Board, 2009b). Out-of-state tuition is more than double the cost of in-state tuition. This discrepancy in pricing puts college out of reach for many undocumented students. To have even the slightest chance of pursuing a college degree, an undocumented student would have to work a high-paying job throughout college, which brings us to the next dilemma. Without paperwork, undocumented students have minimal options when it comes to jobs. The most accessible jobs for undocumented people include working as cooks and dishwashers in restaurants and doing manual labor, construction, property maintenance, and housekeeping. Although these jobs are necessary and respectable, it is hard to "move up the ladder" and make enough money to pay the entire cost of a four-year education, even at a state college, which is usually the most affordable option for higher education. It is nearly impossible for an undocumented person to be a substitute teacher, do an internship at a large company, or get another job where there is room for growth. One of the things I want teachers to know is that undocumented students have dreams and goals. They go to school because they want to get their high school diploma, even if that diploma doesn't mean they are going to get a better job. If you think about it, the fact that undocumented students persist in school and complete high school says something about how much they and their families value education, because,12 unlike U.S. citizens, even if they do well in school, there are still many formidable barriers preventing them from attending college or obtaining a good job. Most of the undocumented immigrants I know work at a few places that hire undocumented people, such as restaurants or cleaning services. Undocumented students hope for a brighter future and, like my friend Yolanda, wish that schools would do more to help them achieve their goals.

RECOMMENDATIONS FOR TEACHERS WORKING WITH UNDOCUMENTED STUDENTS

As shown in Yolanda's story, my personal experiences, and teachers' lack of support for the DREAM Act on our survey, it seems that many teachers hold stereotypical views of undocumented students. Even those teachers who may be supportive have done little to include the experiences and histories of undocumented students in the curriculum. Drawing heavily from my examination of the education of undocumented Latino youth, I have come up with several suggestions for teachers committed to improving their ability to teach these students.

To be more successful in educating undocumented Latino youth, teachers need to change the curriculum to include the experiences and perspectives of immigrant students. This can be done in several ways. For example, teachers can create more room for students to share their own immigration narratives, as Campano (2007) did in his classroom. These stories are just as informative and compelling as anything on an academic department's required reading list. In addition, there are a host of things going on in the community that affect undocumented students that can be brought into the classroom to support student learning, which should be the goal of school. My teachers often act as if they are not interested in the lives of their Latino students outside school. If students and their families live in fear of ICE raids, it is going to be hard to focus in class. Teachers should work with students to address questions like these: if this is a country founded on immigration, why are so many people against immigration now? Is it because most new immigrants are Latino? If the entire southwestern United States was once part of Mexico, taken by the United States after the Mexican-American War (Acuña, 2004), should Mexicans have the right to come north? How has U.S. economic policy fueled immigration—both legal and illegal—from Latin America to the United States? Students care about many issues, like immigration, that can be directly related to the state and district learning standards.

I recently learned that one of the purposes of education is to prepare people to participate in a democratic society (Dewey, 1916; Freire, 1970/2000, 2004; Giroux, 2005). Education should be about helping students learn more about how the system works and working with them to develop a voice to speak up against issues they find troubling or in favor of ideas they support. If educating citizens to think critically is the espoused goal of school, then it follows that teachers would help us learn more about immigrant rights and how to navigate a system that is often hostile to immigrants. Paulo Freire used the word *praxis* to refer to this process of thinking about and acting on the world in order to change it (Freire, 1970/2000). Building on the work of Freire, I believe a primary focus of schools should be to help us develop the skills we need to make the world better for all people.

Many kids grow up in this country and dream about all of the things they want to be: doctors, lawyers, businesspeople, and so on. Immigrant children who were brought to this country by their parents without the proper documentation also have dreams, but their dreams are much harder (and sometimes even impossible) to achieve because of poor-quality K–12 education and limited opportunities for higher education. If reintroduced and passed into law, the DREAM Act could help. It would create more options for college and open pathways for undocumented students to become citizens. Schools can and do play a large role in structuring opportunities for students. In their current form, most schools do little to acknowledge and meet the needs of undocumented youth. With support from teachers and administrators, following some of the suggestions that I have outlined here, undocumented students will eventually be able to make their dreams a reality.

7

MY HOME LANGUAGE IS NOT "A PROBLEM"

with Natasha Martinez, High School Student

⊕

Hola. Espero que te guste mi capítulo. I thought I would start this chapter in Spanish, since speaking Spanish in school was the focus of my research. My school has many students, including myself, who speak Spanish at home and who learned or are learning English as a second language. Speaking more than one language should be considered a positive skill to be admired, but many teachers I have encountered treat speaking languages other than English as harmful or destructive. Some teachers get angry when we speak Spanish in classroom or in the hallways of the school because they do not understand what we are saying. Bilingual students shouldn't be penalized for their ability to communicate in a variety of languages; rather they should be praised and held up as a model for monolingual people to emulate.

It is clear that many teachers lack knowledge about the benefits of bilingualism. The literature regarding bilingualism, which I will explore in more detail later, suggests that bilingual students have greater "cognitive flexibility" (Cummins, 1976; Diaz, 1985), meaning that we use more of our brains than monolingual people. Being bilingual, in my opinion, is a valuable skill that should be supported by schools. I often serve as a translator for family and people in my community who need assistance. One time my cousin got sick, and I had to go with him to the hospital to translate. The nurse said I was "bright" for being able to communicate in both English and Spanish. By contrast, most of the teachers I have interacted with don't see my bilingualism as something valuable but rather as a problem or liability. In this chapter, I share a few of my experiences as a bilingual student, examine some of the research literature regarding bilingualism, and offer recommendations for teachers working with bilingual students.

MY EXPERIENCES AS A BILINGUAL STUDENT

I grew up speaking Spanish, and it continues to be the primary language of communication in my home. From the time I was born until I was in third grade, I lived in Mexico, and my classes were all in Spanish. I came to the United States in the middle of the 1999 school year, and my parents enrolled me in elementary school. I entered a bilingual education class and was taught in both Spanish and English. That was really important in helping me to master the knowledge and skills I needed to progress with my classmates while simultaneously learning English. When I transitioned from the bilingual program into an English-only class, after only one year of bilingual education, I struggled. Looking back, one year of bilingual education was not enough to support my transition into an English-only class, nor did it help me refine my academic abilities in Spanish. I was fortunate to have a good teacher, Mr. Smith, during my second year of school, the only teacher outside the bilingual program who supported my bilingualism. In his class I didn't feel as if I had to give up my home language to learn a new language. Unfortunately, many of the teachers I have encountered have not been as supportive as Mr. Smith; most have restricted my use of Spanish in school. Although language discrimination isn't just practiced by teachers, schools are one of the places it happens most often and most systematically.

It is hard to adequately describe how passionate I feel about retaining my Spanish language and being bilingual. Spanish is the language that my parents use to tell me they love me and teach me about God, and it is the language that connects my family here in the United States with my loved ones in Mexico. I also appreciate English and the value of the language in the U.S. context. But sometimes I feel like I want to say things that the English language doesn't capture; the feeling and meaning behind what I am saying can only be said in Spanish. One time in class I was speaking with my friends in Spanish, and the teacher called us out and told us that speaking Spanish wasn't allowed in his class. I am not the type of student who would talk back to or disrespect a teacher. I was just not raised that way. My friend, who is more vocal in these matters, asked the teacher why he banned the use of Spanish, a language spoken by more than one-third of all of the students in the school and all of the students in that particular class. The teacher said, "I don't care if you all speak Spanish. I don't, so you can't." It is not our fault the teachers don't understand Spanish. There is so much focus on our learning, yet there is much that teachers should have to learn and don't. If teachers are going to work in a school with a huge Spanish-speaking population, they should consider learning to speak the language as well. It not only would allow them to monitor what we are saying and calm their concerns, but, more important, it would also allow them to provide more support for our learning. For example, if we don't understand something in class, the teacher could try to explain it in Spanish, which might help us grasp the concept more effectively.

Many teachers act as if speaking Spanish is equivalent to cursing or using foul language. A common argument offered by teachers to support the suppression of Spanish is that we might be saying inappropriate things and/or talking about them. This line of thinking is flawed logic. Many white students talk about teachers and curse when they speak English, but teachers don't outlaw the use of English just because some kids use that language to say inappropriate things. So what is the difference? I think the difference is that we are Latino and speak Spanish, and teachers can identify with the white English-speaking students more easily. Many of my friends want to learn to speak English better, but they also want to retain their own language and have the freedom to use it across contexts. I don't think that is too much to ask.

THE RESEARCH LITERATURE REGARDING BILINGUALISM

The personal story I have related and the many other experiences that I don't have space to share here suggest that stifling students' language use and bilingualism can negatively affect our desire to connect with teachers and do well in school. I hope that these stories serve as a wake-up call for educators who have not thought enough about this issue or have not heard a student's perspective on it. In addition to personal narratives, there is a wealth of research literature in the form of books, journal articles, and reports that clearly demonstrates the value of supporting the use of multiple languages in schools.

Research suggests that supporting the use of multiple languages can have a positive impact on academic achievement in variety of sub- jects, including math. According to University of London researcher Charmian Kenner, "When children were allowed to use their mother tongue as well as English, they seemed to grasp mathematical concepts such as division and multiplication more easily" (BBC News, 2007). A comprehensive study of eight years' worth of data regarding the achievement of English learners (ELs) in bilingual programs versus those in English immersion programs clearly supports using the stu- dents' native language in schools. J. David Ramírez, Sandra Yuen, and Dena Ramey (1991) have found that those students who were educated in their native language did better in school and had more promising futures than those English learners who were immersed in English and whose native language wasn't used in instruction. This study is very significant because, according to Jim Cummins (1992), it was created and supported by a group of researchers with conflicting beliefs about bilingual education. Therefore, it is difficult to dismiss the findings as biased.

More recent data also make a connection between bilingualism and academic achievement. In a study of 2,167 Mexican and Mexican American students attending U.S. schools, Amado Padilla and Rose- mary Gonzalez (2001) found that students in their study that were enrolled in a college prep track who received some form of English as a second language or bilingual education had higher grade point averages than other, similarly tracked students who did not receive any second language instruction.

There are different ways to support students' use of multiple languages. One is by creating bilingual education programs. Most bilingual programs are transitional, meaning the goal is to get students immersed into English-only classes as quickly as possible without giving attention to developing students' primary language. Although there may be some benefits to this approach, I think the goal should be for all students to learn to speak multiple languages. Important research by Ester de Jong (2002) highlights the effectiveness of two-way bilingual programs for learning multiple languages and supporting the academic achievement of English language learners. In her study of a two-way bilingual program in Massachusetts, de Jong (2002) concluded that the school, because of its approach to teaching and learning in multiple languages, met the academic achievement goals for the English-dominant as well as the EL students. If our education system really valued multilingualism, there would be more two-way bilingual programs in schools.

Prejudice and discrimination based on language, or linguicism, is alive and well in the United States and transcends schools. It is a big issue in our society, especially because the Latino population is growing so quickly. There is even an effort to make English the official language of the United States. Although having English as the official language may not seem problematic, it is part of a backlash aimed at Spanish speakers, the largest minoritized language group. Jason Irizarry and John Raible (2009), in a chapter describing the climate for English learners, challenge this movement and highlight the potential impact on Spanish speakers like myself and my family. They wrote:

> Efforts to mandate one official language fail to recognize the multilingual history of the country. Written in 1777, the Articles of Confederation, the country's first constitution, were disseminated in English, French, and German (Crawford, 1999). However, more than two centuries later, as the United States has become increasingly linguistically diverse, proponents of English-only legislation believe government documents should be available in only one language. Certainly proposed English-only legislation presents serious implications for all ELLs; given the predominance of people in the United States who speak Spanish as a primary language (the U.S. is home to the second largest Spanish-speaking population in the world), it would have a disproportionate, adverse affect on the burgeoning population of *hispanohablantes.*

I am young and have only lived in one state in the United States, but, from what I have read, schools and states have created policies to stop students from being taught in their native language, even though the research, as I have demonstrated here, ascribes significant benefits to being bilingual and learning in two languages. In

California, Arizona, and Massachusetts, bilingual education has been eliminated (Irizarry and Raible, 2009). As a result, millions of English language learners are not getting the services they need.

Various studies have documented the prevalence of language discrimination. Mariana Souto-Manning published an autoethnographic study (a research project in which the author is the subject of the research) in 2006 that shared her experiences as a bilingual Latina in the United States. In her article, she offers various examples of how people consistently insulted her by sharing prejudiced remarks about being bilingual. She heard these remarks in schools, at work, and even in the hospital when she gave birth to her son. If this is the experience of a highly educated researcher, imagine what it is like for us kids. Many students don't know how to respond to this hostility, and they are pushed out of school.

Supporting students' usage of languages other than English is just common sense to me. To write this chapter I read an array of research studies, and I did not find one study that provided empirical evidence supporting English immersion or challenging the research base supporting bilingual education. Most people would agree that being bilingual is an asset, but for some reason they don't think schools should play a part in helping students become bilingual. If schools are charged with preparing the next generation, they should prepare us for the real world, and the real world doesn't operate only in English. Given that so many students in U.S. schools speak languages other than English and that Latinos are the largest minoritized group in schools, teachers need to support the language(s) of Latinos.

TEACHERS' PERCEPTIONS OF LATINO STUDENTS AND THEIR HOME LANGUAGES

As part of my research with Project FUERTE, my colleagues and I developed and administered a survey to teachers to learn more about their beliefs about Latino students. Teachers' responses to the survey items and one open-ended question reflected their antipathy toward the Spanish language and Latino students and families in general. One teacher commented, "Many [Latinos] do not see academics as very *importante*." In this example, I believe the teacher who made this comment was using Spanish to disrespect us. It is ridiculous that teachers don't let us speak Spanish in school, yet one of them used it to make an insulting comment on the survey. The teachers knew that my fellow student-researchers and I constructed the survey and that we would see the comments, but still they said horrible things like this. Beyond the personal insult, the statement is completely inaccurate. Most of us do care about education. Sure, there are some Latinos who don't care, but there are some students of every race who don't care. The majority of us want to do well in school, go to college, and get good jobs.

Flawed perceptions of language became apparent in other statements made by teachers to answer the survey question: why do you think so many Latino students fail to complete high school in four years? More than half of all the teachers gave answers that blamed students' home language for causing high dropout/pushout rates. Few teachers mentioned anything related to the school curriculum or their teaching. One of the comments read, "Language gets in the way of learning." This response suggests that speaking Spanish prevents us from learning what we need to learn to graduate. We learn through language, so language in and of itself is not a barrier. Recent research suggests that youth who speak a language other than English and have instruction in that language do better than students who are only taught in English (Padilla and Gonzalez, 2001; de Jong, 2006). The teacher who made the ignorant comment suggesting that speaking a language other than English is a hindrance needs to read more on the issue. Until teachers learn more about language acquisition and bilingual education, they will continue to operate based on flawed stereotypes rather than on research and evidence-based practices. Several teachers blamed a language barrier for Latino students' high dropout/pushout rates. The barrier is created by teachers and others school agents who are intolerant of Spanish and other languages.

Language doesn't have to be a barrier. Teachers can use students' home language as a bridge to help them learn English and other languages. I have identified several connections between English and Spanish, and I use this knowledge to help my friends better understand concepts they might be struggling with. Knowing Spanish can sometimes help you to get the meaning of an English word. For example, you can look at the root of an English word, like *edifice,* and connect it to a Spanish word, like *edificio,* to figure out that it means "building." Using cognates to link Spanish and English, which I have done my entire life, is also a strategy supported by research (Howard and Christian, 2002). Words in English that end with "tion" often translate into Spanish as the same word, but they end in "ción." The word *presentation,* for example, in English is translated as *presentación* in Spanish. Just knowing some of these simple things can help teachers teach Spanish-speaking students more effectively.

Many teachers think we don't want to learn English. They are wrong; of course we want to learn English. We know that fluency in English is necessary to be successful in this country. But for whatever reason, they think we are lazy or anti-American. In response to the open-ended question, one teacher went as far as to say, "When my grandparents came to this country from Europe, they learned how to read, write, and speak English, and they encouraged their children to become fluent English speakers and to succeed in an English-speaking country." This statement suggests that Latino parents don't encourage their kids to learn English and that we don't want to learn the language. That is a myth. We want to learn English, but most of us also want to retain our native language. But if you believe Latino families are reluctant or unwilling to learn English, then how are you going to be a good teacher of Latino students? How are you going to positively interact with Latino parents?

Because learning English is a major aspect of education, if teachers see Latino youth and families as averse to learning English, they can conclude that Latinos don't value education. Consequently, many teachers believe, as one teacher wrote, "education is not a top priority in this culture." That is another false overgeneralization. I know many parents who work multiple jobs, and some of them don't have the time to attend parent-teacher conferences or other school-sponsored events. Many parents also don't feel welcomed at the school because teachers and administrators don't speak their language. Just because some parents don't attend meetings or other school-related functions doesn't mean that they don't care about their children's education. My parents don't always make it to parent-teacher conferences, but my mother is always keeping track of me and monitoring my progress in school. She checks to make sure that I do my homework and that I am getting good grades and behaving well in school. She is always telling me about how hard her life is because she didn't finish high school. My mother constantly encourages me to do well in school and not to do bad things out of school. She cares a lot about me, but that may not be easy for teachers to see. Every day when I get home, my mother asks me what I did in school, what happened, and if I worked hard or if I got in trouble. If I tell her I have an upcoming exam, she always asks me how I did when I get home from school the next day. Without a doubt, Latino parents do care about their children. I think the overwhelming majority of parents care about their children, but the ways in which they demonstrate their concern may not be recognized or valued by schools. Many teachers make assumptions without knowing us or our families. Instead of judging a book by its cover, teachers need to metaphorically open the book and read it.

It was hurtful to read all the negative comments teachers made regarding the Spanish language on the survey we administered. When I read their responses, I felt like crying. To be honest, on some level I expected their responses to be negative because I have years' worth of data based on interactions with teachers to confirm that many teachers don't think highly of Latino youth. They treat us poorly when it comes to language, often stifling our expression, so it makes sense that they blamed the lack of academic success experienced by students on our desire to retain our native language without mention of their role in shaping our experiences in school.

DEFICIT PERSPECTIVES OF SPANISH SPEAKERS

One of the most interesting things that I learned in this class is that the United States has a history of speaking and supporting different languages. Language diversity is not a new issue. As I documented in an earlier quote, the Articles of Confederation, the document that established the laws of this country prior to the Constitution, which were written more than 230 years ago, were written in three different languages: English, French, and German (Cockcroft, 1995; Irizarry and Raible, 2009). Why, then, is the country trying to create laws to stop us from speaking Spanish? If the use of multiple languages in the United States was supported hundreds of years ago, why is it a problem now? Many of our recent presidents have spoken Spanish and used their language proficiency to attract Spanish-speaking voters. As the country becomes more Latino as a result of birth rates and immigration, an increasing portion of our population will speak Spanish. I would encourage teachers and others with reservations about supporting multilingualism to look back at U.S. history and realize that speaking multiple languages is very American, not anti-American. All students should speak at least two languages so we can all interact with each other and with people outside the United States. If more people spoke multiple languages, there would be less prejudice against those of us who do.

There are times when I struggle to find the right words to express myself in English because Spanish is my first language. Depending on the context, I sometimes mix the two languages. Most of my friends are bilingual and deal with the same issues, so we often communicate using Spanglish, a mixture of Spanish and English. If we don't know some words in English, we say them in Spanish. Mixing both languages allows people to continue to follow what you are saying because you provide enough context for them to understand the word or phrase in the other language. The benefits of multilingualism are both personal and professional. Knowing two languages (three if you count Spanglish as a language) can help you get a job. I translate for my family and friends during doctor's appointments and other meetings. Therefore, I'm getting good practice for a career that requires speaking two languages, such as a translator or teacher. Given the marketability of these skills and their importance to people in the community, schools should do all they can to support multilingualism. Teachers' perceptions of Latinos, and specifically those Latinos who speak Spanish as their primary language, make parents and kids feel unwanted in school. There are a lot of people, including teachers, who criticize students and parents for not being proficient in English. As part of my research, I learned that it takes, on average, five to seven years to gain academic proficiency in a new language (Cummins, 1992; Crawford, 2004). That means many of us are still in the process of learning. It takes time. Imagine how teachers might feel if I forced them to learn a language faster than their brains can absorb it and then made negative assumptions about them based on their performance in the new language. Latino families are criticized in schools and the popular media for a perceived unwillingness to learn English. My parents have worked hard to learn the language. Both of them understand everything people say, but they are not confident in their English-speaking ability. I wish that teachers could put themselves in our shoes for a while. They would see how hard it is to learn another language and retain your families' language. Language learning and being an "emergent bilingual" (García, Kleifgen, and Falchi, 2008) should be praised and valued instead of vilified.

IF I WERE A TEACHER ...

If I were a teacher, my approach to working with emergent bilingual students would be different from what I have experienced. Instead of marginalizing and rejecting students who speak Spanish, I would make them feel special because I know that they come to school with a valuable skill. I would support them in learning English and share with them the strategies that I used to learn English as a second language. I would want to teach in a two-way bilingual classroom like the one Ester de Jong (2006) described in her research. In this type of classroom, both English and the home language of the student are used, which seems logical but is rarely the case. All kids become bilingual with this approach to teaching. Students don't have to sacrifice learning important content to focus solely on learning English. Consequently, we learn the material and develop the ability to communicate in two languages simultaneously.

There are many teachers who say they care about us, but because of their limited knowledge of language acquisition and how to support emergent bilinguals, they are not as effective as they could be. If I were a teacher and a student came to school not speaking English, I would try to help him or her to understand the material using their language. Since I know Spanish, I could be really helpful to students who speak Spanish at home. I could be the teacher I never had. Latinos are the largest group of people of color, and Mexicans arc the largest group of Latinos. If the students were from Mexico like me, I would be able to relate in ways that some teachers can't. I could make them feel more comfortable, since the way we speak and think might have some similarities. Also I would reflect their culture and include Latinos in the curriculum, so they wouldn't feel left out the way many of us do now.

As a teacher, I would do everything I could to make school more enjoyable and ensure that students connect with the content I am teaching. I believe a good teacher learns from their students as much as the students learn from the teacher. Some teachers act like they know everything and have to be right all the time. I would be open to having students give me feedback on my teaching and would modify my approach based on their suggestions. Having had the opportunity to share my thoughts on the education of Latino students with adults at various conferences, I know that young people have a lot they can teach adults, if adults are willing to listen. Most teachers aren't interested in our perspectives on their work. This is why the curriculum remains culturally unresponsive to the needs of Latino youth and other students of color. Many teachers don't see the value of culturally responsive pedagogy. One teacher even went as far as to say, "[Latino students fail] because they want the curriculum to be about them. That is not right." I am not saying that the curriculum and the ways teachers teach have to focus solely on us, but we should see ourselves reflected there. The curriculum and the ways teachers teach are not neutral. Most teachers want us to change completely, to assimilate, and learn their way. They need to meet us halfway. Under the current system, we have to give relinquish or suppress important aspects of our identities for a chance at school success.

RECOMMENDATIONS FOR TEACHERS AND TEACHER EDUCATORS

Although I am only a high school student, as a result of my personal experiences and extended research on the issue of Latino education, I have important insights that can help teachers and those that train them. In this section I offer three recommendations to help teachers and teacher educators improve their practice. The recommendations may seem simple, but they are still important. Part of the reason Latino students are not succeeding is that teachers don't know how to work effectively with us. I hope that readers take these recommendations seriously because schools need to change if they are going to work in the best interest of Latinos and, more specifically, those of us who speak English as a second language.

My first recommendation addresses how teachers are prepared. I never really thought about how teachers are taught until this year. As part of the Action Research and Social Change class, we examined the required courses for teachers in several teacher education programs. Based on the narrow scope of the teacher education curriculum, I suggest making learning Spanish a requirement for all teachers. So few teachers speak Spanish, yet so many students and families do. Therefore, it makes sense to have Spanish-language courses integrated into teacher preparation. If university-based teacher education programs explicitly fostered multilingualism, then it is more likely that teachers would value it. When the future teachers in these programs graduated, they would enter the profession as bilinguals (or at least emergent bilinguals), making it easier for them to communicate with Latino students and families. After investing in learning another language, teachers would be less likely to develop language policies aimed at curbing the use of languages other than English and alienating us from school. Even if they left teaching and went into another job, as many teachers do (Johnson, Berg, and Donaldson, 2005), their proficiency in Spanish would still be beneficial. The demographic trends in this country forecast increases in the population of Latinos and Spanish-speakers; therefore, learning Spanish should be seen as valuable for teachers as learning English is for us.

Most teachers teach one way, even though youth are unique and have diverse learning preferences. Teachers should learn different ways to teach students and not rely on one method. Some students learn faster than others, and some learn slower, but teachers don't always take our individuality into account. For example, last year in my math class we were taking notes, but the teacher was talking really fast. It was a new lesson, and it was hard to follow. Remember, my brain is working in two languages. I hear the information from the teacher, who is speaking in English. I don't know why, but I automatically translate into Spanish, maybe because I feel more comfortable thinking about hard topics in Spanish. Then I write my notes in a mixture of English and Spanish, like Spanglish. So I didn't capture all the information. At the end of the lecture, the teacher gave us work to do, but I didn't know how to complete it because I didn't fully understand his presentation in class. Processing things in two languages can take more time, but that doesn't mean I can't get it. When I asked for help, he said that it was my fault that I didn't fully grasp the material, and he walked away. Basically, he didn't care to take the time to help me. I am sure he was overwhelmed with other important things, but my education and the education of youth like me should be a priority and is worth the additional investment of time. If teachers had a better understanding of language processing and had different techniques for teaching beyond them talking and us taking notes, these troubling incidents I describe would cease and students would perform better academically.

Many teachers don't focus us as students; they just pay attention to their jobs and concentrate on teaching content. That may sound counterintuitive because in a sense we are their job, but they often view their teaching as separate from students' learning, in my opinion. I have heard teachers say, "I am teaching but you are not learning." Teaching and learning are not mutually exclusive. They are inextricably linked. We need to share responsibility for learning as opposed to placing the entire burden on students, who have little control over how and what they are taught. I am beginning to realize that I have more power and the ability to shape some of my learning experiences. I suggest that teachers and administrators recognize their agency and ability to change things and work with us to transform schools into culturally responsive, multilingual, caring spaces that encourage student growth.

CONCLUSION

As I have documented in this chapter, many teachers see students' home language as a barrier to education. Speaking Spanish at home and at school is viewed as a liability and hindrance in the process of learning English. The research on bilingualism is crystal clear. There are no negative consequences to being bilingual. Students who are taught in their native language usually do better in school (Brisk, 2006; Ramírez, Yuen, and Ramey, 1991; Rossell and Baker, 1996). I contributed to the development of this chapter because I am tired of being treated as inferior by teachers just because I am Latina and speak Spanish. I am hoping that teachers will read this and think more deeply about how they work with Latino students like me who speak Spanish as a primary language. Teachers play an important role in our development, and they have power to shape students' opportunities for school success. I am months away from completing high school, so it might be too late for me to see the changes I describe in the chapter. I pray that things will change for the better in the near future. I want to end this chapter the way I started it—in Spanish. So to all the teachers and professors who train teachers out there: you have a big job in front of you. Buena suerte!

8

WHY AREN'T MORE LATINOS IN COLLEGE PREP COURSES?

A CRITIQUE OF TRACKING AND ACADEMIC APARTHEID

with Taína Vargas, High School Student

⁂

Prior to conducting research regarding how students are placed into classes in high school, I had never realized how I was being tracked throughout my own schooling experience. I just came to school and assumed guidance counselors and teachers had my best interests at heart. I assumed they were preparing me to go to college. It wasn't until recently that I became aware of how my academic career and subsequent life choices are being shaped by the perceptions of my ability held by adults in my school. The worst part of it all was that I have been completely oblivious to how my future education and employment opportunities were being stifled because of my placement in the least rigorous classes offered at my school. I just took the classes I was told by counselors and teachers to take, assuming that if I got good grades, I could go to college. I began writing this chapter as a junior in high school, and, believe it or not, I still had not taken Algebra I, a course required to attend most four-year colleges. It turns out that I was not enrolled in or on track to take many of the classes that I needed to be able to pursue postsecondary education.

Instead of Algebra, I am currently enrolled in Consumer Math. The goal of the class is to learn how to balance a checkbook and do other simple math. It is ridiculously easy. I have been named student of the week in the class several times, but that isn't worth much because Consumer Math isn't a college-prep course. I have already taken three years of classes and only have one year left to enroll in all the college-prep classes I should have had already.

This chapter takes a closer look at tracking as a way of organizing education in high school. It documents how tracking has been used to limit opportunities for many Latinos and examines how tracking can influence how Latino students think of themselves.

GETTING ON TRACK

Guidance counselors and teachers often direct Latino students into certain classes based on what they think about us—thoughts that are often negative and based on deficit thinking (see Chapter 2). Teachers and counselors often rely on standardized test scores to make decisions about grouping students, which I think is dangerous for a host of reasons. Our performance on standardized tests, which may be culturally and linguistically biased (Gándara and Contreras, 2009; Helms, 1992; Malgady, Rogler, and Costantino, 1987), often doesn't represent our true capabilities as students. The questions and prompts on these tests are more closely related to the experiences of white suburban students and often disconnected from the lived experiences of Latino youth and other students of color. If I have to write an essay about a camping trip, it is not going to be very good if I have never gone camping (at least not as good as the one written by the student who goes camping every summer). Moreover, we are held accountable for our performance on these tests, yet the district cannot guarantee that we had qualified teachers to help us master the materials or that the content is even presented to us in ways we can understand.

Rarely do people look at how putting students into certain academic tracks can cause students to lose interest. Or when students realize that the classes they have taken are not going to prepare them for college or a good career, they lose interest in school and stop putting in the effort they need to do well. Once you get placed on a particular track, like the fundamentals level in my school, which is the lowest level, it is hard to move up to another track. All students deserve the chance to enroll in higher-level classes for their own personal development as well as to prepare them to participate in this knowledge-based economy, in which the majority of new jobs require a college degree. Almost 14 million job openings between 2004 and 2014 have been and will continue to be filled by workers with a bachelor's degree or higher (Crosby and Moncarz, 2006). More of us have to go to college because there aren't enough jobs out there for high school graduates and even fewer for those who have not completed high school. Many of the factory jobs that supported high school graduates and dropouts/pushouts from previous generations don't exist in this country anymore. This erosion of manufacturing jobs is visible in my town, where there are several empty factories that are just abandoned and in disrepair or that have been converted into apartments. President Barack Obama recently established a goal for the United States to once again have the highest proportion of college graduates in the world by 2020 (Carey, 2009). If half of all Latinos continue not to graduate from high school, and if many of those who do graduate are not prepared to go to college, our country will never be able to reach this goal. The future success of the country is predicated on the academic success of Latino youth.

UNPACKING TRACKING

As our research team began to brainstorm issues that we wanted to study, one of my friends in the class posed the question, "Why is it that when you walk by a class, it is either all white or all Latino?" I had never thought about it before, but he was right. In most of my classes there are hardly any white students, even though they account for close to half of the student body. At that moment, Dr. Irizarry said, "We are going to go on our first field trip," and we began to walk up and down the halls of the school, peering in at each class through the door windows. We got some nasty looks from teachers along the way, but that was a small price to pay to learn a valuable lesson.

When we returned to the classroom, we started to do an informal tally of students by race/ethnicity. It was clear that students were being segregated. Just the thought of separating the Latino students from the white students was enough to get me angry, but then my anger and frustration were elevated to a new level when another one of my friends in the class observed, "The white kids are in the higher classes, and we are in the lower." "That's messed up," I yelled out. Then I started to think about it more critically and shared what I had come to believe: white students are just smarter than us Latinos. It seemed like a logical reason to support our disparate tracks within the school. That is why they are in the higher-level classes, and we are in the lower-level classes. Dr. Irizarry tried to challenge my thinking, saying that our placement in classes wasn't necessarily reflective of how smart we are and that tracking is often based on false data or biased opinions that disproportionately hurt students of color. But I didn't want to believe that because if that were true, it meant my school didn't want the best for me; in fact, it created a system to keep me down. This issue sparked a huge discussion, which was more like a heated debate. Our entire class agreed that we weren't all going to achieve consensus regarding the root causes of racialized patterns in class placements right then, but we did conclude that we needed to conduct more systematic research.

Academic Tracking

Tracking is the grouping of students based on their perceived ability level (Oakes, 2005). The overrepresentation of Latinos in the lowest, least rigorous tracks of my school suggests that larger forces are at play. Beyond the perceptions of school officials, there are also policies in place that contribute to relegating us to the lowest tracks. In order to enroll in a higher-level course than the one in which they are originally placed, students need signatures from all their current teachers and a counselor or administrator. Because few of us have meaningful relationships with teachers, we don't get the benefit of the doubt when trying to enroll in upper-level courses. If teachers do not know you or your work, they could just deny your request. This policy keeps many Latino students in low-level classes. Tracking isn't unique to our school; researchers have studied the racialized patterns of class placement for many years. Pedro Noguera (2003) argues that racial biases held by teachers and other school agents influence decisions about student grouping and classes and that Latinos remain in low classes as a result. It is clearly the case at my school. Also, students who speak Spanish as a first language are often relegated to lower-track classes (Harklau, 2000) or overrepresented in special education programs (Artiles et al., 2002; Cummins, 1989; Hosp and Reschly, 2004). On the other end of the spectrum, Latino students are underrepresented in honors and advanced placement courses (Conchas, 2006; Noguera, 2003; Valenzuela, 1999). Because this happens on such a large scale in schools across the country, it makes me think that it isn't by chance or accident.

Research by Antwi Akom (2003) extends previous work by John Ogbu (1978) and others and speaks to the ways that school success is linked to a "white identity" or "acting white." Akom (2003) studied a group of black female students who were able to resist what he refers to as "academic apartheid," experiencing school success without compromising their identities. In this case—academic apartheid—a term that I chose to appropriate for the title of this chapter, refers to the ways in which access to high-level classes and opportunities for school success more generally are often denied to students of color through various policies and institutionalized practices. As a result, classes are segregated by race and/or class. Fueled by our walk through the hallways of my school to examine the distribution of students of diverse backgrounds, after consulting the research literature regarding academic tracking, my desire to dismantle the system of tracking and advocate for high-quality educational opportunities for all students began to foment.

Although I experienced tracking every day, prior to this project I had not realized how big an issue it is and how it affects students of color. Much of the literature that I read for this project suggests that schools that serve students from lower socioeconomic strata and youth of color often provide them a poor-quality education, limiting their life choices (MacLeod, 2005; Noguera, 2001; Duncan-Andrade and Morrell, 2008). As a result of poor-quality education, many students remain stuck in a cycle of poverty. Most of these students will end up being poor too. Similarly, schools that serve middle-class and upper-class kids typically offer them a higher-quality education than they offer us to ensure that they have the knowledge and skills necessarty to progress onto college and secure jobs that help them stay in the middle and upper classes.

Social reproduction (Bourdieu, 1977; MacLeod, 2005; Duncan-Andrade and Morrell, 2008) is evident in my school, but I always assumed the assignment of students into classes was random, not intentionally discriminatory. The more we discussed social reproduction theory, the more my coresearchers and I were able to identify the role that schools play in shaping opportunities and structuring inequality among students based on race and class. All the pieces started to fit together—tracking Latino and other students of color into low-level classes that don't prepare them for college, keeping the curriculum focused on white European culture, providing less funding for city schools versus suburban schools, eliminating bilingual education programs—all these forces contribute to making education a less-than-positive experience for many Latino students. The data suggest that schools are not preparing most Latino students for college but rather for low-wage jobs (Cammarota, 2008). Social reproduction theory offers me a new perspective for understanding why so many of my fellow Latino students fail to complete high school. Although often described as "dropouts," students who leave school should be referred to as "pushouts" as well to reflect the role of schools in co-constructing their departure (Brown, 2007). When students leave high school, they have few career options. The impact of dropout/pushout is even more harsh for females, who are left with fewer options than their male counterparts and consequently struggle to survive economically (National Women's Law Center and MALDEF, 2009).

Data Collection

Building on our curiosity around how students are grouped and assigned to classes, we designed a project to critically examine tracking at our school. First, we asked the guidance department for a class list for each class offered at our school with students identified by race/ethnicity. Our request was denied. We then asked if we could just get class lists and then we would come up with a system to figure out the race/ethnicity of the students ourselves. Again our request was denied. After some creative thinking, we came up with a new plan. My coresearchers and I decided to cut out the "middle man" and go directly to teachers. We approached teachers and asked if we could conduct a brief, informal study of students' racial/ethnic identities to extend what we were learning in our Action Research and Social Change class. We were interested in how students identified themselves, but we were also interested in the level of the class in which the students were enrolled. We created a color-coded sticker system and asked students to place the sticker (or multiple stickers) corresponding to their racial/ethnic identities on their hands. We then took a photo of their hands, returned to our classroom and tallied the results.

Our sticker project allowed us to gather empirical data to examine the racial/ethnic breakdown for each of the different classes and unveiled a system of academic apartheid within the school. More than 85 percent of the students in advanced placement (AP) courses were white. More than 75 percent of the students in the college prep courses we visited were white. More than 75 percent of the students in the fundamentals-level courses in our sample were Latino. Given that approximately half the students in the school are Latino and approximately half are white, you would expect the classes at each level to be more racially/ethnically balanced. While these racialized patterns may seem obvious to some, having empirical evidence to support our claim and our efforts to dismantle tracking helps to bolster our position.

One of the ways that the system of tracking remains intact and unchallenged is by limiting students' ability to select their classes. Our programs of study are largely determined by guidance counselors, without significant input from students and their families. We don't even get our class schedule until we show up for the first day of classes. Once we arrive for the first day, the environment is completely chaotic because we are learning for the first time what courses we have and often there are mistakes in the schedule. One student I know was given fourteen study hall periods to start the year, and it took more than a month to fix his schedule and get him into classes. By the time he started most of his classes, he was far behind the other students. Teachers' and counselors' opinions about what Latino students are capable of are often very far from reality. I remember one time a teacher told one of my friends that he was "wasting his time in school" and that he would never be able to go to college. He asked why she thought that, and she said it was because he isn't "college material," whatever that means.

THE PSYCHOLOGICAL IMPACT OF TRACKING

Tracking practices at our school separate students into fundamentals, college prep, honors, and AP classes. By creating these differential levels, schools are limiting opportunities for many students to pursue postsecondary education and good careers. Students in fundamentals-level courses are not expected to go to college and are not pushed in this direction by teachers, counselors, and other school personnel. When students are tracked into low-level classes and treated as if they

141

are unintelligent, they often start to internalize these messages about their academic ability. My experiences in the least rigorous academic classes offered at my school had me convinced that Latinos were not as smart or as capable as white students. In one of our first classes for the research project, we were asked to describe what a researcher looks like. All of us described an old white person, most often a man. None of us saw ourselves or any Latinos as researchers. Our narrow conceptions speak volumes and demonstrate the depth of our sense of intellectual inferiority and the superiority we ascribed to white people.

It is important to recognize not only the harmful effects of tracking in terms of future college admissions and employment, but also how these practices influence the identities that we develop as students in the present. Sonia Nieto and Patty Bode (2008) note that tracking can be a major factor in the development of students' "classroom personalities." I know this to be true from my own experiences in schools. Being in all the lowest-level classes, I didn't identify with my "student self" very much; my other identities, those valued outside school, became more important. As time went on, my desire to excel academically diminished, and I became content with just getting by.

Now, after engaging in this collaborative research project, I have a stronger self-concept and a more positive appraisal of my abilities. This experience has challenged me to work hard and learn new skills. For example, we learned to conduct research, analyze data, and present it at professional education conferences. Before this class, I never would have thought that I could do any of these things. I am pushing back against my label as a fundamentals-level student and forging new identities as a scholar and change agent.

TEACHERS' PERCEPTIONS OF TRACKING

One of the questions on the survey we administered to the faculty and staff at our school asked teachers for their level of agreement with the following statement: "Tracking is an effective practice for organizing education." More than 82 percent of all teachers agreed or strongly agreed with the statement. Tracking is still supported and extolled as an effective practice in so many schools, despite the fact that research has demonstrated that tracking can be harmful to students.

There is a wealth of research that speaks to the negative long-term effects of tracking, yet many teachers prefer tracking because they see it as a way to make their jobs easier. In their study of student and teacher perceptions of tracking at a predominantly Latino school, Rosina Wright-Castro, Rosita Ramirez, and Richard Duran (2003, p. 9) reported that teachers claimed that "ability grouping allowed them to better meet students' needs" and that "reducing the variability of students' ability levels made it easier for them to adjust assignments accordingly." Although teachers argue that tracking better serves their students' needs, the research literature is relatively void of empirical studies that connect tracking to increased learning gains. To the contrary, there is convincing evidence to suggest that students in low-ability-track classes do not perform as well as so-called low-achieving students in mixed-ability classes on achievement tests (Braddock and Slavin, 1992). In short, the research literature confirms my personal experience and suggests that tracking is a flawed practice that doesn't promote schoolwide achievement and is potentially harmful for the students relegated to the lowest tracks.

It is important for Latino students to be challenged and held to high standards, but it is equally vital that all students are provided with the support they need to reach those goals. With expanded opportunities and increased support in schools, Latinos would be able to more accurately demonstrate their academic capabilities, and teachers would be less likely to dismiss them as "culturally deprived," or "at risk," troubling labels that serve to justify for many the denial of access to academically rigorous courses. As part of our research, we viewed the film *How We Feel: Hispanic Students Speak Out,* in which Latino students share their perceptions about school. Sadly, the students featured in the documentary had a lot in common with us, even though they were interviewed almost twenty years ago. They described feeling uncared for by teachers and being discriminated against in school. I really related to one student who said that her teachers thought all Latino students had "attitude problems." She continued by saying that the teachers weren't necessarily wrong but that they didn't realize these students' "attitudes" resulted from being constantly ignored, controlled, or mistrusted by the teachers. I feel like I have been labeled this way by some of my teachers.

Having access to upper-level classes, however, addresses only one aspect of a larger systemic problem. The culture and climate of schools serving Latino students need to change as well. The dominant perception of students enrolled in low-level classes is that they are lazy or incapable of learning. The teaching in fundamentals-level classes revolves around completing worksheets and lacks meaningful, hands-on assignments. Teachers in these classes often modify their teaching to reflect their low expectations for students and don't create learning experiences that help students develop higher order thinking skills. The "dumbing down" of curricula for Latino students and other students of color is not unique to our school; it has occurred in schools across the nation for years. Recent research has documented that students in low-ability classes have less exposure to course content and receive lower-quality instruction than students in middle- or high-level classes or even mixed classes (Oakes, 2005; Oakes, Rogers and Lipton, 2006). If tracking were dismantled and all students were offered high quality educational experiences, the future for Latino youth would be more promising.

I AM MORE THAN YOU THINK I AM

The past two years have been full of life-changing events. Becoming a student-researcher and critically examining my own educational experiences has changed my life and the way I think about myself. In addition to developing an identity as a Latina scholar, I also became a mother during this time, which has also heightened my awareness of the educational opportunities available to Latinos. I want the best for my daughter, and for her to have a chance at a great life, schools need to work better for her than they have for me and so many other Latinos. I don't want her to have to endure what I have gone through in schools. Prior to having my daughter, school was difficult, and it is even more difficult now as I try to balance being a student and a parent. My daughter provides me with motivation to do well personally and to transform the education system for future generations. When people look at me, especially now that I am a teen mother, they don't see the next teacher, nurse, or other type of professional. In some ways, people see me as a walking stereotype. I have to deal with the prejudice against Latinos, women, and teen parents that exists in our society. But I am more than a stereotype or a label. I am a strong young Latina who is committed to doing all I can to expand educational opportunities for Latino students.

Right now my school is segregated into two groups: students of color, most of whom are Latino, and white students. Eliminating tracking would promote integration, which I thought was a goal in our society. Our classes would look a lot different than they do now. We would have students of diverse backgrounds in all our classes, and consequently our learning experience would be enhanced. De-tracking would create more opportunities for cross-cultural interactions. It would also offer many Latino students in our school the opportunity to show how smart they really are, thus debunking the stereotypes about our perceived lack of intellect or motivation. Finally, with the elimination of tracking, we would have the chance to add "student" to the many identities we have. Currently, school is a place where many of us are just passing time but never really have the opportunity to develop our intellect. If classes were more evenly balanced in terms of race/ethnicity, it would lead to a greater balance in all aspects of school. Inaction results in the maintenance of the status quo, where the majority of Latino students continue to be underserved by schools. We cannot delay efforts to transform the education of Latinos. Too many lives depend on it.

Many people, including teachers and students, think that the system is too big and too powerful to be changed. Proponents of academic tracking argue that high-achieving students would be held back if they had to learn with students who are currently in the lower tracks. Yet there are examples where de-tracking has worked. Some school districts are beginning the process of de-tracking, including the schools in Stamford, Connecticut. In the 1960s–1970s, Stamford schools sorted students into as many as fifteen different levels. Right now there is a system of three to five levels at each of the four middle schools in the district. These levels are going to be replaced in the near future by a two-tiered model in which the top quarter of sixth graders will be enrolled in honors classes and the rest in college-prep classes. As the *New York Times* reports, though some parents are opposing the shift, the superintendent and other stakeholders argue that tracking has played too large a role in maintaining the status quo, which is unfair to kids and their families (Hu, 2009).

Off-Track: Classroom Privilege for All (1998), a video documenting a de-tracked class in action, highlights a world literature course in a New Jersey high school and provides powerful evidence to support providing all students with access to quality learning opportunities. During an interview in which she offers a poignant rationale for eliminating tracking, Professor Michelle Fine notes, "We don't need public education to reproduce social, class, and race discrepancies. We've got a larger society that's more than happy to do that. The task of public education is to interrupt those discrepancies and create a broader set of opportunities for everybody" (Hancock Productions, 1998).

More schools should consider a de-tracked approach. It would require a change in thinking among many educators, but ultimately eliminating tracking would provide all students with a more well-rounded, academically rigorous education and increased opportunities upon the completion of high school. Students decide on their level of investment in school based on their appraisal of the opportunity structure available to them. I also think that being actively prepared to attend college would encourage more Latinos to remain in school and would diminish the dropout/pushout rate. As it stands now, many of us who are stuck in the lower tracks don't see college as an option. Even if we do well in our classes, we are not taking the appropriate prerequisite courses for college and are largely unprepared to complete college-level work.

Because schools marginalize Latinos by funneling them into lower-level classes, many of us have lost our self-esteem and confidence to do well in school. With the elimination of tracking, Latinos will feel more confident about their abilities and potential for academic growth. I used to feel that white students were way smarter than me because they were consistently placed in higher-level classes. Once I began to research tracking, my perspective started to change. Through my research, I learned that my perceptions were inaccurate. Latinos are as smart as anyone else; we just have fewer opportunities to show how smart we really are.

Conducting research regarding the education of Latinos has led me to think more critically about the need for more Latino teachers. Although the Latino population is growing rapidly, we continue to be underrepresented in the teaching profession. If the teaching force continues to be homogeneous and overwhelmingly white, the cultural conflicts Latino students like me experience daily will persist, and dropout/pushout rates for Latino students will continue to soar. For this reason, I am considering going to college to get my bachelor's and master's degrees to become a teacher myself. Not only do I think that it is important for future generations of Latino students to have teachers who can understand them, but I also think that my white coworkers would be able to learn a lot from me.

Novice as well as veteran teachers have much to learn about Latino students. As part of this project, I have begun to think about myself as an emerging expert in Latino education. I can draw from my personal experiences, and I have also been formally studying the education of Latinos for two years. At school, I always thought the teacher was the only one with knowledge and that I was there solely to receive it. I now recognize that I, too, possess valuable knowledge, and the educators can also learn from me. After our conference presentations, many of the audience members approached me to talk and ask questions about our work. Having people demonstrate interest in me and my work has made me feel important in a way that I have never felt in school.

RECOMMENDATIONS FOR TEACHERS

To the teachers and future teachers who are reading this book, I hope that this chapter has extended your knowledge about academic tracking, heightening your sensitivity to the experiences of students relegated to the least academically rigorous tracks of their school. Indeed, grouping students by their perceived ability level may seem like a logical way to organize schools or an easier way to teach. But what happens to the students who are tracked into low-level classes and not prepared for college? How are our futures compromised by your decisions? Many schools have been tracking students for years, and only some are starting to experiment with new methods of organizing the delivery of instruction. So what can teachers do until then? First of all, if you are teaching a "low-level" class, try to make it exciting and challenging for those students. I know some teachers like to save their energy for the high-level or advanced placement classes because they think they can do more with those students, but those of us in fundamentals-level classes are filled with untapped potential and are waiting to be challenged and engaged academically. Young people are especially insightful. We can tell if a teacher is just getting through our class but is really looking forward to the honors class that comes in next period. I would also encourage teachers to use action research with their students and have them participate in a similar study of tracking practices at their school. For example, in math classes, teachers can have students use real data to expose tracking and show how it is largely based on race. Students can learn important math skills while using real data to change potentially harmful policies at their school.

Second, schools need to make sure that all students are prepared to attend college and are informed about the college admissions process. Because we aren't labeled as "college material" according to our placements in classes, teachers and administrators assume that we are not interested in college at all. Tell us when the SATs are scheduled, or when the college fair will be and help us access them. In our school, many students are left out of these conversations because teachers and counselors assume that we are apathetic about our education, an assumption that is fundamentally flawed. Students will rise to the level of expectation set for them (Merton, 1948). The expectation should be that all students prepare for college to ensure that they have options after graduation.

Third, teacher education programs should prepare teachers to work with Latinos. This is an underexamined issue that affects the quality of education for Latino students. If I were a college professor training teachers to go out into classrooms and work with Latino youth and families, I would have my students experience Latino people, language, and culture in settings outside school. There are many ways to accomplish this goal, but traditional approaches have not been sufficiently successful. Immersion experiences, in which someone puts him or herself into a completely new environment for a certain length of time, can be very powerful, but they have to be done appropriately, accounting for the differential power relations that govern interactions between Latino families and teachers in schools. Moreover, immersion experiences shouldn't be focused on extracting information and returning to the ivory tower. I don't want people to come to my community just to study us like we are laboratory animals. I think teachers should naturally spend time in Latino neighborhoods, and they will learn a lot as a result. Sometimes I think teachers don't relate to us because they are scared of what they don't know. Those who are charged with preparing the next generation of teachers should require their students to step out of their comfort zones and get to know us.

Finally, teachers should allow their students to inform their practice and seek input from students regarding how to improve their teaching. I feel strongly that many teachers are interested in improving their practice and helping students achieve, but they often feel like they don't have the power to make change within their schools. As a Latina high school student, I know how that feels. I can relate to feeling like decisions about me are being made without my input all the time. Teachers are knowledgeable about teaching, but they are rarely included in shaping national and local policy related to education. Both Latino students and their teachers are marginalized by larger policies within schools, and collectively we can work to dismantle the oppressive forces that limit their teaching and stifle our learning.

NO LONGER SILENT

When I was first invited to contribute to this chapter on tracking, I thought I had nothing to say. My voice was silenced as a result of my experiences in school. For a long time, I was made to feel as if I were dumb. Now I am starting to feel like I have a voice. This chapter is one way for me to assert that voice. I hope that by sharing my experiences with tracking, locating them within the larger body of research, and calling upon teachers to dismantle this oppressive practice that readers will be inspired to raise their voices in solidarity with and in support of Latino youth and other students who have been underserved by schools.

9

THE COLOR OF JUSTICE
RETHINKING SCHOOL DISCIPLINE
AND EXCLUSION
with Ramiro Montañez, High School Student

۵

It all started one fall afternoon in the cafeteria of my school. I was sitting with a group of friends, as I usually do, discussing our plans for getting together after school. We were speaking in Spanish because that is the first language for most of us. When we get together, we like to speak in the language with which we are most comfortable, especially when we are having fun and joking around. All of a sudden, out of nowhere, this white student from a nearby table threw some yogurt at me and my friends, shouting, "English!" We were angry, but we have had a bunch of run-ins with school security and administrators in the past and knew that they always side with the white students. We assumed that if we reacted by throwing food back, we would be the ones in trouble. Still, we had to do something. So one of my friends went over to a teacher and let her know what happened. She acted like she was too busy to deal with it and told him to go sit down. I then went over to that table and told the offending students to chill. They laughed at me and told me to shut up and sit down. At this point one of the white kids pushed me with two hands. I retaliated by punching him in the face. Immediately the security school guards came rushing in and tried to restrain me. They took me and my friends to the principal's office and did not even question any of the white students who started the entire incident. As I waited in the office to find out my punishment, I thought to myself, here we go again.

I know that hitting someone is wrong and against school rules. However, this could have all been avoided had an adult intervened. There is a growing tension between Latino and white students at my school, and school personnel do nothing to address the problem. In fact, I would go as far as to say that they actually add fuel to the fire and exacerbate it by targeting Latinos and turning a blind eye to the negative behaviors of white students. In this case, we asked a teacher for help, and she was unwilling to do anything. Also, as seen in his screaming at us to speak English, the student who threw the yogurt took issue with us speaking Spanish in the cafeteria. We get criticized all the time by our teachers for speaking Spanish, and there is an anti–Spanish language and anti-Latino feeling in the school. Teachers and administrators do nothing to help improve the climate of the school for Latinos and then treat us harshly when we try to assert ourselves and get respect in the few ways that we can. As I look back on this incident, as well as several other similar incidents that I or my Latino friends have experienced, I realize that the way school administrators deal with discipline issues marginalizes us and depresses our interest in school.

This chapter takes a closer look at school discipline and exclusion policies, with special attention given to racial/ethnic differences in the ways that students are disciplined. I draw from some of my personal experiences with school security and administrators in my high school as well as the research literature on the topic to show how Latinos and other students of color are pushed out of school by discriminatory discipline practices. In addition, I share some of the findings from my original research on the racialized aspects of school discipline to clearly demonstrate that these practices are not random, neutral, or colorblind. Finally, I discuss what scholars have referred to as the "school-to-prison pipeline" (Christle, Jolivette, and Nelson, 2005; Wald and Losen, 2003; Edelman, 2007), the pathway from schools to prisons for students who are marginalized and pushed out of school as a result of the racist application of discipline policies. Instead of physically punching back, as I did in the cafeteria, this is my verbal jab to speak back to those adults who tried to push me out of school. Through the recommendations that I share at the conclusion of the chapter, I hope that future and current teachers and administrators will read this, feel my pain, learn from the research, and change the ways they discipline students to create a more equitable and just system, resulting in a better school climate for all students.

THE COLOR OF SCHOOL DISCIPLINE: A LOCAL PERSPECTIVE

Based on my experiences, discipline policies in school are applied differently, depending on the racial/ethnic or linguistic background of the student. Latino students don't have the same freedoms that white students in my school have. Teachers, administrators, and school security let white students do essentially whatever they want. There is an assumption that white students are well intentioned and Latino students and other students of color are nefarious and in need of being controlled. No matter what we are doing, our motives are assumed to be negative. In contrast, white students are always given the benefit of the doubt, even when they are doing something wrong. Racial discrimination is evident in every aspect of school life.

One of the most vivid examples of the differential treatment of Latino students can be seen in the classroom. I can't even count how many times that I have been reprimanded by teachers for asking classmates for assistance in understanding something after a teacher has refused to help me. I came to the mainland United States from Puerto Rico when I was fourteen. I speak English reasonably well, but I still have some trouble getting everything teachers are saying, especially when they are going really fast. Sometimes, I just need them to slow down or repeat something. I suspect that I am not the only one who feels that way. I have, like a good student, raised my hand and asked for teachers to clarify a point. Most often, they will say something like "I went over that already" or "If you can't keep up, that's your problem." I feel that most of my teachers are too focused on getting through the lesson quickly and less concerned with having all the students learn what they are trying to teach. It is sometimes just easier for me to lean over to a bilingual classmate and quietly ask for help. When I do so, teachers have scolded me for talking during class. When I tell them that I am actually trying to learn what they are teaching, they get frustrated with me and kick me out of class. My choices are either to stay quiet and not learn to my potential or ask a friend for help and take the chance of getting in trouble and asked to leave the class.

Getting kicked out of class, which happens all the time to Latino students at my school, doesn't seem to be the most effective punishment. When we are excluded from class, we have no chance to learn from the teacher or our peers. Consequently, we aren't exposed to important course content, making it even harder to follow the next lesson, and it creates a never-ending process of catch-up. When we are excluded from class, we often wander the hallways and become the target of security guards and administrators that patrol the halls. The hallways of the school are another site where the differential treatment of Latino students is evident. When Latino students are in the hallways—going to the restroom, working on a project, or going to our locker to get something for class—we are often asked to show a pass and are questioned about our intentions. In my experience, when white kids walk in the hallways, they are not subjected to the same scrutiny. Adults in the building assume that white students should be moving through the hallways as part of the school day and don't give them any negative attention for doing so. In contrast, they think that we should be glued to our seats all the time and that if we are moving around, there is a problem. We are constantly watched while we are in school, making it feel like prison sometimes.

Another area where we are monitored more intensely and disciplined more harshly than white students is the enforcement of the dress code. I attend a public school, and we are not required to wear uniforms, as was the case when I attended school in Puerto Rico. Here students have the freedom to choose what they wear to school, assuming they observe some rules. My school doesn't allow students to wear or even carry a hat in the hallways, and teachers and staff are always telling students who wear baggy pants to pull them up. I have asked adults in the building about the policy, and they say that they are trying to prepare us for the real world and that you can't dress certain ways at work. That might be true, but there are still differences in which dress code offenses they choose to focus on. The school dress code policy states that you cannot wear a hat in school, and that policy has recently been extended to prohibit even carrying a hat in the hallway. My friends and I wear fitted hats to school; it is the style for many urban youth of color. Our lockers are not safe places to store our belongings, so conflict emerges when we choose to wear hats to and from school, inevitably needing to bring them into the school building with us. The focus on curbing our use of hats, even targeting us for carrying them, seems ridiculous to me, and the dress code, guised in efforts to prepare us for the world of work, seems to target the styles of dress employed by Latinos and other youth of color. It has not gone unnoticed by my colleagues and me that a group of white students in my school paint their hair different colors, wear heavy metal T-shirts, and have piercings all over their faces, and there is no policy that aims to curb their forms of self-expression. If school officials are really enforcing the dress code to prepare us for the workforce, then they need to say something to this group of students as well. Sporting blue hair and earrings on your face will diminish your chances of getting a job more than baggy pants or a hat.

Another example that highlights the "color" of school discipline is the language that is used between administrators and students during official and unofficial discipline hearings and investigations in the school. During the questioning following the incident I described at the beginning of this chapter and throughout all of my encounters with the administrators in my school, I was spoken to and expected to speak only in English. Whenever you are about to get in trouble, you get anxious and worried; you feel a bunch of emotions, including anger, disappointment, and sadness. English is my second language, and whenever I get emotional, Spanish comes to my brain first, so that is what I speak. However, I can't speak Spanish in these meetings because none of the administrators would understand me. Some administrators also overtly express the anti-Spanish language sentiment I referred to earlier. Once my friend was being questioned about an incident he had with a teacher. He was fortunate that the only Spanish-speaking guidance counselor in the school was in the meeting with him and one of the principals. He started to tell his side of the story and express his feelings in Spanish, hoping the counselor would translate for him. Before she had a chance to, the administrator said, "This is my country. When you come here you speak English." My friend is Puerto Rican, so he is an American citizen by birth, and this is technically his country too. In legal terms, moving from Puerto Rico to any U.S. state is the same as moving from California to Texas. In addition to brushing up on U.S. history, this administrator also needs to address his bias against the Spanish language. By only allowing English to be spoken during school discipline hearings and investigations, many Latino students aren't allowed to fully express their perspectives and feelings, further alienating them from school.

THE COLOR OF SCHOOL DISCIPLINE: A NATIONAL PERSPECTIVE

I used to think that the adverse treatment of Latino students was unique to my school. After conducting research on the issue of school discipline, I found that the differential treatment of whites and students of color in matters of school discipline is not specific to Rana High School but rather is a national issue. My observations of racial/ethnic differences in school discipline are confirmed by William Drakeford (2004), who conducted research on the racial disparities in school discipline. According to Drakeford, Latino and African American students are overrepresented in harsh disciplinary actions such as school suspensions and expulsions. White students, he concluded, were more likely to receive school-based punishments such as in-school suspension and had a much lower rate of being suspended from or kicked out of school.

Similarly, Russell Skiba and his colleagues suggest that students from lower socioeconomic strata, those of us who are eligible for free and reduced-priced lunch, are at a greater risk for being suspended (Skiba et al., 2002). Most of the Latinos at my school come from low-income families, so we are targeted because of our race and socioeconomic status. Skiba and his colleagues' study of middle-school disciplinary data found that students were disciplined differently based on their race and gender, with male students of color most likely to be given harsh disciplinary sanctions. I don't think that students of color act out at school without provocation; rather, students sometimes engage in disruptive behaviors in response to their experiences in school. This theory is supported by the work of Pedro Noguera, who argues that those students most often suspended from schools have some of the greatest academic and emotional needs (Noguera, 2003). According to Noguera, increasing the rate of suspensions and expulsions to gain control of learning environments that may be chaotic does little to improve the quality of education for students. He writes, "Schools that suspend large numbers of students, or that suspend small numbers of students frequently, typically find themselves so preoccupied with discipline and control that they have little time to address the conditions that influence teaching and learning" (Noguera, 2003, p. 347).

Increases in the prevalence of suspensions can be connected to the implementation of zero-tolerance policies in schools (Noguera, 2003; Wald and Losen, 2003), which make suspension and expulsion mandatory for certain offenses. Since the early 1990s, many school districts have adopted a zero-tolerance approach to school code violations. As a result, the number of students suspended annually from school has nearly doubled since 1974 (from 1.7 million to 3.1 million). In addition, it is much more common for police to patrol in schools, and new laws have been enacted mandating referral of children to law enforcement authorities for a variety of school code violations (Wald and Losen, 2003, p. 10).

Although there are definitely some offenses that require students to be removed from school, such as bringing a weapon onto campus, zero-tolerance policies have been overused and at times implemented without taking important factors into account. It seems like schools are more concerned with punishing students, especially Latino and African American males, and maintaining a reputation of being tough on students than they are with addressing the conditions that influence students to act in ways that might get them suspended or expelled in the first place. These studies, as well as others (Brown, 2008; Monroe, 2005), confirm that the overrepresentation of minority students receiving harsh disciplinary actions is not limited to my school but is a common practice in schools across the United States. Many studies about racial disparities in discipline practices focus on African Americans, and less is known about the experiences of Latinos. With these studies as a backdrop, I initiated a study of the overrepresentation of Latinos in in-school suspension, which is discussed in what follows.

SCHOOL DISCIPLINE AND LATINO YOUTH

Motivated by my personal experiences and inspired by the research literature on school discipline and exclusion, I collaborated with several of my colleagues (who are also featured prominently in this book) to conduct original research examining the application of school discipline with Latino youth. I began by interviewing the members of the research collaborative. Almost without exception, the Project FUERTE student-researchers shared multiple examples of being discriminated against and treated more harshly than white students by teachers, security, and administrators. Most of my colleagues had at some point been kicked out of class, sent to in-school suspension, and/or suspended from school and had seen white students receive lesser punishment (or no punishment at all) for the same alleged offenses. The fact that these are our perceptions and experiences should be enough to convince adults working in schools to reexamine their practices and policies. Unfortunately, because we are young—and also because we are Latino—many people don't believe our stories. When we have pointed out the negative differential treatment of Latino students to teachers and administrators, they say we are making excuses or looking for the easy way out. They become wildly defensive if you suggest that race is somehow influencing their interactions with Latino students. So we figured the best way to demonstrate how Latino students were being disproportionately excluded from class was to conduct a study that documented the racial/ethnic texture of the in-school suspension room over time.

The racial makeup of the in-school suspension room was included as part of our study of race and tracking, as students are tracked out of classes as well as into different course levels that prepare them for different futures. Because youth who are being removed from class and treated as troublemakers share commonalities along the lines of race and social class, it seems logical to broaden our understanding of tracking beyond college prep and fundamentals-level classes to include the exclusion of students from classes through school discipline policies. To begin, we had to develop research questions and methods for collecting data necessary to answer them. We wanted to know: Are there racial/ethnic differences in the composition of groups facing in-school suspension? If there are patterns of racial/ethnic overrepresentation, do they persist over time? To address these burning questions, we used the same method we used to expose the racial discrimination in academic tracking (see Chapter 8).

We visited the in-school suspension room at twenty-five random times between late October and early June. Most often, we collected data on the demographics of the students being held in in-school suspension on Monday afternoons or Wednesday mornings, during the time our class met. We averaged just over two visits per month. Each time we visited the in-school suspension room to collect data for our class project, we read a brief introduction describing the research and invited students to participate. We then asked willing participants to identify themselves by race/ethnicity as white, Latino, African American, and/or other. They picked a sticker color that corresponded to their group and put their hands in circle. We then took a picture of their hands with stickers to tally the results. Our method allowed for students to identify with more than one group, and each student got to select his or her group identification, instead of us picking for them or identifying them for the purposes of the research. Of course, this method is not perfect. We only collected data on Monday afternoons and Wednesday mornings, so the composition of the room could have changed throughout the day. Nevertheless, the trends we uncovered are extremely provocative and disturbing.

Our findings confirmed what we already suspected. Latino students are excluded from class and placed in in-school suspension at much higher levels than white students. Since Latinos represent about half of the student population, you would expect them to represent about half of the students in in-school suspension. We had twenty-five data points, and not once did the racial/ethnic composition of the group approach proportionate representation. When we analyzed the results of all twenty-five visits collectively, we found a 5 to 1 ratio, with five Latinos for every one white student confined to in-school suspension. We found Latino students represented every time we went to the room, but there were several times when we found no white students at all. Overall, Latino students were overrepresented by approximately 500 percent among students suspended but forced to serve their suspension in-house.

Initially, I cracked jokes when we approached the room and made believe I was taking bets from my classmates who were helping me collect the data. "I predict 2 to 1 Latinos this time," one of my classmates would say; "3 to 1," I would reply. During the first few visits, we would all laugh because it was so obvious that Latino students were being targeted and suspended at such high rates. We would act professionally once we arrived at the room and then enjoy a collective laugh again once we left. As time went on and the pattern of Latino overrepresentation became more visible, it became less funny. Soon it turned so serious that we were angry about going to the in-school suspension room to collect data and wanted to end the data collection process. After ten visits, we figured we already had sufficient data. But we continued. We wanted to ensure that we made the most convincing argument, and the only way to do that was to collect data until the end of the school year. Each time we returned to our classroom to discuss what we had observed that day, the conversations increased in intensity. I am usually shy and not very talkative, but this issue really disturbed me and motivated me to speak out. I always thought the treatment of Latino students by teachers and administrators was problematic, but I never understood how these practices were institutionalized.

My understanding of Latino youths' exclusion from school through the disproportionate application of school discipline policies was enhanced through conversations with classmates around our findings. Our discussions were typically filled with passion, and we often challenged each other. The data were clear; Latino students are grossly overrepresented in in-school suspension. When asked to come up with potential explanations for our findings, one of my colleagues said with a big smile, "Because Latinos like to show off and act crazy. You know how we do." Another member of the group commented, "We want attention, so we act up sometimes." Building on this comment, another colleague added, "Acting up is sometimes the only way you can get teachers to hear you. Even if you are going to get in trouble, you have to get your feelings out." First, many of us confined our responses to personal reasons or individual personality or cultural traits as a rationale to explain our findings. As our discussion progressed, and as we started to use research literature on school suspension to support our arguments, we shifted our focus from oversimplified, individual explanations to include a more critical examination of the role of the larger system in the racial/ethnic composition of in-school suspension. I became increasingly aware of how cultural misunderstandings and a lack of cultural sensitivity contributed to pushing Latino students out of the classroom and into negative situations that lead to suspension. In addition to the example cited above—not being able to communicate with adults in the building in the language many of us feel most comfortable in—I think that many teachers and administrators are scared of us. As one teacher told me, "You look like a thug, and you will probably end up in prison!" I am a good person, dedicated to my family and respectful of adults who treat me respectfully. As a result of my research, my understanding of the racialized aspects of school exclusion are now expanded to include both individual and institutional factors.

I often feel angry in school, sitting through classes in which I am not learning anything and teachers and security are constantly watching my every move. Sometimes I want to snap. When I do have a disagreement with a teacher, I have a short fuse because I am holding in years of hurt feelings about things that have happened to me in school in the past and how poorly prepared I am for the future. What used to seem laughable now clearly paints a serious picture. There is nothing funny about excluding one group of students from school and making it harder for them to learn. But before I became more critical of my schooling experiences, I was unaware of the larger consequences of being kicked out of class or getting suspended.

THE IMPACT OF SCHOOL DISCIPLINE AND EXCLUSION

Research reaffirms what I suspected—suspending students isn't an effective practice (Mendez, 2003). Suspending students doesn't improve their behavior; it only disconnects students further from school and makes it harder for them to complete their work and learn the material. While our methods for collecting data and our willingness to critique practices within our own school may seem novel, our findings are not new (see Children's Defense Fund, 1975). In my experience, many teachers, especially those working in schools like mine where there is a mounting pressure to get kids to pass the state tests, have little patience. They tend to shift the pressure they feel onto us, stressing us about improving our test scores and making sure that our school makes adequate yearly progress (AYP) (No Child Left Behind Act, 2002). I am impatient with teachers because of the ways in which I have been made to feel in school, and I think many teachers feel stress because of the pressure put on them by school and district administrators. Whenever things don't go smoothly, whether students aren't "getting it" and are in need of extra help students are focused on something other than learning, many of our teachers are quick to kick us out of class. Most suspensions occur when the confrontation emerging from getting kicked out of class escalates. By removing us from class, they find temporary relief and can absolve themselves from their responsibility for our learning, attributing our low test scores to our discipline issues.

Suspending students, especially those that are already struggling academically in schools, makes it harder for students to pass their classes, proceed to the next grade, and eventually graduate. More-over, the suspension system, at least in my school, is flawed. When we get sent to in-school suspension, we have to stay there and are not allowed out of the room, except for one bathroom break. You just have to sit there all day. You are supposed to do your work, but the person monitoring you is not supposed to let you out to get the work you missed from your teacher, so most of the time you just sit there doing nothing, looking at the wall. If you know you are going to be in in-school suspension and can plan ahead to get your class assignments, many teachers get aggravated because they say you are making more work for them. It is no-win situation. The person monitoring the room just keeps you captive there as if you were in a holding cell in prison. Even when you do have the work you need for the day, the teacher in the room may not know that content and can't help you understand it and complete the assign-ment. Spending time in in-school suspension results in significant gaps in students' learning. There has to be a better way to discipline students and resolve conflict within schools.

Students who get suspended regularly are less likely to graduate from high school. Schools that have high rates of suspension, like mine, also have high dropout/pushout rates. I am only a teenager, and I can see the correlation between school suspensions and dropout rates. You would think that the adults in my school would come to the same conclusion and develop methods of improving student behavior that don't involve keeping young people out of the class-room and disrupting their learning.

School suspension is a short-term solution; it gets the student out of the class for a period of time and gives the teacher a break from that student. There is rarely an opportunity to resolve the issue that is the cause of the suspension. When you return to class after being suspended, the problem that led to the incident still exists and usu-ally leads to another conflict and subsequent suspension. The brief respite for teachers comes at a high price for the students who are excluded from learning with their classmates. Even those students who get suspended but are able to persevere through graduation often have lower achievement rates. As you can imagine, it is hard to keep up with the work when you have extended absences.

When students receive an out-of-school suspension, the school is supposed to work with them to ensure they get the work that they will miss. In my experience, the school sends a letter home letting you know that they will mail you the work, but they never do. The first time I was suspended I didn't know the rules, and nobody explained them to me. After not receiving any of my work in the mail from teachers for several days, I went to the school to try to get my assignments so I wouldn't fall too far behind. I stopped into the office to let them know what I was doing, and they started yelling at me and telling me if I didn't leave the building that second they were going to call the police and have me arrested. There was never any thought put into how I was going to keep up with my classes. When I returned, the teachers refused to help me and said I had to figure it out on my own. Basically, I had to teach myself if I wanted to learn. If I have to teach myself anyway, what is the point of going to school?

Repeated conflicts with school staff often result in feelings of alienation, increased absenteeism, and dropout/pushout. What happens to those students who do not finish school? Well, for many students of color, leaving school before they graduate often puts them on a path to prison. Right now there are more than three Latinos in prison for every one in a college dorm room (Associated Press, 2007), a ratio similar to that we found in the in-school suspension room. Latinos represent one of the fastest-growing populations in local, state, and federal prisons and jails. According to a recent report from the Pew Hispanic Center, the percentage of incarcerated Latinos increased from 16 percent in 2000 to 20 percent in 2008, while the population of Latino adults in the United States increased by only 2 percent, from 11 percent to 13 percent during that time period (Lopez and Livingston, 2009).

Approximately 85 percent of inmates don't have a high school diploma (Fields, 2008). That is not to say that every person who drops out will end up in jail, but there is definitely a correlation between going to jail and not having a high-quality education. Our society invests more financial resources in incarcerating inmates than it does to educate students in K–12 schools. In my state (and this holds true for most states), we spend three times as much money, on average, to keep a person incarcerated for a year as we do to educate one student for a year. You could say that Latinos and African Americans, who represent more than three-quarters of the prison population nationwide, are more valuable and worthy of investment in jail than in K–12 schools or colleges. If more money and time were invested in the education of students of color, the need for prisons would be greatly diminished.

There are few well-paying jobs for people who do not possess a high school diploma, so many people, including several of my friends, have to hustle on the streets to make a living and put food on the table. Many of my friends work jobs "off the books" in construction or as farm hands in the tobacco fields and apple orchards in the area, but those jobs are usually temporary and don't provide enough money to support a family. You are forced to make tough choices, and sometimes these choices put you on the wrong path. Timothy Black (2009) conducted an ethnographic study in which he followed three Puerto Rican brothers for eighteen years, trying to better understand the relationship between education and work for Latino men, and he argues that changes in society, including the loss of manufacturing jobs, the elimination of unions, and poor-quality education, led the participants in his study to troubled lives filled with dead-end jobs, bouts with unemployment, and, for two of the men, significant time in prison. Black suggests that prisons provide economic development for our country and that African American and Latino men are valuable as inmates because they provide jobs for people, most of whom are white, working in the prison industry.

The school-to-prison pipeline is real. Schools play a significant role in shaping students' experiences and preparing them to assume certain roles in life. When students are educated well, they have options for work and/or higher education. When they are not, their options are limited to jobs as low-wage laborers, which are insufficient to support a family. High dropout/pushout rates, which stem from high school suspension and exclusion policies, suggest that Latino students are not being educated well. As the numbers of Latino student dropouts/pushouts has increasee, so has the presence of Latinos in prison. We need to create a pipeline of Latinos into college and promising careers, not into prisons. Teachers and administrators are the ones who currently create and implement discipline policies, so they need to be actively involved in changing them.

RECOMMENDATIONS FOR TEACHERS

Because I have been suspended from school several times, receiving both in-school and out-of-school suspensions, and because I have researched this topic for almost two years for this project, I am in a good position to offer recommendations to teachers and administrators on how to address the problems created by excluding students, especially Latino students, from school. I don't think that many researchers can say that they have been on both sides of the proverbial fence, experiencing suspension personally on multiple occasions and studying it formally as a researcher as well. Based on my research, the first thing that I would suggest to adults working in schools is to allow students to co-construct the rules and the consequences for breaking them. When we come to school, the rules that are instituted to govern our behavior and the consequences for breaking them have already been established. Many times students don't think the rules make sense, as demonstrated in the uneven application of the dress code at my school. Having students work with the adults in the building to make the rules will increase the likelihood that students will follow them. As a result, discipline problems will decrease, and, I think, academic achievement will increase.

I would also recommend that students work with the adults in the building to come up with consequences for breaking rules. Students are less likely to think they have been treated unfairly when they (or their friends) are the ones who developed the consequences applied in response to inappropriate behavior. Many students harbor ill will toward the school and many teachers because they feel they have not been treated fairly. Consequently, there is a lot of friction between teachers and students. The climate of schools would improve if students were treated more fairly. If I were a principal, I would even have a student panel that was involved in enforcing the discipline policies. It is our school, so we should have a say in running it.

I have also seen a lot of negative and disrespectful behaviors from teachers that go unnoticed and unpunished by administrators. Teachers will often say horrible things to us like, "I hate teaching in this school," "None of you are going to make it in life anyway," and "Latinos are lazy." I am not making this up. I hear these types of things from teachers all the time. Also, some teachers get in your face and start yelling at you disrespectfully. These behaviors should not be allowed either because they create a hostile environment for students. I think that there should be a process whereby students could be involved in disciplining teachers who don't follow the rules or who don't treat students with respect.

The district should provide training for teachers, security guards, and administrators who work with Latino youth and other students of color. First, they need to read the literature on school suspension, learn about the overrepresentation of students of color, and become familiar with strategies to interact more appropriately with Latino students. Most significantly, they have to realize that the literature says that suspension is harmful to student learning, hence pushing many students of color out of school. The adults in our school need to become more familiar with our experiences. Whenever we conduct presentations and share our stories and the information from our project, audience members are shocked to hear that schools have been less than supportive of Latino students. Discrimination is evident to anyone who cares to notice. Ask students what their experiences have been and help them explore how the policies in their school have affected them.

Finally, and perhaps most important, adults in schools need to work to make schools fundamentally different from prisons. When we are constantly watched and harassed and put in a room for days without the ability to move around or engage in academic work, we are in prison, not in school. School should be a place for learning, critical thinking, and personal development. Honestly, for many of us, none of this is happening. We are not learning, we are not encouraged to think or express ourselves freely, and our development is stifled. The school-to-prison pipeline begins with schools, and schools have the potential of offering more positive, alternate pathways for youth. To do so, school discipline and exclusion policies need to be reexamined.

PART 4

NO HAY BIEN QUE DE MAL NO VENGA

THE TRANSFORMATIVE POTENTIAL OF YPAR

⤺

This final section focuses on the transformative potential of Youth Participatory Action Research (YPAR). Thus far, many of the chapters have documented harsh, oppressive conditions that serve as "limit situations" (Freire, 1970) for Latino youth, impeding their personal and academic development. Certainly the data are alarming, and the situation is dire. However, we remain hopeful. Although not systematically implemented across most districts or states, YPAR has emerged as a promising practice with the potential to improve the educational experiences and outcomes for students of color and other groups of marginalized students. A growing body of research has documented the benefits of this innovative approach to working with youth who have been underserved by schools (see, for example, Torre, 2005; Torre and Ayala, 2009). The contributions to this section speak to the impact of YPAR on individual students as well as on a white teacher and aspiring teacher educator who participated in the multiyear project.

The students' participation in YPAR allowed them to challenge institutional forms of oppression and simultaneously create new identities and possibilities for themselves. The harsh conditions we rightfully bemoan and condemn, while implemented to oppress, became the fodder for our classes, the subject of our analysis, and the vehicle to academic achievement. As the refran above points out, good frequently can and often does emerge from less than desirable situations. Out of these negative conditions has emerged a group of more critically conscious students, poised to transform the field of education and eager to change the world.

10

FROM THE "EXCEPTION" TO THE "NORM"

RESEARCH AND PERSONAL REFLECTIONS ON YOUTH PARTICIPATORY ACTION RESEARCH

with Anthony Acosta, Undergraduate Student

❧

Growing up, I was my mother's pride and joy. Because I excelled in most classes, I was always referred to as the "exception" and praised by teachers and adults in my community. When I heard people reference my alleged exceptionality, I thought it was a good thing; I figured that I was being recognized for my academic excellence. Perhaps I was, but I didn't think about what being personally referred to as the exception said about other Latinos who were, metaphorically speaking, the rule. My understanding became more complicated when I overheard my fifth-grade teacher talking to one of her colleagues. She said, "Thank God for Anthony. Who would have thought that there is finally one Hispanic who actually may have a future?" At the time, her words confused me; I didn't know any better. It felt like praise, but even back then I suspected there was more to it. As the years passed, I felt as if teachers continued to see me as the exception, as the hope for my race. There was a lot of pressure placed upon me. I knew there was no way I could fail and let everyone down. I felt as if I were the last hope for all Latinos. There is, as they say, a flip side to that coin. While I received praise from teachers and was held up as the future of the race, my friends received little support, and there was little expectation that they would graduate from high school, move on to college, and eventually get good jobs.

The pressure started to get to me in middle school. I began to feel alienated from my Latino peers. Teachers singled me out in what they thought was a positive way, but it drove a wedge between me and my friends, so I began to act up in class and purposely perform poorly on assignments. As I lost teachers' praise and respect, I was comforted by feeling less alienated from my friends. Eventually, teachers stopped singling me out for praise and treated me like everyone else, which was just as much of a problem. I guess I never really felt comfortable as a Latino child in school, and teachers didn't see how holding low expectations for other Latinos had a negative impact on me, a smart and high-achieving Latino student.

At a parent-teacher conference later that year, my teachers shared their concerns about my academic performance and told my mother I was not reaching my potential. Once again elevating me and my potential while disparaging my Latino classmates, they told her I was "different from the others" and should "spend more time with the white kids in the class because they will be successful in life." One teacher went as far as to suggest that my friends "had no futures" and weren't going to succeed academically. I, on the other hand, had been blessed by teachers, for reasons I didn't fully understand, as "the golden child." I thought many of my friends had as much, if not more, potential than I did. We lived in the same neighborhood, attended the same schools, and had families that were very similar. Yet I was put on a path to academic success, and they were put on a path leading to the tobacco fields that surround the outskirts of my community. Teachers wanted me to be the exception; I wanted academically successful Latinos to be the norm. I was young, but already I had developed strong feelings about being Latino, and my personal identity was strongly connected to my ethnic identity as a Puerto Rican.

As far back as I can remember, I wanted to do well in school and in life. My family taught me to value school and to try to make the most out of life. However, my desire to do well in school was equaled by my strength of identification with my community. Kids like me should never have to choose between academic success and connection with our communities, friends, and families. That is why I chose to write this chapter, which describes my research regarding the educational aspirations of Latinos and the impact that conducting this research has had on me. My aim is to share the voices of the participants in my research to clearly demonstrate that Latinos want to do well in school and that schools too often don't support their growth. It is also important to note that school had more meaning for me once I started to learn about my community and saw how I could use what I was learning to change teachers' practice and the policies that shape educational opportunities for Latinos.

COMPARING TEACHER AND COMMUNITY PERSPECTIVES

The personal story that I used in my introduction was not an isolated incident. As a Puerto Rican male, I am constantly presented with stereotypes about my group. To many people who don't know me, I may be perceived as a "thug" or "hood" because of my style of dress. The common perceptions of urban Latinos are that we don't do well in school, have children out of wedlock, and are out to make fast money, even if that means doing something illegal. This is simply not the case. I have been working various jobs since the age of sixteen. I do not work because I want the money, though it is a nice perk, but more as a way to help support myself and my family and to gain work experience that will be necessary for me to survive once I graduate from college and enter the "real world."

I interact with other Latino males daily, and the overwhelming majority of them want to do well in school and come from families in which education is highly valued. Despite working more than fifteen hours a week throughout high school, I was still able to take four advanced placement courses, graduate at the top of my class, and gain admission into a branch campus of the University of Connecticut, where I am currently a pre-pharmacy major with a 3.8 grade point average. Once teachers got to know me, they realized that I didn't fit into their stereotypical profile. They held me up as the exception but still held on to their negative perceptions of Puerto Rican and other Latino males, generally speaking.

My research, which I began when I was a senior at Metro High School, sought to provide additional data points for teachers to better understand the aspirations of Latino males and the goals and expectations that members of the Latino community have for this group of students. The public perceptions of Latino males are not completely fabricated out of thin air; they are based on some data, the one side of the story about Latinos that *does* get told. If you watch the news or look at the data regarding the academic performance of Latinos, you will notice a trend. Both can be interpreted as largely negative. Anytime a Latino male does something wrong, it seems to make the news, and the reporters always make sure to share the fact that it was a Latino who committed the offense.

Similarly, academic achievement data for Puerto Ricans is also largely depressing. More than half of all Latino males fail to complete high school in four years (U.S. Department of Education, 2009), and Puerto Ricans have some of the lowest rates of academic achievement among Latinos in the United States. Even though they generally speak English and are U.S. citizens, whether born on the island of Puerto Rico or the mainland United States, Puerto Rican youth between the ages of sixteen and twenty-four have the lowest rates of school enrollment and employment compared to other groups of Latinos (Treschan, 2010). A recent report released by the Community Service Society of New York found that Puerto Ricans in that city were unemployed and out of school at twice the rate of Mexicans (Treschan, 2010). These trends are not limited to New York, the site for that study; the undereducation and underemployment of Puerto Ricans is a huge problem in my community as well. I have often wondered why so many Latino students drop out of school. I don't believe high dropout rates among Latinos can be attributed to low aspirations or poor work ethics. Most Puerto Rican males (and females) that I have met, both inside school and out, have high aspirations and desire a more promising future. There is no denying the fact that the dropout rate for this group is extremely high, but why? I think simple explanations like "They don't care about school" are insufficient to explain away these gaps in achievement. To unpack the possible reasons for Latino male underachievement in schools, I sought out several sources of data. The most important data source for my study was my community, which is home to one of the largest Latino populations (by percentage of residents) on the East Coast.

My personal experiences with teachers' perceptions of my community, coupled with the data regarding deficit perspectives of Latino students presented throughout this book, led me to co-construct a study to learn more about Latinos' views on education. Wanting to move beyond teachers' stereotypes of Latino males and guided by a passion to include Latino voices in the discourse on education, I interviewed Latino members of my community, asking two simple questions: (1) What do you want for your sons and/or the Latino males in this community? and (2) Why do you think so many Latino males have not succeeded in school? In what follows, I share some of the responses of different members of my community as well as my analysis of each.

Padres/Parents

Because Latinos' lack of success in school is most often blamed on Latino culture, it made sense to me to start with elders in the community, those who typically pass on Latino culture to their children. In addition, many teachers refer to low parental involvement as the reason Latinos don't do well. Interviewing parents first allowed me to get at the heart of the issue and learn more about parents' aspirations for their male children. My friends attend a variety of schools in and around our city, and they have had different experiences in school. Some have experienced school success; others have left school prematurely. Because I had a relationship with this group of parents, I thought they would be more than willing to share their honest perspectives; therefore, I decided to include them as participants in my research. In total, I interviewed eight parents. The interviews were conducted in whichever language the parent was most comfortable speaking. Some interviews were in Spanish, others in English, and some in a mixture of the two. During the interviews, I took notes and tried to record the main ideas the parents conveyed, at times trying to quote their exact words. At the conclusion of each interview, I read them what I had written to check its accuracy. One of major themes that emerged from my interviews with parents was the significant value they assigned to education. The words of Pedro's mother sum it up. She said, "¡Educación es lo más importante en la vida!" (Education is the most important thing in life!)

Other parents had similar thoughts on the importance of education for their children. Rafael's father, one of three fathers included in the group of parents interviewed, went into more depth, saying: "What are you going to do without *una educación*? Nothing. What kinds of jobs are out there for you if you don't have education? What do they pay? If you want to do good in life, you need to have an education. That is the bottom line. You either get an education or you get a bad job or probably no job." As I stood there listening to Mr. Rodriguez, I remember the way that his voice trembled and the power of his words. It seemed that he wasn't just responding to the questions but also channeling his experiences in school and his desire for change into his response. Equally passionate about education, Señora Suarez, my friend Damien's mother, said:

> Growing up on the island [of Puerto Rico], my family had a *finca* [farm]. My parents stressed school and hard work, but we always knew that we would eat and put food on the table. We live *en la ciudad* [in the city] now. There are no fincas here. You don't work; you don't eat, *mi amor* [my love]. Or, you have to do what you gotta do to get money for your family and that gets our boys in trouble. That's why so many of them [Latino males] are locked up. They need a chance to succeed in this life and education is that chance.

Señora Suarez echoes the arguments forwarded by many researchers of the U.S. Latino experience, even though she hasn't read their books. Julio Cammarota, in his powerful book *Sueños Americanos* (2008), writes:

> Latinos have some of the lowest educational attainment rates, implying that they will tend not to meet the basic credential requirements for entrance into the high-skill and high-paying job markets ... work options for young Latinos without college degrees become limited to a single alternative: a job in the expanding low-wage service sector. (Cammarota, 2008, 24)

The parents confirm what Cammarota found in his study, and they fear that if their children don't do well in school, jobs at fast food restaurants and department stores are waiting for them. Although there is nothing wrong with working in these jobs per se, they tend not to pay well and have little room for advancement.

Several of the parents cited racism as a barrier to quality education. Many of them asserted that educational opportunities for their children are limited because they are Latinos. For example, Señora Quiñones, my friend Joey's mother, said, "This city never wanted us here. The schools have always treated us bad. *Tú sabes* [you know]." Señor Portes, Freddy's father, commented, "*El racismo* [racism], Tony. That's a big part of it." Parents' aspirations for their children, as seen in these responses, were high. They wanted the best for their children, and they viewed education as important for living a full life and for basic survival. They also acknowledge the pervasiveness of institutional racism in the lives of Latino families and how it hinders their children's opportunity for a quality education.

The Domino Players

The parents I interviewed have known me most of my life. I didn't want people to think that the parents' answers would be like mine because we are so close. Also, I thought that other people would provide different but equally important perspectives. Expanding the research sample, I interviewed a group of four men who regularly meet to play dominoes in front of a bodega in my neighborhood. I thought that capturing male perspectives on Latino male achievement would add a layer of complexity to the narrative, so this group of men who have a long history in my community seemed like a perfect group to interview. Again, none of the people interviewed said anything that came close to having low expectations or aspirations for Latino males. Like *los padres* that I interviewed, the men shared high aspirations for their children. One said, "Of course we want our boys to do good in school. In Puerto Rico, school is stressed. Look how many people there go to college compared to here. There is something about this place that doesn't allow us to do good." Another one of the men followed up with, "Like any [other] group, Latinos want their kids to do better than we did." The best point, in my opinion, was offered by the third member of the group that I interviewed. When I asked him, "How important is education for Latinos?" he responded:

> We have been fighting for education for a long time. Have you ever heard of ASPIRA? That organization has been fighting [the system] for a long time. People around here are always trying to make the schools better for our kids. Why would we fight like that if we didn't care? We care more than many other groups. They don't have to fight for their rights. We do.[1]

The Church Ladies

The final group that I interviewed was made up of five Latina women at my church. Some of the women were friends of my mother, so I knew them well. Others I had heard of only by name. When I told them that I was doing research for a school project about Latino education and the high rate of dropout among Latino males, they were all excited to share their opinions. Like the other participants in the study, they stressed having high aspirations for Latino males in their families and in the community. Doña Ana was the mother of two boys, one who was attending college and one who had dropped out of high school. Hers was a very interesting case because you had two completely different educational trajectories between siblings. I would assume that both kids were raised similarly, hearing positive things about the value of school from Doña Ana. Nevertheless, her two sons took two completely different paths. Her insight into the dropout crisis demonstrates how schools can shape the futures of Latino boys. Commenting on why she thought her boys had such different educational outcomes, she shared:

> Alejandro was my oldest. He went to [City] High School. That school is really big. He didn't like it there, but there was no other choice. I couldn't afford Catholic school. Nobody there cared about him, not the teachers, not the principal. School wasn't easy for him. Then when Johnny went to junior high school, he got into the magnet school. There the kids wore uniforms; there was discipline and respect. The teachers there knew him and looked out for him. I think the kind of school you go to and the way people show you *cariño* [care] has a lot to do with it.

Doña Clara also had two sons, both of whom were still attending high school but were struggling academically. She commented:

> *Mis hijos* [my sons] have had a hard time with school. My oldest gets suspended all the time. I don't have the answers, Tony, but maybe your project can help because you're right, too many of you are not graduating and going to college. I don't know what the answer is, but I do know that I want them to do good, get good grades, graduate and go to college or get a job.

I could really feel Doña Clara's pain. As she spoke to me, I could see tears start to come to her eyes. It was a tough subject because for these ladies, the dropout rate wasn't just a statistic about other people's kids. With all of the negative variables associated with failing to complete school, this topic was deeply personal.

The three other women from the church all had children, and they all stressed how important getting a good education was to "help the family move forward," "to do what you want in life," and to "be able to raise your kids right." Again, in contrast to the dominant narrative regarding the value of education in Latino communities, Latino families do have high aspirations for their children. All these perspectives, including comments from parents and members of the community, clearly attest to the importance Latinos assign to education. The parents' comments also reveal that many of the participants believe that there is a system that is operating against Latino males, pushing them out of school. The responses of the participants, as well as books and articles I read for this project, made me think differently about the dropout situation in the Latino community.

RESEARCH ON DROPOUTS/PUSHOUTS

My interest in the issue of dropouts and educational aspirations among Latino families peaked when I read *Ain't No Makin' It* (2005) by Jay MacLeod. MacLeod followed two groups of youth who lived in a housing project. One group was comprised mostly of youth of color; the other group consisted primarily of whites. The youth of color believed in the promise of school and viewed education as vital to social mobility. They believed that if they worked hard in school, they could make it in life and have a good job. Having experienced generational poverty, the white youth didn't place high value on attending school, and they did not assert themselves academically. In fact, they caused trouble in school and constantly cut classes. As you can imagine, the white kids who didn't try hard wound up with low-paying jobs that made it hard for them to move up the social ladder. As many people do when they have few options, several turned to using and selling drugs. What was surprising was that the youth of color with whom MacLeod interacted endured the same outcomes as the white youth who didn't put forth as much effort. The author returned to the housing project where the youth lived ten years after first meeting these two groups of boys to see what they had made of their lives. It was shocking to learn that the outcomes for the two groups were relatively equal, despite their differences in aspirations, with most working in low-paying jobs and several having served time in prison. Becoming aware of the social reproductive function of schooling prompted me to think of the application of this theory to describe the experiences of Latino males in my city.

I have been a resident of Hartford all my life. I was in the Capital City school system until I completed the fifth grade, when I transferred to Metro High School, a magnet school that went from sixth to twelfth grade and comprised students from six different districts. Capital City is one of the poorest in the United States, and because schools are funded mostly through property taxes, the amount spent on kids' education in Capital City is less than in the suburbs. Also, whenever you have high levels of poverty and people striving to make it with little opportunity, you also have social problems like violence. My city is ranked as one of the most violent cities in the United States. What role do schools play in shaping these conditions? What role should they play in helping to fix them?

Michelle Fine's research in *Framing Dropouts: Notes on the Politics of an Urban Public High School* (1991) also influenced my thinking. In her research with students at a large urban comprehensive high school in New York City, she shows how schools play a large role in molding students' opportunities to learn and succeed. By including the perspectives of students in her research, she paints a different picture of dropouts and shows how negative interactions between students and schools lead many students to leave school. Instead of depicting dropouts as lazy students who don't want to do the work necessary to succeed in school, she argues that youth who drop out are often the students who are most critical of schools. However, in addition to being critical of the poor quality of education they are receiving, they are also the least likely to conform and just "play the game."

Another area of research related to my work is the education of Puerto Ricans on the island of Puerto Rico. As I said earlier, the dropout rate for Puerto Ricans in U.S. schools is ridiculously high. As a result, many teachers have concluded that Puerto Ricans don't succeed in school because their culture doesn't value education. In addition to the stories told by my participants (above), the data regarding the academic achievement of Puerto Ricans on the island of Puerto Rico also paint a different picture. In 2005, more than one in five people on the island of Puerto Rico over the age of twenty-five had a bachelor's degree or higher, an increase of more than 20 percent since the 2000 census (U.S. Census, 2007). High school completion rates for Puerto Ricans on the island are significantly higher than for those of us on the "mainland" United States. Therefore, since Puerto Ricans on the island and on the mainland share a culture, the Latino dropout crisis cannot be reduced to oversimplified explanations such as "the culture doesn't value education." I believe that as a minority group in the U.S. mainland context, we are treated badly, whereas on the island most of the elected officials, teachers, principals, and so on, are Puerto Rican, so students there know that Puerto Ricans can achieve academically.

What I learned from my interviews in the community; through reading the work of scholars who have studied the issue of dropouts, especially research with a focus on the disproportionate dropout rates among Latino and African American youth, and data regarding the academic achievement of Puerto Ricans on the island has significantly shaped my thinking about the issue. I now realize that U.S. schools create opportunities for a select few students and leave the majority behind. As one who was treated like the exception—one of the few Latinos who could succeed, according to my teachers—I now understand why I was singled out for special treatment. Certainly, kids have to take responsibility, and many make the most of dificult situations, but it is hard when the goal of the system is to allow only a few students to succeed. I hope that through this research and other efforts to improve education for Latinos, kids like me will no longer be the exception but the norm.

THE IMPACT OF PARTICIPATION IN COLLABORATIVE RESEARCH

This project has not only influenced my thinking on the topic of Latino male academic achievement, but also it has made me think about myself and the process of schooling differently. According to Horace Mann, the founder of the common school movement, schools were designed to be the "great equalizer," meaning it shouldn't matter if you are poor or rich, white or a student of color; if you want to learn and achieve, and you are willing to put forth the effort, you can achieve success. Because of social stratification and school funding patterns, however, if you do not live in the right neighborhood or fall into the right district, then you can be forever stuck in a brutal cycle of undereducation and poverty. I feel that I was really lucky to be selected through a lottery to attend an interdistrict magnet school and did not have to attend my neighborhood middle and high schools. My local high school is classified as a dropout factory, meaning that more than 40 percent of the students who begin in ninth grade never make it to the twelfth grade. The magnet school I attended for the second half of my education, Metro High School, wasn't perfect, but there was an expectation that all students, including Latino males, could and should do well in school. Instead of being singled out as the only Latino with a chance of going to college, I got the sense from the administrators and the teachers that we could all go to college. I wasn't singled out as the exception but rather treated as the norm.

Teachers did not look at my baggy pants and fitted Yankee cap tilted to the side as signaling a lack of intelligence. They didn't judge me based on my physical appearance or view me through a deficit lens. Instead they provided me with what all students need—opportunity and support. During my senior year, I was able to take four Advanced Placement courses. It is unfortunate, but I know that these opportunities would not have been available had I attended my assigned zone school.

The difference between my experiences in traditional and magnet schools is made evident not only through the course offerings but also in the quality of instruction I received. Before I transferred to Metro High School, I was always "taught to the test." My state requires that all students deomonstrate a mastery of English, reading, and mathematics measured by standardized tests we have to take over the course of our schooling, beginning in the third grade. Most schools in my community have built their curriculum solely around passing this test. Consequently, classes like science and social studies, which are not required for the exam, were omitted from curriculum. Every morning teachers would bore us to death by using Success for All (SFA), a scripted program designed to improve our scores on the test. I don't know how good it was for improving our test scores, but I do know that it did nothing to make me like reading or writing. In fact, it made me hate reading and start to dislike school. Coming to school every day to learn how to pass a test results in many kids losing enthusiasm for school, thus fueling the premature departure of students from school.

I am really appreciative of the opportunity to attend MHS. However, I think it is problematic that my access to a quality education that prepared me for college and life was dependent on a lottery. I think about all the kids whose names weren't chosen during the lottery drawing and wonder where they are today. Maybe some of them made it, but probably, based on the statistics, most didn't. I could have been one of those statistics if not for the luck of the draw. It is unfair that the achievement of Latino males is based more on luck than hardwork or intelligence. As students, we don't get to influence the hiring of qualified teachers, the curriculum they implement, and, for the most part, what schools we attend. All kids should have the opportunities that I have had, and they shouldn't have to leave their neighborhoods or home district to get them.

One of the most interesting parts of this work has been interacting with other high school students, college students, and a university professor on a collaborative research project. Each of us took responsibility for a different aspect of the research, and all had to contribute to the larger project. As part of our efforts to inform the work of teachers, one of the research teams explored the experiences of successful teen mothers. Typically, girls who get pregnant in high school are treated like outcasts. The common perception is that teen mothers cannot complete their studies and pursue promising careers. My colleagues wanted to move beyond the discourse of pregnancy prevention, although prevention is certainly important, and identify women who have been able to achieve academic and personal success despite starting a family while still in high school. My colleagues were not trying to take the responsibility off the teen parents and place it elsewhere; they were trying to show that having a baby while still in high school, though difficult, doesn't portend a predetermined negative fate. Their project included voices that we never hear—those of successful teen mothers. It is important for girls who do get pregnant to see models of success, not just examples of failure. Just hearing these new perspectives made me rethink my stereotypes about teen mothers. If someone like me, who is connected to the community, still holds stereotypes that shape how I think about people in my community, then most certainly people who have little experience here or who only hear about us on the news are going to have stereotypes that need to be challenged. Because the publicized examples of failure outnumber and overshadow stories of success, I believe that it is imperative for educators to have increased interaction with successful Latino males and learn strategies that help lead to school success.

Another important outcome of my participation in this collaborative research project has been a shift in my perceptions of my future.

I always thought that I would be successful and have a high-paying job. I am on my way to that goal. Prior to this project, I thought making money was the most important thing in life. Now I realize that part of my responsibility is to make the world, starting with my community, a better place. I used to picture leaving Capital City and moving to a big house in the suburbs and never looking back. That is the model of success that is held up for youth of color from urban communities. Now I see how flawed that thinking was. Certainly I want to make a good living, but I also want to do something with that money and with my time for the community.

Finally, throughout school, the focus has always been on me as an individual. We take individual tests, get individual grades, and try to reach individual goals. By working on this group research project, I have begun to see the importance of working with others to achieve communal goals as well. The project was enriched because we each got to make an original contribution, and in the end it looked like something different and better than any individual effort. Of course, we had struggles and internal drama at times, but I learned a valuable lesson in teamwork. It is hard for an individual to change the system, but as a member of a group, you can change the world. All of us—students, teachers, families, principals, the community, politicians, and others—have the capacity to transform schools for Latinos and other youth the question remains, do we have the moral courage to do so?

11

BORDER CROSSING
PERSPECTIVES FROM A WHITE TEACHER
AND TEACHER EDUCATOR
Aja E. LaDuke, Graduate Student[1]

ॐ

I began my teaching career just as the No Child Left Behind Act (NCLB, 2002) took hold in public schools. Finally stepping into my very own classroom, I felt well prepared by my teacher education program. I was well versed in writer's workshop methods and facilitating reading groups with elementary students, as well as other innovative empirically supported techniques for literacy instruction. I was initially encouraged to use these tools at my disposal, but over time I noted that more and more valuable professional development time was devoted to rewriting our curriculum to conform to scripted reading guides with discussion questions made to "sound like the test." The myopic focus on test preparation contradicted everything that I had learned in college and graduate school about effective approaches to teaching and learning, in literacy and all content areas. I became increasingly frustrated as new initiatives designed to meet the requirements of NCLB continued to appear across the curriculum and in some cases reduced time for certain content areas altogether—that is, those that were not "on the test." I returned to graduate school, thinking that earning a doctoral degree would put me in a better position to effect change in K–12 education, to remedy these disservices to our students as I had come to understand them. Upon enrolling in a doctoral program, I had no idea the depths to which my experiences, both social and academic, would change my thinking about education and society in general so drastically and so emotionally. Never would I have predicted that my graduate work, and specifically my graduate assistantship with Project FUERTE, would show me another view of K–12 education entirely, one that revealed even more flawed policies, structural inequities, and disservices to students above and beyond the "test prep pedagogy" (Rodríguez, 2008) that had angered me and prompted me to return to graduate school in the first place. In this picture, significant gaps in my preparation as an educator were now not only visible, but glaring.

This chapter documents shifts in my identities, namely my racial identity and professional identity as a teacher, resulting from two years of collaborating with and learning from Latino youth. In addition, I will explore the ways in which my participation in the Youth Participatory Action Research (YPAR) collaborative served as a teacher education experience for me and therefore holds potential for preservice teachers. Like the Latino youth researchers who became my new teachers, offering me unique perspectives on teaching and teacher education, I was engaging in a process of introspection and finding a new voice with which to speak out in solidarity against injustices toward Latinos in U.S. schools. I will discuss how engagement with youth in this powerful way could take shape as an alternative or addition to traditional education programs, which often fail to adequately prepare teachers to work effectively with students of culturally and linguistically diverse backgrounds. Finally, I call for teachers to be open to shifting their identities and positively embracing the Latinization of U.S. schools.

SHIFTING THE FOCUS

Though my background was with elementary school students, my involvement in Project FUERTE and immersion in the high school environment increased my comfort level within it. Though we had established relationships and routines, there were still many moments that made me stop to think about my role as the only white participant in this Latinocentric collaborative. On one afternoon I walked into the classroom and placed my multiple bags down, as I would at the beginning of any other Action Research and Social Change class. For this class meeting, the students were going to process their experiences delivering a presentation at a professional conference the week before. These conversations, in which members of the research collaborative would share their thoughts about the direction and outcomes of the project, were common throughout class meetings. For the first half of class, students' comments focused primarily on the presentation, reflecting on their emerging sense of confidence as public speakers and intellectuals, questions from the audience they struggled with or found interesting, and their general sense of amazement with the dramatic juxtaposition between how they are positioned in school and their role as researchers in the project. During a pause in the conversation, they shifted the focus onto the adult members of the research collaborative, commenting, "You get to ask us a bunch of questions about what we think; we want to know what you think." To me, this shift in focus— from the adults pushing the youth to be more introspective to the youth probing into our feelings—was a sign that the students were enacting identities as researchers and intellectuals in a school setting that often suppressed their intellect and individual identities. They had taken the skills they had developed as a result of being interviewed several times by university researchers and through conducting their own interviews for their research and applied them in this real-world context.

The student-researchers asked the adults, among other questions, "What were you thinking on the first day you met us?" At that point, I was fully immersed in the project and accustomed to coming to Rana High School (RHS) at least twice a week over a period of several months for class sessions and extra meetings supporting our work, so I really had to force myself to think back to the very first day that we had arrived to meet our class members. I was caught a bit off-guard and gave a generic answer, referencing my great antici-pation of what was to come as well as feelings of trepidation that are common when embarking on any new experience. After I responded to their question, I asked my coresearchers what they thought I was thinking about them on that first day. Smiling and laughing, they said things like, "I bet you thought we were going to steal your purse or something." I laughed but then thought more about it. Maybe some small part of me was bothered—had they really thought that about me? I remained in that emotional space for about a minute and then jumped back into my head and the lessons I had learned from the students. They had been mistrusted, dismissed, forgotten, emotionally beaten down, and disrespected by teachers, the overwhelming majority of whom are white females like me. The truth is, upon beginning my participation as a graduate student, I wondered if I would be impeded by my whiteness and lack of experience crossing lines of cultural and linguistic difference in a school setting. I worried that the students might not accept me, especially because of their experiences with teachers who looked like me. I quickly learned that in order for them to accept me as a member of the research collaborative, I was going to have to perform my identities in ways that differed from the majority of teachers they had encountered. I was going to have to figure out ways to share power and join them as equal partners in the struggle for educational equity.

Much of what the students uncovered through their research pointed to teachers' lack of cultural understanding and competence among teachers working with Latino youth. From what I observed in my more than eighteen months at the school, they were right! Nevertheless, their proclamations about their teachers made during class discussions, such as "White teachers don't care," still hit home, hurt, and touched me profoundly. Although they were constantly challenged to qualify their statements and allow room for variability—directly connected to their desire not to be lumped together and stereotyped *themselves* by teachers—my heart often ached during these discussions. I shared the students' pain as they coded the teachers' overtly racist survey responses, which reinforced the idea that white teachers really only cared about white students. I wondered if it was possible for my care for them to compete with the barrage of negative comments they read. As the only white member of the team, it was not the only time that I felt insecure about my racial identity and the impact that my presence might have on the group.

When asked the question about my first impressions of the students, as discussed above, I didn't mention my concerns, including my fear that the student-researchers would not be able to see past my whiteness and give me a chance to prove that I was different from their teachers—to show that I had been actively working to "unbecome White" (Clark and O'Donnell, 1999) or perform my whiteness in ways that allowed me to connect with people of color (Raible, and Irizarry, 2007). In hindsight, I realize that I withheld this information in an effort to mask my vulnerability. I think my reluctance to be vulnerable stemmed not only from the ways in which I have been socialized to perform my racial identity but also from the ways in which I was prepared to perform the role of teacher. My teacher education program, lauded across the country and ranked highly in *U.S. News and World Report*, had failed to take into account that I was not just a teacher but a white teacher. Because of race-based privileges, unearned resources that individuals receive based on their membership in the dominant racial group, white people do not have to acknowledge their whiteness and the benefits associated with being white.

I often felt feelings of insecurity and doubt, wondering if, despite relationships we had built over hundreds of hours of interaction, the students would always see me as an outsider, imposter, or intruder. On some level, while trying to avoid being the typical white teacher they had encountered throughout their schooling and research—one who remains disconnected from students—I had done exactly that by not being honest with them and failing to be critically introspective in that moment as the "interviewee." It was not until I was able to shift the focus from studying students and remaining preoccupied with what they thought about me to looking at myself that I was able to fully integrate myself into the group. In a real sense, the students became my teachers, offering me valuable lessons about my personal and professional development that were absent from my teacher education program.

As teachers, we are trained to focus on students, and rightfully so. However, focusing solely on students, without concurrent efforts to improve one's ability to cross lines of cultural difference or consider the role that power plays in shaping interactions in and out of the classroom, can be as problematic as not centering students in our work at all. Teaching is a shared act between students and teachers. If there is no evidence of teaching, there is no evidence of learning. My vision of quality teaching has been strongly influenced by the work of Paulo Freire (1970/2000), who described teaching as a reciprocal act in which teachers and students shift roles and share power. My philosophy of education was just that—a philosophy—until the student-researchers forced me to confront my whiteness in ways that I had not contemplated prior to this project.

CROSSING BORDERS WITHIN THE COLLABORATIVE

We all make mistakes, and I admit that not sharing my initial fears to my coresearchers was one of mine. We all make them, teachers and students alike. To be effective educators, we have to be willing to admit them, whether it is not knowing the answer to a student's question in class or recognizing the underlying assumptions we hold about cultural and linguistic differences. To learn—and at times, unlearn—we have to be able to make mistakes, to be vulnerable, and even to be uncomfortable. I had to unlearn much of what I had been taught as part of my formal training as a teacher. As a preservice teacher, I was encouraged to take advantage of opportunities to learn *from* my cooperating teacher, as well as opportunities to try different lessons and strategies *on* my students. Opportunities to learn from students and their families remained unexplored and undervalued. Through my work in Project FUERTE, I was immersed, for the first time in a formal academic context, in another culture. The linguistic codes and "repertoires of practice" (Gutierrez and Rogoff, 2003) were sometimes unfamiliar and even jarring. My racial identity, as well as my role as a graduate student, initially positioned me as an "outsider" in the collaborative. During several of the earlier class meetings, I asserted myself in the hope that students would get to know me and welcome me into as a full participant in the research collaborative. Much of my energy was initially dedicated to "proving myself" and gaining acceptance, working largely from a paradigm that positions adults above youth in the social hierarchy. It was not until I opened myself up to be taught by students that I was able to begin to traverse cultural barriers and develop new understandings about myself, and myself in relation to others.

As a white person in a society that exalts whiteness, navigating schools that are most often governed by white, European, cultural norms, I rarely have to think about my identities. I can determine the contexts I enter and the borders I choose to cross or not cross. That is not the case for my colleagues of color, including the youth-researchers. Cultural border crossing—that is, crossing lines of cultural and linguistic difference—is a part of their lived experience, and they often have to think about which identities to perform in which contexts on a daily basis. They have developed the ability to read situations and evaluate these contexts and then make decisions about how to "perform" themselves in that moment.

Despite five years of university-based teacher education, bachelor's and master's degrees in education, multiple internships, and years teaching in my own classroom, I still had significant gaps in my preparation. In my years of teacher preparation I had been asked to reflect on myself and my practice plenty of times, to the point at which my classmates and I would joke, "Oh no, here comes another reflection." I was asked to ponder who I was as a teacher, what my teaching philosophy was, how I felt about the schools that I had worked in as an intern or student teacher, how successful a particular lesson was, and so on. Though I rolled my eyes at them, these reflections actually served me well in practice. Yet they were largely insufficient for preparing me to work in a school comprised primarily of students of color. Somehow I had missed the class that would ask me to dig deeper into my own assumptions, the parts of myself that were not so easy to face. Through participation in this research project, I realized these shortcomings and became increasingly frustrated with myself and with the years I had invested in higher education to get to this point in my career. Maybe I would have taught differently had someone asked, "Do you lower your expectations for students whom you think have 'troubled home lives'?" or other questions that might have provoked unsettling answers, before I had entered my own classroom. Instead, this process of critical introspection and subsequent border crossing was instigated by the very young people I entered the teaching profession to serve and emerged naturally within the context of the research collaborative.

To be certain, reading stories of urban schools and narratives emerging from the youth navigating these spaces can be an especially powerful learning tool. I first became familiar with the plight of urban youth of color in urban schools through texts like *Savage Inequalities* (Kozol, 1992) and *Literacy with an Attitude* (Finn, 1999), both widely popular books that have undoubtedly profoundly influenced the perspectives of teachers across the country. These texts, however, when not accompanied by border crossing into those spaces described so poignantly in prose, are largely insufficient for improving one's ability to work in urban schools.

Adults in school typically occupy positions of power over students, thus significantly influencing interactions across lines of difference. As significant as the immersion experience itself was, the unique role I played within the research collaborative was also crucial in creating a space for me to develop a greater understanding of myself as teacher and as a person more generally. I was not the instructor of record for the course in which the research project was embedded, nor was I a high school student or university intern. My role as a graduate assistant, a position largely unfamiliar to the students, allowed me to occupy an ambiguous space where I did not have to facilitate student learning or take responsibility for issues of grading, classroom management, or other tasks typically undertaken by the teacher. I could dedicate all my time to reflecting on and making meaning of my experiences, which distinguished me from the high school students who were taking a full complement of classes and working part-time jobs. I had the privilege of observing and interacting with the student-researchers from a unique standpoint. I watched them navigate through contexts and decide which identities to perform and which languages to use to enact them. I stood with them and shared their pain as they confronted racism daily in their interactions with adults in the school and marveled at their resilient spirit as they continuously bounced back after these events with renewed vigor to continued to pursue a high school diploma.

Schools do not exist in isolation, and the racism and other forms of discrimination that plague Latinos and other people of color in society at large also permeate these settings. For the first time, these encounters became deeply personal because they targeted people that I care for immensely. Although I identified with individuals who had experienced discrimination represented in texts and images in the popular media, my level of investment was heightened and the feelings of hurt and anger that accompany discrimination were intensified after I crossed borders and developed authentic relationships across lines of difference. The research project became our collective outlet to challenge and combat oppression and offer a new vision for the education of Latino youth—one informed by Latino youth themselves.

"DISCOVERING THE WATER"

For many educators and policymakers, the plight of Latino students struggling to successfully complete high school is completely foreign. As evidenced by the stories of the student contributors, many teachers are like fish living in blissful ignorance, to use Kelly Maxwell's (2004) metaphor, and have yet to "discover the water." Just inhabiting the same physical space as students doesn't necessarily result in understanding the sociopolitical and sociocultural contexts students have to navigate to achieve school success. Often hidden or suppressed are the struggles of Latinos to maintain a sense of self, particularly around their ethnic identities, while navigating spaces that are dominated by the "overwhelming presence of whiteness" (Sleeter, 2001). Those of us for whom this context seems natural foten take for granted the curve on which many students embark to learn the cultural norms associated with school. Many teachers may also unknowingly reify these norms and alienate students they believe are unwilling to completely assimilate and shed their cultural identities.

Conversely, the Latino students in the research collaborative are always aware of "the water" when they are in school. Each day they confront explicit and implicit messages that they need to change who they are within those walls to have a chance at academic success. I was aware of the privileges—particularly those around race and class—that I brought with me into this setting, and I had a general sense of the experiences of Latino youth navigating school from important works such as *Subtractive Schooling* (Valenzuela, 1999) and *Puerto Rican Students in U.S. Schools* (Nieto, 2000), among others, but my experience on this project was unique in that I had the opportunity to metaphorically stand in the water with Latino youth. As teachers search for ways to improve their practice with Latino youth, they must find ways to stand with their Latino students, share collective experiences—triumph as well as tragedy—and allow these experiences to inform their lives and their teaching practice. Being the only non-Latino member of the research collaborative was germane to this experience. For the first time in a professional setting, I was in the numerical minority, and I was not in the position of power. Although I have worked in settings where students of color outnumbered white teachers and students, I was always in a leadership role with a significant amount of status. Because of the collaborative, redistributive nature of YPAR, this was not the case in Project FUERTE. As the sole non-Latino participant in a research collaborative examining the education of Latinos, I was not the expert, and I lacked the valuable emic perspectives that the youth brought to the work. The convergence of crossing borders, relinquishing power, and developing a stance of solidarity with the youth allowed me to experience "the water," or the sociopolitical and sociocultural contexts of Latino education, in new, highly personal ways that would not have been possible without this experience. Moving beyond statistical portraits of Latino youth and growing to love this group of Latino students allowed me to bear witness to their brilliance, be enlightened by them, and forge a commitment with them to address the education of the largest group of students of color in U.S. schools more effectively in my work as a teacher and teacher educator. As a graduate student, I had read about dropout statistics and the conditions of urban schooling, and it affected me enough to commit to studying these areas in greater depth. But to some degree I could return to my regular student life—my white, middle-class, monolingual "American" life. After "discovering the water," I no longer feel like I have that luxury, nor do I have nostalgia for it. When I hear statistics or anecdotes about Latino youth, I immediately conjure up images of my colleagues in the research collaborative. The numbers and stories take on a new life and inspire me to act.

NAMING WHITENESS

Just as white teachers need to acknowledge the disconnect that can exist between their understandings of the experiences of Latino youth and the daily lived realities of students, it is also important to acknowledge how students' experiences in schools are shaped by whiteness (Wise, 2005) and efforts to subjugate the cultural identities of people of color within schools. Although students may see people of color represented in the popular media, they have little access to people of color in professional positions in the schools they attend and/or in the curriculum. When the perspectives and contributions of people of color are included, they are typically treated in a tokenistic fashion, relegated to certain months of the year (Banks and Banks, 2004; Gay, 2000; Lee, Menkart, and Okazawa-Rey, 1998). As asserted by Christine Sleeter (2001), most students of color attend schools that exalt white culture and values, although that is not stated explicitly, while the cultures and contributions of youth of color are ignored or, even worse, maligned. Lisa Delpit (1995) credits this to a deeply rooted but often hidden sentiment held by white teachers that their students of color are "other people's children." That is, there is a contradiction between how white teachers invest in their own children's education and the quality of education they provide for students in urban schools.

As evidenced by an array of studies, when potential teachers are participating in diversity, foundations, or multicultural education classes that require them to reflect critically on their own identities through the lenses of power and privilege, they are resistant and uncomfortable with the process, as it is often characterized by cognitive dissonance (Ahlquist, 1991; Assaf and Dooley, 2006; Clark,

1999; Galman, 2006; Ladson-Billings, 1996; LaDuke, 2009; Ryan, 2006). This dissonance is often due to the fact that many white students in teacher education programs have not had to face their own whiteness (Weiler, 1988). The privileges that accompany being white, such as representation in the curriculum, often remain hidden (Howard, 1999; McIntosh, 1989; Wise, 2009). Furthermore, they may never have been asked to think of themselves as raced or classed, or as having their own distinct culture, and have learned to adopt a colorblind outlook that allows them to move through many contexts, schools included, without having to talk directly about race (Irvine, 2003; Milner, 2006; Sleeter, 2001).

Resistance in its many forms, and as enacted by students of color, shows that the colorblind approach is not effective (Kohl, 1994; Ogbu, 1992). In contrast, studies of effective teachers of students of color in general and of Latino/a students in particular (Irizarry, 2009; Irizarry and Antróp-González, 2007; Ladson-Billings, 1994; Raible and Irizarry, 2007) reveal that teachers who have been successful with these populations not only acknowledge differences among students but also between themselves and their students, often involving admitting to and acting on one's own areas of disconnect. For example, in John Raible and Jason Irizarry's study (2007), two white teachers were profiled as successfully navigating diverse communities and providing quality, culturally responsive instruction for their students within them. These teachers made intentional decisions to become more connected to Latino/a communities and specifically to their students' community. One teacher attended a predominantly Latino/a church in the community in which masses took place only in Spanish. Another made an effort to recognize the ways in which her students expressed their identities through variations of English, such as Ebonics or Puerto Rican variations of Ebonics. The role of language is important to note here and will be discussed in more detail in a subsequent section, but it is also crucial to point out the willingness of these two teachers, both white, to physically enter nonwhite communities to unpack the "funds of knowledge" (Moll et al., 1992) within them. Although the authors document the various sites from which the participants drew to inform their identities, it is important to note that teacher education coursework and field experiences were not listed. Rather, it was through the individual's personal development, which certainly has implications for professional practice, that they came to know more about the community and their students and to use this knowledge to drive their curriculum.

PERFORMING WHITENESS IN THE CONTEXT OF LATINIZATION

Joining with Latino students in a collective endeavor required me to perform my whiteness (Clark, 1999; Gillespie, Ashbaugh, and DeFiore, 2002; Howard, 1999) differently, particularly in the context of the Latinization of U.S. schools. This shift does not signify trading in whiteness for another identity, but rather intentionally deciding to enact an antiracist/ally identity on behalf of and with students and people of color. White teachers, including me, have been able to live in the water without feeling it. We can easily explain away situations that confront us with anti-Latino sentiment by treating them as the exception rather than being indicative of larger, more encompassing issues. For example, the anti-immigrant/anti-Latino sentiment expressed through recent legislation in Arizona targeting individuals who are suspected of being in the country without the appropriate documentation and the proposed elimination of ethnic studies in the state's public schools do not solely speak to the cultural climate in one state. Rather, the disproportionate targeting of Latinos for negative treatment is evident across the country in policies as well as everyday racial microaggressions (Sólorzano, 2001) that Latinos have to endure. The process of Latinization, as noted in Chapter 1, has been highly contested. As white teachers, we can bury our heads in the sand and choose to ignore the inevitable or, as many in Arizona have done, work to create policies that curb the tide of Latinization and reify narrow conceptions of whiteness whereby individuals in the dominant racial group use their power to continue to suppress racialized others and maintain hegemony. As the demographics of the country continue to shift, white teachers need to shift with them. We are presented with a wonderful opportunity to embrace our interconnected futures and allow Latinization to enrich our lives and inform our practice.

Every day, teachers have the opportunity to learn from Latino students, yet, in part because of an increased focus on student outcomes with significantly less attention to the learning experiences being offered to students, we do not explore these opportunities as often or with the enthusiasm necessary to support Latino students and transform our teaching practices. A major disconnect between white teachers and Latino students is that teachers are not trained to traverse these cultural boundaries and recognize and value the unique skills and experiences Latino students do bring to school. Instead of valuing the "cultural wealth" (Yosso, 2005) that Latino youth possess, educators often define students by what they lack, whether it be financial resources, fluency in Standard English, or the like. Teachers are in the unique position to see and hear how students move between and across contexts and negotiate issues of languages with cognitive and social flexibility—an impressive feat to be certain, yet they are not taught how to value it, to *really* see it and to allow themselves to be transformed by it. Most often, teachers are socialized in a way that tells them, when they hear Spanish or variations of the English language in their classrooms, to steer students away from them, as if they were an interruption of learning. In reality, the opposite is true. It is an opportunity for learning for the teacher—an opportunity that is lost over and over again in the majority of schools serving Latino youth.

Although teacher preparation programs are doing much to incorporate technology education and new literacies into their curricula, teachers need to be trained to "read the world," per the theorizing of Freire (1970). Navigating issues of language and participating in a variety of discourse communities is a familiar and natural practice for many students and people of color and can represent another form of new literacies to be acquired by white teachers. Against a backdrop of anti-Latinization sentiment, it is interesting to see how K–12 schools and schools of education that prepare teachers have readily embraced the rise in technology use as advancement and have created coursework and integrated experiences into existing courses to make sure that students developed the twenty-first-century skills they need to be successful in an increasingly technological world. In contrast, transforming the curriculum to create opportunities for teachers to refine their skills to more appropriately meet the needs of the rapidly increasing population of Latino students in U.S. schools has received significantly less attention. As teachers work to understand and improve their practice, culture must be as important a consideration as course content, and certainly these are not mutually exclusive categories. Performing whiteness within the context of Latinization in ways that foster connections with Latino students and support their development requires teachers to acknowledge the pervasiveness of white supremacy, allow themselves to be transformed through their interactions with individuals and communities across lines of cultural and linguistic difference, and take action to ensure that Latino youth, and all students, learn the skills they need to excel personally and professionally.

LASTING IMPRESSIONS

I still have much work to do to be the person and teacher I hope to become. This journey has been rewarding in ways that transcend words. After spending two years learning from the student-researchers, I have discovered new ways to perform my white identity as well as new strategies for engaging with Latino youth in the process of teaching and learning. More important, I have developed relationships that will last a lifetime, and I will be forever grateful to the youth researchers for their generosity and contributions to my personal and professional development. As I complete my doctoral studies and embark on a career as a teacher educator, the next few months of my life will be filled with accomplishment and uncertainty. No accomplishments that I accumulate in the years to come will surpass becoming, as one of the students dubbed me during a presentation, an "honorary Latina," an unanticipated reward from my border-crossing experience.

Earning the status of an "honorary Latina" from my coresearchers means even more to me than receiving a doctoral degree. I plan to honor this title and live up to the massive responsibility placed upon me, just as I plan to uphold all the rights and privileges granted to recipients of the doctorate. The doctoral degree represents a point of completion, an end to my formal education, but my honorary insider status with this group is a point of departure, the beginning of a lifelong journey.

EPILOGUE
YPAR AS A SHARED JOURNEY
AND DESTINATION

↪

Tell me whom you walk with, and I will tell you who you are.
—Spanish *refran* (translated)

Each chapter in this book brings to life issues that arise as marginalized Latino students journey through school in pursuit of an education that prepares them for what they view as the "real world." At times, as the voices of the students that permeate this text suggest, students feel alone on this journey, completely disconnected from their teachers and other school personnel. They report feeling forced to navigate alone the often foreign and occasionally hostile terrain of school. Some students are triumphant on their solitary journeys, successfully completing their K–12 schooling despite a lack of support or connection to the institutions they attend or those that govern them. Many others, as evidenced by the alarmingly high dropout/pushout rates among Latinos, never reach their final destination.

As teachers, administrators, researchers, policymakers, and others search for ways to ameliorate academic outcomes for Latino youth and others traditionally underserved by schools, they often fail to include those constituents most directly affected by their policies and practices—namely, Latino youth and their communities. In doing so, teachers and administrators often walk alone, although unnecessarily. If we are to effectively respond to the Latinization of U.S. schools and significantly improve Latino student achievement, then students, their communities, teachers, and other school agents need to walk together on a shared journey with a common mission. Joining together, as the refran that opens this epilogue suggests, has an impact on all parties. We are identified by those individuals and groups with whom we metaphorically walk. Thus far, most schools have been reluctant to join with Latino students and families to develop an agenda based on interest convergence, points of accord between the goals of families and schools, or a collective plan of action to address the undereducation of Latino youth. The goal of this book has been to forward the perspectives of one particular but representative group of Latino youth on the education they receive. The students' voices presented here are offered in the hope that readers will begin or continue to "walk with" Latino youth on a shared journey toward educational equity and social justice.

YOUTH PARTICIPATORY ACTION RESEARCH

Youth Participatory Action Research (YPAR) has emerged as an exciting and effective approach to engaging youth in transformational resistance (Solórzano and Delgado Bernal, 2001), a struggle to simultaneously transform oneself and the educational system. A variety of studies have recently documented the benefits of YPAR in working with youth and other marginalized populations (Morrell, 2004; Fine and Torre, 2006; Cammarota and Romero, 2006; Duncan-Andrade and Morrell, 2008; McIntyre, 2009; Payne and Hamdi, 2009). Interestingly, many of these studies document the findings of YPAR projects that were based *outside* public schools, typically in institutions of higher education and/or community-based organizations. Grounding YPAR in the actual schools students are actively navigating, I argue, is also necessary if the social reproductive function of schools is to be disrupted and replaced with a model that facilitates academic and personal success for all students.

As several of the student-researchers observed, the mere thought of conducting research can be intimidating because research is typically viewed as the domain of the highly credentialed ruling elite. Historically, researchers have sought to maintain a distance from their subjects in order to preserve their objectivity in learning more about the issue or individuals under investigation. Conversely, YPAR departs from these rigid and occasionally problematic notions of research by meaningfully integrating and placing value on the emic (or "insider") perspectives of those most directly affected by the problem under investigation. Although much of the traditional research on the schooling experiences of Latino youth and other groups underserved by schools is done with students positioned as the objects of research, YPAR includes students not only as informants but as coresearchers with important insights that can inform all aspects of the research process. Stressing the intersections of valuable emic perspectives and collective investment in social change, Jeff Duncan-Andrade and Ernest Morrell (2008) note, "Participatory action research is valuable because it brings in populations that are often alienated within the traditional research paradigm, but it is also important because these populations often have the best vantage point and the greatest vested interest in the work itself" (Duncan-Andrade and Morrell, 2008, p. 108).

YPAR is not solely a research methodology, although it goes without saying that it constitutes a systematic and rigorous approach to empirical inquiry. YPAR is also useful as an ideology that represents a paradigmatic shift in thinking about the researcher's relationship to research participants. That is, YPAR represents a more humanizing approach to research, in that it attempts to honor the local knowledge and perspectives of participants. Moreover, YPAR explicitly uses research to inform actions aimed at challenging and dismantling oppressive conditions. Hence, YPAR is not solely focused on the academic goals of generating publications to inform a particular body of research literature, although a wealth of important scholarship, typically coauthored with youth members of the research collaboratives, has emerged from these efforts. Rather, in the hands of youth themselves, YPAR can serve unapologetically as a tool for social change. In this sense, research is reclaimed as an indelible right of all people and used to transform their unsatisfactory conditions in the present (see Appadurai, 2006). This focus on research as a tool for emancipation is germane to YPAR. Other approaches to research may claim a liberatory focus, but the development of multigenerational collaboratives (Torre and Fine, 2008) connected by an explicit commitment to social action (O'Leary, 2004; Cammarota and Fine, 2008) is unique to YPAR, insofar as it has developed in recent years.

YPAR can also be used as a pedagogical strategy to work with youth to develop and refine the academic and interpersonal skills necessary for academic success as well as active participation in a democracy. YPAR as a pedagogical approach accomplishes several of the espoused goals of school, including but not limited to academic achievement and parental/community involvement. In contrast to approaches to teaching and learning that remain within the confines of the school, focusing solely on the teaching of material that often feels disconnected from the sociocultural realities of students' communities, YPAR connects schools and communities in ways that have, for many schools, heretofore been unattainable. Parental and community involvement are reconceptualized through YPAR. Instead of emphasizing a strict adherence to the prescribed curriculum frameworks, YPAR focuses on the youth, begins with the issues of importance to them, and then uses research-related activities as the venue for teaching important skills. Students' investigation of the issues they identify as important and meaningful transcends the walls of the school and the rigid, prescriptive curricula many youth in urban schools are forced to endure. The community becomes integrated into the work of the school through the practice of YPAR. That is, students and other members of the community participate actively in the research, defining the directions and the implementation of the work. Additionally, the funds of knowledge (Moll et al., 1992) that exist in urban communities are honored and leveraged to inform the work of the collective research team.

This book emerged from YPAR as a pedagogy rooted in student engagement and a shared sense of purpose. At the inception of the project, most of the student-authors self- identified as being apathetic about school. Many shared stories of losing enthusiasm over time; they talked about feeling very enthusiastic about learning during their elementary school years and the ways in which that fervor for school waned as they progressed through high school. Over time, most of the student-authors became disengaged from school and shifted their educational aspirations to reflect how they were positioned within school. Instead of trying to do well academically and move on to college, they lowered their expectations merely to, as one student put it, "hopefully graduate."

This loss of hope and sense of diminished expectations are evident in the following excerpt from an interview conducted with a student at the inception of the project in which he was asked about his educational and career aspirations:

IRIZARRY: What do you hope to get out of school and how do you think school might help you accomplish your goals?

STUDENT: I know that you want me to say I want good things, that I want to be something in life, but I can't really say that. You know what I mean? Of course I want to be somebody, but I don't know. It's like ... without education, you really can't make it. Right now I am in school, but I am not getting an education. You know what I mean?

IRIZARRY: What role, if any, has the school played in shaping your belief about what is possible for you in the future?

STUDENT: A big role. I am not smart here. I never feel like myself here. Sometimes it is like nobody sees me. Maybe if things were different, I might feel different.

This student's alienation from school makes sense, given the cumulative effect of his experiences in schools to date. Why would teachers expect students to invest heavily in institutions that often render them invisible and silence their voices? When students feel actively engaged as equal partners in teaching and learning and when their identities are affirmed, however, both the value they place on education and their personal and professional aspirations are transformed and reflect what becomes possible with adult support. In an interview conducted at the end of the school year, coinciding with the culmination of the first year of the project, the same student responded differently to the same question, signaling a change in the ways in which he thought about himself in relation to school:

STUDENT: I want to go to college for either teaching or engineering. I know that I am way behind on my credits and I have a lot of work to do, but I am going to do it.

IRIZARRY: When we first spoke about fourteen months ago, you answered very differently. Why the change?

STUDENT: I don't know. I feel different about myself, about the world ... you know. For the first time in my life, I feel smart, like I have something to say. I feel free. I don't know how to explain it, but before this project, I wasn't like ... free. I am here [in school] for a reason now—to help myself and to help others.

It is not hyperbole to point out how the repositioning of students from passive consumers to active producers of knowledge, facilitated by youth participatory action research pedagogy, empowered students with a newfound sense of freedom. According to Maria Torres-Guzmán (2009, p. 5), freedom requires "access to all of the resources (linguistic, social, and cognitive) at one's disposal." This newfound freedom to assert oneself simultaneously as a Latino and as a scholar, as a student and as an activist, and as a member of multiple linguistic and cultural communities created the conditions under which students could develop and perform new identities. The YPAR approach represents a departure from the skill-and-drill "banking method" (Freire, 1970/2000) pedagogies that dominate the education of many Latino students. New approaches that center students' experiences, engage them as meaningful partners in teaching and learning, and address their sociocultural and sociopolitical realities allow students to experience varying degrees of liberation. As partners in the YPAR process, teachers, too, can become liberated from the shackles of oppressive mandates and assessments that often strip them of the freedom to utilize all the linguistic, social, and cognitive resources at their disposal and that often force them to adopt and implement practices that may not be in the best interests of students.

SPANGLISH VOICES

Latinization is currently leaving an indelible mark on this country, transforming outdated notions of nationhood and shaping the future of the United States. Latinization will and should influence the work of teachers and the function of schools. We are all undergoing transformation and transmogrification, albeit in different ways. Our repertoires of practice (Gutiérrez and Rogoff, 2003), which describe individuals' and groups' histories of engagement in cultural practices and move away from the concept of static traits—and the knowledge base and cultural contexts that inform them—are influenced by our interactions within our racial/ethnic groups as well as interactions across lines of cultural and linguistic difference, resulting in hybrid identities and cultural practices that reflect the various sites and communities from which we draw and that shape our identities. Latinization, undoubtedly, is shaped by the context in which it occurs and by complementary and/or competing forces that influence how the process unfolds. Sometimes the process of Latinization can be peaceful and harmonious, with students and schools engaging in mutually edifying and enriching cultural exchanges that positively influence both parties. As evidenced by many of the interactions between Latino students and schools documented within this book, at other times the cultural collisions or *choques* (Torre and Ayala, 2009) between students and their teachers are more abrupt and even violent, negatively influencing students and teachers alike, alienating them from one another, and ultimately adding to the chasm of cultural division. Whatever the tone or tenor of the interaction, teachers and students alike are affected, whether positively or negatively.

As distinct cultural frameworks, worldviews, identities, and histories come into contact with one another in schools, new hybrid identities emerge. An example of the outcome of these cultural exchanges and *choques* is Spanglish, a hybrid language form mixing English and Spanish and identified by many of the student authors. Although some language purists and others detest Spanglish, citing its failure to honor the conventions of either English or Spanish, it nevertheless represents the product of a cultural exchange where one's own linguistic practices can be asserted while gradually incorporating a new language into one's repertoire. Hybrid language practices represent one possible product of cultural exchanges, but the notion of cultural hybridity, or Spanglish in this context, as a heuristic for understanding and positively responding to Latinization, is even more comprehensive. Instead of asking (or requiring) that one group completely shed its identity in favor of conforming to more dominant forces, Spanglish represents the obvious confluence of two linguistic and cultural systems as a result of the inevitable *choques* caused by individuals from different cultural backgrounds coming into contact.

Efforts to transform the education of Latino students should not focus on changing students' cultures or "fixing" students to make them more "American." *Choques* resulting from an assimilationist framework can make schooling feel like a subtractive experience for Latino youth (Valenzuela, 1999). In contrast, developing interactions and pedagogies that support additive approaches to education, in which students and their teachers are encouraged to shape and be shaped by the environments they co-inhabit and co-construct, represents the first step on the journey toward a quality education for Latinos. Fostering positive cultural exchanges requires teachers, students, administrators, families, and others to learn new modes of communication, allowing for the cultivation of distinctly Spanglish and other voices, whereby students and teachers have the freedom to speak, be heard, and have their identities affirmed.

A SHARED JOURNEY AND DESTINATION

As the teacher and lead author of this text, I have had the privilege of accompanying this group of students for part of their journey through high school. We have worked collaboratively over several years, becoming enmeshed in each other's lives. Through my sustained interactions with the students over time, I have been able to map changes in their attitudes toward school, celebrate academic and personal successes, and sometimes even grieve losses and failures with them. From my vantage point, the experience has been overwhelmingly positive. I have been profoundly affected by our interactions and hope that I am becoming a better teacher, teacher educator, researcher, and person as a result. Through my formal interviews with the participants, I have learned a great deal about their experiences, their aspirations, and what will be necessary in order to transform the preparation of teachers to work more effectively with Latino youth. However, the most important lessons—those times when the impact of youth participatory action research were most visible—occurred as I walked with students and observed them in action, collecting and analyzing data together and presenting our findings to audiences at local community gatherings and at professional academic conferences.

Of the many stories from our years of working together, one anecdote stands out in particular. For me, the moment encapsulated in this anecdote symbolizes the transformative power of YPAR, both as a research methodology and as pedagogy. For this reason, I offer the story as an appropriate and hopefully inspiring way to close this book.

After presenting some of the research included in this book at a conference for educators and policymakers, one of the audience members posed a question to the students, who were seated in the front of a large room: What is the most important thing you learned from this project?

The students, as had become customary, looked at each other to see who wanted to field the question. Answering questions from adults in the audience, as one can imagine, can feel quite intimidating, even for the most seasoned presenter. Even so, with each presentation the students became more confident, and several even came to relish the opportunity to share their thoughts and respond to questions, while others remained more passive, allowing their colleagues to do most of the talking. Taína, who was usually reserved and quiet during the question and answer portions of the presentations, asserted herself and was designated to field that question.

"What is the most important thing you learned from this project?" the audience member repeated.

"I learned that we Latinos are not dumb, like I thought," Taina replied, with a proud smile engulfing her face. "We are smart." She continued, "I learned that by myself, it is hard to change things, but if teachers work together with students, we can do anything."

In the end, Taina's declaration effectively summarizes better than anything I could write as a researcher the power of Youth Participatory Action Research. Furthermore, her words emphasize the potential for transforming educational opportunities and outcomes when teachers and students embark on a shared journey with a shared destination.

NOTES

⊸

INTRODUCTION

1. Located in a rural area of the state, the community has a population of less than 30,000. However, it is often referred to as "urban" because a large percentage of residents are people of color and poverty is pervasive.

2. The term *Latino,* which is often used interchangeably with *Hispanic,* is used throughout the text to refer to people who identify themselves as being descended from and connected to cultural communities in Mexico, Puerto Rico, the Spanish-speaking Caribbean, and other regions of Latin America. I acknowledge that solely using the masculine form of the noun to refer to both men and women can be problematic, and many scholars have utilized Latino/a to be more inclusive. However, this form isn't perfect, narrowing the construction of gender to two categories. As scholarship on Latinos continues to grow, we need to develop terminology that accurately describes and affirms the identities of this diverse group.

3. The backlash against Latino students, and Latino immigrants in particular, that fosters the internalized oppression referenced here parallels a global assault on immigrants. For a more comprehensive discussion of how internalized inferiority is part of a larger, dominant ideology that is predicated on a fear of the "other" that transcends national boundaries, see Habermas, *Europe: The Faltering Project* (2009).

4. I use the term *minoritized* to suggest that although Latinos may share status as members of a historical numeric minority group, in many cases they constitute the majority of the student body within the schools they attend. Research has documented that numerous urban school districts are more segregated now than during the heyday of the civil rights movement, leaving many youngsters

in our nation's cities to attend predominately brown and black schools. In a growing number of communities across the United States, students of color can hardly be said to constitute minorities when their community populations are overwhelmingly comprised of people of color. *Minoritized* captures the ongoing political and social issues that racialize Latinos in predictable, frequently stereotyped, ways.

5. Data extrapolated from the U.S. Census Bureau report *Educational Attainment in the United States* (Washington, DC: 2007).

6. For more information on the positioning of youth of color as disposable, see Giroux, 2000; 2010.

CHAPTER 1

1. Not all Latinos are immigrants. For example, Puerto Ricans born on the island of Puerto Rico are citizens of the United States and are free to travel without restrictions within the country's borders. Although the experiences of Puerto Ricans moving from the island to the mainland share many of the characteristics of immigration from other Latin American countries, not the least of which are nativism and linguicism, their citizenship status offers certain rights and privileges not available to other immigrant groups. I use "(im)migrants" to connote the differences that exist among Latino immigrants/migrants and to signal the complexity of Latino immigration.

2. See Juan Flores, *From Bomba to Hip Hop: Puerto Rican Culture and Latino Identity* (2000); Raquel Rivera, *New York Ricans from the Hip Hop Zone* (2003); and Jeffrey Ogbar, *Hip-Hop Revolution: The Culture and Politics of Rap* (2007) for a more detailed discussion of the role of Latinos in the formation and proliferation of hip-hop.

CHAPTER 5

1. This chapter was written when Kristina Nieves was completing high school; she is now a college student.

CHAPTER 10

1. ASPIRA is a grassroots organization dedicated to the development of the educational and leadership capacity of Hispanic youth. It was established in 1961. See http://www.aspira.org/manuals/what-aspira.

CHAPTER 11

1. Aja LaDuke was a doctoral candidate at the time this chapter was written. She has since completed her degree and is currently employed as an assistant professor in teacher education at the College of Saint Rose.

REFERENCES

⋄

INTRODUCTION

Shor, Ira. 1992. *Culture Wars: School and Society in the Conservative Restoration.* Chicago: University of Chicago Press.

CHAPTER 1

Achinstein, Betty, and Julia Aguirre. 2008. Cultural match or culturally suspect: How new teachers of color negotiate sociocultural challenges in the classroom. *Teachers College Record,* 110(8): 1505–1540.

Acuña, Rodolfo. 2004. *Occupied America: A History of Chicanos,* 2nd ed. New York: Harper and Row.

Anzaldúa, Gloria. 1999. *Borderlands/La Frontera,* 2nd ed. San Francisco: Spinsters/Aunt Lute.

Banks, James A., and Cherry A. McGee Banks, eds. 1989. *Multicultural Education: Issues and Perspectives.* Boston: Allyn and Bacon.

Bowker, Michael. 2009. Hispanic executives continue their rise to power amid a shaky economy. *Hispanic Business Magazine,* January 28, 2009. http://www.hispanicbusiness.com/rankings/corporate_elite/2009/1/28/hispanic_executives_continue_their_rise_to.htm.

Brisk, María Estela. 2006. *Bilingual Education: From Compensatory to Quality Schooling,* 2nd ed. Mahwah, NJ: Lawrence Erlbaum Associates.

Cammarota, Julio, and Augustine Romero. 2006. A critically compassionate pedagogy for Latino/a youth. *Latino/a Studies* 4(3): 305–312.

Center for Immigration Studies. 2003. *Where Immigrants Live: An Examination of State Residency by Country of Origin in 1990–2000.* Report, September 2003. Washington, DC.

Cepeda, María Elena. 2001. Columbus effect(s): Chronology and crossover in the Latin(o) music boom. *Discourse* 23(1): 63–81.

Cochran-Smith, Marilyn, Danne Davis, and Mary Kim Fries. 2004. Multicultural teacher education research, practice, and policy. In *Handbook of Research on Multicultural Education*, 2nd ed., ed. James Banks and Cherry McGee Banks (pp. 931–975). San Francisco: John Wiley.

Cockcroft, James. 1995. *Latinos in the Making of the United States: The Hispanic Experience in the Americas*. New York: Franklin Watts.

Crawford, James. 1999. *Bilingual Education: History, Politics, Theory, and Practice*. Los Angeles: Bilingual Education Services.

Cummins, Jim. 2000. *Language, Power, and Pedagogy: Bilingual Children in the Crossfire*. Clevedon, England: Multilingual Matters.

English First. 2009. *About English First*. Retrieved January 4, 2010, from: http://englishfirst.org/englishfirst/

Farley, Christopher J. 1999. Latin music pops. *Time*, May 24, 1999, 74–79.

Freeman, Rebecca. 1998. *Bilingual Education and Social Change*. Clevedon, England: Multilingual Matters.

Freire, Paulo. 1970/2000. *Pedagogy of the Oppressed*. New York: Herter and Herter.

Garcia, Eugene E. 2005. *Teaching and Learning in Two Languages*. New York: Teachers College Press.

García, Ofelia, Jo Ann Kleifgen, and Lorraine Falchi. 2008. From English language learners to emergent bilinguals. In *Equity Matters: Research Review No. 1*. New York: Teachers College, Columbia University.

García-Nevarez, Ana G, Mary E. Stafford, and Beatriz Arias. 2005. Arizona elementary teachers' attitudes toward English language learners and use of Spanish in classroom instruction. *Bilingual Research Journal* 29(2): 295–318.

Glazer, Nathan, and Daniel P. Moynihan. 1963. *Beyond the Melting Pot: The Negroes, Puerto Ricans, Jews, Italians, and Irish of New York City*. Cambridge, MA: MIT Press.

Gort, Mileidis, Wendy Glenn, and John Settlage. 2007. Teacher educators' efforts to self-improve in the area of linguistic and cultural diversity: Al andar se hace camino. Paper presented at the annual meeting of the American Educational Research Association, Chicago, April.

Grant, Carl A., and Christine E. Sleeter. 1994. *Making Choices for Multicultural Education: Five Approaches to Race, Class, and Gender*. New York: Merrill.

Gutiérrez, Kris D., Jolynn Asato, Mariana Pacheco, Moll, Luis C., Kathryn Olson, Eileen L. Horng, Richard Ruiz, Eugene E. García, and Teresa L. McCarty. 2002. "Sounding American": The consequences of new reforms on English language learners. *Reading Research Quarterly* 37: 328–343.

Huntington, Samuel P. 2004. The Hispanic challenge. *Foreign Policy* 141: 30–45.

Irizarry, Jason G., and John Raible. Forthcoming. Beginning with *El Barrio*: Learning from exemplary teachers of Latino students. *Journal of Latinos and Education* 10(3).

Irwin, Judith W. 1996. *Empowering Ourselves and Transforming Schools: Educators Making a Difference*. Albany: State University of New York Press.

Kochhar, Rakesh; Suro, Rakesh, and Tafoya, Sonya. 2005. *The New Latino South: The Context and Consequences of Rapid Population Growth*. Washington, DC: Pew Hispanic Center.

Kossan, Pat. 2009. Court eases rules on English learner program. *Arizona Republic*, June 25, 2009.

Laó-Montes, Augustín. 2001. Mambo montage: The Latinization of New York City. In *The Latinization of New York*, ed. Augustín Laó-Montes and Arlene Dávila. New York: Columbia University Press.

———. 2008. Reconfigurations of empire in a world-hegemonic transition: The 1898 Spanish-Cuban-American-Filipino War. In *Revisiting the Colonial Question in Latin America*, ed. Mabel Moraña and Carlos Jaurequi, 209–240. Madrid: Iberoamericana.

Lipman, Pauline. 2004. *High Stakes Education: Inequity, Globalization, and Urban School Reform*. New York: Routledge.

Lopez, Mark Hugo. 2008. *How Hispanics Voted in the 2008 Election*. Report, November 2008. Washington, DC: Pew Hispanic Center.

MacDonald, Victoria M. 2001. Hispanic, Latino, Chicano, or "Other"? Deconstructing the relationship between historians and Hispanic-American educational history. *History of Education Quarterly* 41(3): 365–413.

———, ed. 2004. *Latino Education in the United States: A Narrated History from 1513 to 2000*. New York: Palgrave Macmillan.

MacDonald, Victoria M., and Karen Monkman. 2005. Setting the context: Historical perspectives on Latino/a education. In *Latino Education: An Agenda for Community Action Research*, ed. Pedro Pedraza and Melissa Rivera, 47–73. Mahwah, NJ: Lawrence Erlbaum.

Merton, Robert K. 1948. The self-fulfilling prophecy. *Antioch Review* 8: 193–210.

Milner, H. Richard. 2010. What does teacher education have to do with teaching? Implications for diversity studies. *Journal of Teacher Education,* 61(1–2), 118–131.

Minaya-Rowe, Liliana, ed. 2002. *Teacher Training and Effective Pedagogy in the Context of Student Diversity*. Greenwich, CT: Information Age Publishing.

Montero-Siebuth, Martha, and Edwin Meléndez, eds. 2007. *Latinos in a Changing Society*. Westport, CT: Praeger.

Nieto, Sonia. 2000. Puerto Rican students in U.S. schools: A brief history. In *Puerto Rican Students in U.S. Schools,* ed. Sonia Nieto, 5–39. Mahwah, NJ: Lawrence Erlbaum.

Nieto, Sonia, and Patty Bode. 2008. *Affirming Diversity: The Sociopolitical Context of Multicultural Education*. Boston: Pearson.

Oppmann, Patrick. 2009. Rogue minutemen leader held in fatal home invasion. June 23, 2009. http://www.cnn.com/2009/CRIME/06/23/arizona.slaying.minutemen/index.html?iref=allsearch.

Parsad, Basmat, Laurie Lewis, and Elizabeth Farris. 2001. *Teacher Preparation and Professional Development: 2000* (NCES 2001-088). Washington, DC: U.S.

Department of Education, National Center for Educational Statistics. Retrieved September 25, 2003, from http://nces.ed.gov/pubs2001/2001088.pdf.

Perez, Bertha, and María Torres-Guzmán. 1996. *Learning in Two Worlds: An Integrated Spanish/English Biliteracy Approach*. White Plains, NY: Longman.

Pitts, Byron. 2009. Immigrant's murder sheds light on PA town. CBS News, December 16, 2009. http://www.cbsnews.com/stories/2009/12/16/eveningnews/main5988073.shtml

Podgursky, Michael, and Mark Ehlert. 2007. *Teacher Pensions and Retirement Behavior*. Report, April 2007. New York: CALDER Urban Institute.

Quiocho, Alice, and Francisco Rios. 2000. The power of their presence: Minority group teachers and schooling. *Review of Educational Research* 70(4): 485–528.

Raible, John, and Jason G. Irizarry. 2007. Transracialized selves and the emergence of post-white teacher identities. *Race, Ethnicity, and Education* 10(2): 177–198.

Sheets, Rosa H. 2004. Preparation and development of teachers of color. *International Journal of Qualitative Studies in Education* 17(2): 163–166.

Suro, Robert, Rick Fry, and Jeffrey Passel. 2005. *Hispanics and the 2004 Election: Population, Electorate, and Voters*. Report, June. Washington, DC: Pew Hispanic Center.

Tung, Rosann, Miren Uriarte, Virginia Diez, Nicole Lavan, Nicole Agusti, Faye Karp, and Tatjana Meschede. 2009. *English Learners in Boston Public Schools: Enrollment, Engagement, and Academic Outcomes*. Report, April. Boston: Mauricio Gaston Institute for Latino Community Development and Public Policy in collaboration with the Center for Collaborative Education.

U.S. Census Bureau. 2008a. *An Older and More Diverse Nation by Midcentury*. Report, August 14. Washington, DC.

———. 2008b. 2008 American Community Survey. http://factfinder.census.gov/servlet/STTable?_bm=yand- geo_id=01000USand-qr_name=ACS_2008_1YR_G00_S1601and-ds_name=ACS_2008_1YR_G00_andlang=enand-redoLog=false.

U.S. Department of Education, National Center for Education Statistics (NCES). 2006. School and Staffing Survey (SASS), 2003–2004, Public Teacher File.

U.S. Department of Justice, Federal Bureau of Investigation. 2008. *Hate Crime Statistics, 2008*. Report, November 2009. Washington, DC.

Valdés, Guadalupe. 2001. *Learning and Not Learning English: Latino Students in American Schools*. New York: Teachers College Press.

Valli, Linda, and Daria Buese. 2007. The changing roles of teachers in an era of high-stakes accountability. *American Educational Research Journal* 44(3): 519–558.

Valenzuela, Angela. 1999. *Subtractive Schooling: U.S.-Mexican Youth and the Politics of Caring*. Albany: State University of New York Press.

Villegas, Ana M., and Tamara Lucas. 2002. *Educating Culturally Responsive Teachers: A Coherent Approach*. Albany: State University of New York Press.

Wortham, Stanton, Edmund Murillo, Jr., and Enrique Hamann, eds. 2002. *Education in the New Latino Diaspora: Policy and the Politics of Identity.* Westport, CT: Ablex Publishing.

Zinn, Howard. 1999. *A People's History of the United States,* 2nd ed. New York: Harper and Row.

CHAPTER 2

Antróp-González, René, William Vélez, and Tomás Garrett. 2005. Donde están los estudiantes puertorriqueños/as exitosos? [Where are the academically successful Puerto Rican students?]: Success factors of high-achieving Puerto Rican high school students. *Journal of Latino/as and Education* 4(2): 77–94.

Anyon, Jean. 1981. Social class and school knowledge. *Curriculum Inquiry* 11: 1–42.

Brick, Michael. 2010. Texas school board set to vote textbook revisions. *New York Times,* May 20. http://www.nytimes.com/2010/05/21/education/21textbooks.html

Cammarota, Julio, and Augustine Romero. 2006. A critically compassionate pedagogy for Latino/a youth. *Latino/a Studies* 4(3): 305–312.

Cockcroft, James. 1995a. *Latinos in the Making of the United States: The Hispanic Experience in the Americas.* New York: Franklin Watts.

———. 1995b. *Latinos in the Struggle for Equal Education.* New York: Franklin Watts.

Coalition for Achievement Now. 2009. *Connecticut Achievement Gap Remains Country's Worst, National Assessment Shows.* http://www.conncan.org/matriarch/MultiPiecePage.asp Q PageID_E_297_A_PageName_E_MediaRoomNewsReleaseOct142009.

Darling-Hammond, Linda. 2000. Teacher quality and student achievement. *Education Policy Analysis Archives* 8(1): http://epaa.asu.edu/epaa/v8n1.

Duncan-Andrade, Jeffrey, and Ernest Morrell. 2008. *The Art of Critical Pedagogy: Possibilities for Moving from Theory to Practice in Urban Schools.* New York: Peter Lang.

Flores-González, Nilda. 2002. *School Kids/Street Kids: Identity Development in Latino Students.* New York: Teachers College Press.

Fry, Rick. 2008. *One-in-Five and Growing Fast: A Profile of Hispanic Public School Students.* Washington, DC: Pew Hispanic Center.

Gándara, Patricia, and Frances Contreras. 2009. *The Latino Education Crisis: The Consequences of Failed Social Policies.* Cambridge, MA: Harvard University Press.

Herrnstein, Richard, and Charles Murray. 1994. *The Bell Curve.* New York: Free Press.

Howard, Tyrone C. 2003. Who receives the short end of the shortage? America's teacher shortage and implications for urban schools. *Journal of Curriculum and Supervision* 18(2): 142–160.

Irizarry, Jason G., and René Antróp-González. 2007. RicanStructing the discourse and promoting school success: Extending a theory of culturally responsive pedagogy for DiaspoRicans. *Centro Journal of Puerto Rican Studies* 19(2): 36–59.

Kirkland, David. 2010. "Black skin, white masks": Normalizing whiteness and the trouble with the achievement gap. *Teachers College Record.* http://www .tcrecord.org, ID Number 16116, date accessed 11/4/2010.

Kozol, Jonathan. 1992. *Savage Inequalities: Children in America's Schools.* New York: Crown.

Ladson-Billings, Gloria, and William F. Tate. 1995. Toward a critical race theory of education. *Teachers College Record* 97(1): 47–68.

MacLeod, Jay. 2005. *Ain't No Makin' It: Aspirations and Attainment in a Low-Income Neighborhood,* 2nd ed. Boulder, CO: Westview.

Moll, Luis C., Cathy Amanti, Deborah Neff, and Norma González. 1992. Funds of knowledge for teaching: Using a qualitative approach to connect homes and classrooms. *Theory into Practice* 31(2): 132–141.

Montero-Seiburth, Martha. 2005. Explanatory models of Latino/a education during the reform movement of the 1980s. In *Latino education: An agenda for community action Research,* ed. Pedro Pedraza and Melissa Rivera, 99–156. Mahwah, NJ: Lawrence Erlbaum.

Nieto, Sonia. 1999. *The Light in Their Eyes: Creating Multicultural Learning Communities.* New York: Teachers College Press.

———. 2000. Puerto Rican students in U.S. schools: A brief history. In *Puerto Rican Students in U.S. Schools,* ed. Sonia Nieto, 5–39. Mahwah, NJ: Lawrence Erlbaum.

Padilla, Laura M. 2001. "But you're not a dirty Mexican": Internalized oppression, Latinos, and law. *Texas Hispanic Journal of Law and Policy* 7(59): 65–73.

Patton, Michael Q. 1990. *Qualitative Evaluation and Research Methods,* 2nd ed. Newbury Park, CA: Sage.

Rodríguez, Louie F. 2008. Latino school dropout and popular culture: Envisioning solutions to a pervasive problem. *Journal of Latinos and Education* 7(3): 258–264.

Rolón-Dow, Rosalie. 2005. Critical care: A color(full) analysis of care narratives in the schooling experiences of Puerto Rican girls. *American Educational Research Journal* 42(1): 77–111.

Sleeter, Christine E. 2001. Preparing teachers for culturally diverse schools: Research and the overwhelming presence of whiteness. *Journal of Teacher Education* 52(2): 94–106.

Valenzuela, Angela. 1999. *Subtractive Schooling: U.S.-Mexican Youth and the Politics of Caring.* Albany: State University of New York Press.

Yosso, Tara. 2005. Whose culture has capital? A critical race theory discussion of community cultural wealth. *Race, Ethnicity, and Education* 8(1): 69–91.

CHAPTER 3

Antróp-González, René, William Vélez, and Tomás Garrett. 2005. Donde están los estudiantes puertorriqueños/as exitosos? [Where are the academically successful Puerto Rican students?]: Success factors of high-achieving Puerto Rican high school students. *Journal of Latino/as and Education* 4(2): 77–94.

Conchas, Gilberto Q. 2006. *The Color of School Success: Race and High-Achieving Urban Youth.* New York: Teachers College Press.

Dee, Thomas S. 2005. "A teacher like me: Does race, ethnicity, or gender matter?" *American Economic Review* 95: 158–165.

Dilworth, Mary E. 1992. *Diversity in Teacher Education: New Expectations.* San Francisco: Jossey Bass.

Flores-González, Nilda. 2002. *School Kids/Street Kids: Identity Development in Latino Students.* New York: Teachers College Press.

Freire, Paulo. 1970. *Pedagogy of the Oppressed.* New York: Herter and Herter.

———. 2004. *Pedagogy of Indignation.* Boulder, CO: Paradigm.

Gay, Geneva. 2000. *Culturally Responsive Teaching: Theory, Research, and Practice.* New York: Teachers College Press.

Howard, Gary. 1999. *We Can't Teach What We Don't Know: White Teachers, Multiracial Schools.* New York: Teachers College Press.

Irizarry, Jason G., and René Antróp-González. 2007. RicanStructing the discourse and promoting school success: Extending a theory of culturally responsive pedagogy for DiaspoRicans. *Centro Journal of Puerto Rican Studies* 19(2): 36–59.

Irizarry, Jason G., and John Raible. Forthcoming. Beginning with *El Barrio*: Learning from exemplary teachers of Latino students. *Journal of Latinos and Education* 10(3).

Irvine, Jacqueline J. 2003. *Educating Teachers for Diversity: Seeing with a Cultural Eye.* New York: Teachers College Press.

Leadbetter, Bonnie J., and Niobe Way. 1996. *Urban Girls: Resisting Stereotypes, Creating Identities.* New York: New York University Press.

Milner, H. Richard. 2006. Preservice teachers' learning about cultural and racial diversity: Implications for urban education. *Urban Education* 41(4): 343–375.

Morrell, Ernest, and Jeffrey R. Duncan-Andrade. 2002. Promoting academic literacy with urban youth through engaging hip-hop culture. *English Journal* 91(6): 88–92.

Nieto, Sonia, and Patty Bode. 2008. *Affirming Diversity: The Sociopolitical Context of Multicultural Education.* Boston: Pearson.

Reyes, Xaé A., and Diana Ríos. 2003. Latinos, education, and the media. Special issue, *Journal of Latinos and Education* 2(1): 3–11.

Rolón-Dow, Rosalie. 2005. Critical care: A color(full) analysis of care narratives in the schooling experiences of Puerto Rican girls. *American Educational Research Journal* 42(1): 77–111.

Sleeter, Christine E. 2001. Preparing teachers for culturally diverse schools: Research and the overwhelming presence of whiteness. *Journal of Teacher Education* 52(2): 94–106.

———. 2006. *Un-standardizing the Curriculum: Multicultural Teaching in the Standards-Based Classroom.* New York: Teachers College Press.

Solórzano, Daniel G., and Dolores Delgado Bernal. 2001. Examining transformational resistance through a critical race and LatCrit theory framework:

Chicana and Chicano students in an urban context. *Urban Education* 3: 308–342.

U.S. Department of Education, National Center for Education Statistics. 2008. *The Condition of Education, 2008.* Washington, DC.

———. 2004. Schools and Staffing Survey, 2003–2004, Public School Teacher, BIA School Teacher and Private School Teacher Data Files. Washington, DC.

Vavrus, Michael. 2002. *Transforming the Multicultural Education of Teachers.* New York: Teachers College Press.

CHAPTER 4

Cammarota, Julio, and Augustine Romero. 2006. A critically compassionate intellectualism for Latina/o students: Raising voices above the silencing in our schools. *Multicultural Education* 14(2): 16–23.

Center for the Study of Biracial Children. 2006. *Myths and Realities.* http://csbchome.org/?p=5.

González, José Luis. 1993. *Puerto Rico: The Four-Storeyed Country and Other Essays.* Princeton, NJ: Markus Weiner.

Hamilton, Brady E., Joyce A. Martin, and Stephanie Ventura. 2009. Births: Preliminary data for 2007. National Vital Statistics Reports 57(12). Hyattsville, MD: National Center for Health Statistics.

Howard, Gary. 1999. *We Can't Teach What We Don't Know: White Teachers, Multiracial Schools.* New York: Teachers College Press.

Irvine, Jacqueline J. 2003. *Educating Teachers for Diversity: Seeing with a Cultural Eye.* New York: Teachers College Press.

Kozol, Jonathan. 2005. *The Shame of the Nation: The Restoration of Apartheid Schooling in the U.S.* New York: Crown.

McIntosh, Peggy. 1989. White privilege: Unpacking the invisible knapsack. *Peace and Freedom* (July–August): 10–12.

Misra, Ria. 2009. Louisiana justice of the peace Keith Bardwell refuses to marry interracial couples. *Politics Daily,* October 16, 2009. http://www.politicsdaily.com/2009/10/16/louisiana-justice-of-the-peace-keith-bardwell-refuses-to-marry-i/.

Nieto, Sonia. 2000. Puerto Rican students in U.S. schools: A brief history. In *Puerto Rican Students in U.S. Schools,* ed. Sonia Nieto, 5–39. Mahwah, NJ: Lawrence Erlbaum.

Orfield, Gary. 2001. *Schools More Separate: Consequences of a Decade of Resegregation.* The Cambridge, MA: Harvard University, Civil Rights Project.

Pollock, Mica. 2003. *Colormute: Race Talk Dilemmas in an American School.* Princeton, NJ: Princeton University Press.

Sleeter, Christine E. 2001. Preparing teachers for culturally diverse schools: Research and the overwhelming presence of whiteness. *Journal of Teacher Education* 52(2): 94–106.

Zentella, Ana Celia. 1997. The Hispanophobia of the official English movement in the U.S. *International Journal of the Sociology of Language* 127: 71–86.

CHAPTER 5

Antróp-González, René, William Vélez, and Tomás Garrett. 2005. Donde están los estudiantes puertorriqueños/as exitosos? [Where are the academically successful Puerto Rican students?]: Success factors of high-achieving Puerto Rican high school students. *Journal of Latino/as and Education* 4(2): 77–94.

Creswell, John W. 1998. *Qualitative Inquiry and Research Design: Choosing Among Five Traditions.* Thousand Oaks, CA: Sage.

Flores-González, Nilda. 2002. School Kids/Street Kids: Identity Development in Latino Students. New York: Teachers College Press.

García, Ofelia, José Luis Morín, and Klaudia Rivera. 2001. How threatened is the Spanish of New York Puerto Ricans? In *Can Threatened Languages Be Saved? Reversing Language Shift Revisited: A Twenty-First-Century Perspective,* ed. Joshua Fishman, 44–73. Portland, OR: Book News.

Gee, James P. 2005. *An Introduction to Discourse Analysis: Theory and Method,* 2nd ed. New York: Routledge.

Kirkland, David. 2006. The boys in the hood: Exploring literacy in the lives of six urban adolescent black males. Ph.D. diss., Michigan State University, East Lansing.

Luttrell, Wendy, and Janie Ward. 2004. The "N-word" and the racial dynamics of teaching. *Harvard Education Letter* (September–October): 4–6.

Martínez, Ramón. 2010. Spanglish as literacy tool: Toward an understanding of the potential role of Spanish-English code-switching in the development of academic literacy. *Research in the Teaching of English* 45(2): 124–145.

Paris, Django. 2009. "They're in my culture, they speak the same way": African American language in multiethnic high schools. *Harvard Educational Review* 79(3): 428–448.

Pérez, Bertha (ed). 1998. *Sociocultural Contexts of Language and Literacy.* Mahwah, New Jersey: Lawrence Erlbaum.

Sankoff, David, and Shana Poplack. 1981. A formal grammar for code-switching. *Papers in Linguistics* 14: 3–46.

Smitherman, Geneva. 1977. *Talkin and Testifyin: The Language of Black America.* Boston: Houghton Mifflin.

Solórzano, Daniel. 2001. Critical race theory, racial microaggressions, and campus racial climate: The experiences of African American college students. *Journal of Negro Education* 69: 60–73.

Torres-Guzmán, M. 2010. *Freedom at Work: Language, Professional, and Intellectual Development in Schools.* Boulder, CO: Paradigm Publishers.

Zentella, Ana Celia. 1997. *Growing Up Bilingual.* Oxford: Blackwell.

CHAPTER 6

Acuña, Rodolfo. 2004. *Occupied America: A History of Chicanos,* 2nd ed. New York: Harper and Row.

Bonilla-Silva, Eduardo. 2006. *Racism Without Racists: Color-Blind Racism and the Persistence of Racial Inequality in the United States.* Lanham, MD: Rowman and Littlefield.

Cammarota, Julio. 2008. *Sueños Americanos: Barrio Youth Negotiate Social and Cultural Identities.* Tucson: University of Arizona Press.

Campano, Gerald. 2007. *Immigrant Students and Literacy: Reading, Writing, and Remembering.* New York: Teachers College Press.

College Board. 2009a. Young lives on hold: The college dreams of undocumented students—why we need the DREAM act. Press release, April 21, 2009, http://www.collegeboard.com/press/releases/204864.html, retrieved April 30, 2009.

———. 2009b. 2009–2010 College prices: Keep increases in perspective. http://www.collegeboard.com/parents/csearch/know-the-options/21385.html, retrieved April 30, 2009.

Congressional Budget Office. 2010. Cost estimate Development, Relief, and Education for Alien Minors Act of 2010. As introduced on November 30, 2010. http://www.cbo.gov/ftpdocs/119xx/doc11991/s3992.pdf

Dewey, John. 1916. *Democracy and Education.* New York: Macmillan.

Erickson, Karla, and Jennifer L. Pierce. 2003. Farewell to organization man: The feminization of loyalty in high-end and low-end service jobs. Paper presented to the Gender, Work and Organization Conference, June 25–27, Keele University, Staffordshire, England.

Freire, Paulo. 1970/2000. *Pedagogy of the Oppressed.* New York: Herter and Herter.

———. 2004. *Pedagogy of Indignation.* Boulder, CO: Paradigm.

Giroux, Henry. 2005. *Schooling and the Struggle for Public Life.* Boulder, CO: Paradigm.

Immigrant Rights Project. 2008. *Immigration Myths and Facts.* http://www.aclu.org/files/pdfs/immigrants/myths_facts_jan2008.pdf#page=1.

Irvine, Jacqueline J. 2003. *Educating Teachers for Diversity: Seeing with a Cultural Eye.* New York: Teachers College Press.

Portes, Alejandro, and Rubén Rumbaut. 2006. *Immigrant America: A Portrait,* 3rd ed. Berkeley: University of California Press.

Raible, John, and Jason G. Irizarry. 2007. Transracialized selves and the emergence of post-white teacher identities. *Race, Ethnicity, and Education* 10(2): 177–198.

Reyna, Christine. 2000. Lazy, dumb, or industrious: When stereotypes convey attribution information in the classroom. *Educational* Psychology *Review* 12: 85–110.

Schmidt, Samuel. 1997. Stereotypes, culture, and cooperation in the U.S.-Mexican borderlands. In *Borders and Border Regions in Europe and North America,* ed. Paul Ganster, James Scott, Alan Sweedler, and Wolf Dieter-Eberwein, 214–299. San Diego: San Diego State University Press.

Shelton, Jim. 2008. City "family day" includes resident ID card signups, protests. *New Haven Register,* September 21, http://www.nhregister.com/articles/2008/09/21/news/a3-nefamilyday.txt.

Watteau, Marie, and Olga Medina. 2009. NCLR applauds the reintroduction of the DREAM Act. Press release. http://www.nclr.org/content/news/detail/56486/.

Yoxall, Peter. 2006. The Minuteman Project, gone in a minute or here to stay? The origin, history, and future of citizen activism on the United States–Mexico border. *University of Miami Inter-American Law Review* 37(3): 517–566.

Zamudio, Margaret. 2002. Segmentation, conflict, community, and coalitions: Lessons from the new labor movement. In *Transnational Latina/o Communities: Politics, Processes, and Cultures,* ed. Carlos G. Veléz- Ibánez, 205–224. New York: Rowman and Littlefield.

Zapana, Victor. 2008. 1 year later, ID card a mixed bag. *New Haven Register,* June 8. http://www.nhregister.com/articles/2008/06/08/past_stories/19918032.txt.

CHAPTER 7

BBC News. 2007. Bilingual classes "raise results." http://news.bbc.co.uk/2/hi/uk_news/education/6447427.stm, March 15.

Brisk, María Estela. 2006. *Bilingual Education: From Compensatory to Quality Schooling.* Mahwah, NJ: Lawrence Erlbaum.

Brisk, María Estela, and Margaret M. Harrington. 2007. *Literacy and Bilingualism: A Handbook for ALL Teachers,* 2nd ed. Mahwah, NJ: Lawrence Erlbaum.

Cockcroft, James. 1995. *Latinos in the Making of the United States: The Hispanic Experience in the Americas.* New York: Franklin Watts.

Crawford, James. 2004. *Educating English Learners: Language Diversity in the Classroom.* Los Angeles: Bilingual Educational Services.

Cummins, Jim. 1976. The influence of bilingualism on cognitive growth: A synthesis of research findings and explanatory hypotheses. *Working Papers on Bilingualism* 9: 1–43.

———. 1992. Bilingual education and English immersion: The Ramirez report in theoretical perspective. *Bilingual Research Journal* 16 (1–2): 91–104.

de Jong, Ester J. 2002. Effective bilingual education: From theory to academic achievement in a two-way bilingual program. *Bilingual Research Journal* 26(1): 65–84.

———. 2006. Integrated bilingual education: An alternative approach. *Bilingual Research Journal* 30(1): 23–44.

Diaz, Rafael M. 1985. Bilingual cognitive development: Addressing three gaps in current research. *Child Development* 56: 1376–1388.

García, Ofelia, Jo Anne Kleifgen, and Lorraine Falchi. 2008. From English-language learners to emergent bilinguals. In *Equity Matters: Research Review No. 1.* New York: Teachers College, Columbia University.

Howard, Elizabeth R., and Donna Christian. 2002. *The Two-Way Immersion Toolkit.* Washington, DC: Education Resources Center, Document Reproduction Service No. ED473082.

Irizarry, Jason G., and John Raible. 2009. As cultures collide: Unpacking the sociopolitical context surrounding English language learners. In *Empowering Teachers for Equity and Diversity: Progressive Perspectives on Research, Theory, and Practice,* ed. H. R. Milner. New York: Palgrave Macmillan.

Johnson, Susan Moore, Jill H. Berg, and Morgaen L. Donaldson. 2005. *Who Stays in Teaching and Why: A Review of the Literature on Teacher Retention.* Boston: Harvard Graduate School of Education Project on the Next Generation of Teachers.

Padilla, Amado M., and Rosemary Gonzalez. 2001. Academic performance of immigrant and U.S.-born Mexican heritage students: Effects of schooling in Mexico and bilingual/English language instruction. *American Educational Research Journal* 38: 727–742.

Ramírez, J. David, Sandra D. Yuen, and Dena R. Ramey. 1991. *Final Report: Longitudinal Study of Structured English Immersion Strategy, Early-Exit and Late-Exit Transitional Bilingual Education Programs for Language Minority Children.* San Mateo, CA: Aguirre International.

Rossell, Christine H., and Keith Baker. 1996. The educational effectiveness of bilingual education. Research in the Teaching of English 30(1): 7–69.

Souto-Manning, Mariana. 2006. A critical look at bilingualism discourse in public schools: Autoethnographic reflections of a vulnerable observer. *Bilingual Research Journal* 30(2): 559–577.

CHAPTER 8

Akom, Antwi. A. 2003. Reexamining resistance as oppositional behavior: The nation of Islam and the creation of a black achievement ideology. *Sociology of Education* 76(4): 305–325.

Artiles, Alfredo J., Beth Harry, Daniel J. Reschly, and Phillip Chinn. 2002. Over-identification of students of color in special education: A critical overview. *Multicultural Perspectives* 4(1): 3–10.

Bourdieu, Pierre. 1977. Cultural reproduction and social reproduction. In *Power and Ideology in Education,* ed. Jerome Karabel and Albert H. Halsey, 487–511. New York: Oxford.

Braddock, Jomills H., and Robert E. Slavin. 1992. Why ability grouping must end: Achieving excellence and equity in American education. *Journal of Intergroup Relations* 20(1): 51–64.

Brown, Tara. 2007. Lost and turned out: Academic, social, and emotional experiences of students excluded from school. *Urban Education* 42(5): 432–435.

Cammarota, Julio. 2008. *Sueños Americanos: Barrio Youth Negotiate Social and Cultural Identities.* Tucson: University of Arizona Press.

Carey, Kevin. 2009. On accountability: Achieving President Obama's college completion goal. *Diverse Issues in Higher Education,* June 11, http://diverseeducation.com/artman/publish/article_12633.shtml.

Conchas, Gilberto Q. 2006. *The Color of Success: Race and High-Achieving Urban Youth.* New York: Teachers College Press.

References

Crosby, Olivia, and Roger Moncarz. 2006. The 2004–2014 job outlook for college graduates. *Occupational Outlook Quarterly* (Fall): 41–57.

Cummins, Jim. 1989. A theoretical framework for bilingual special education. *Exceptional Children* 56: 111–120.

Duncan-Andrade, Jeffrey, and Ernest Morrell. 2008. *The Art of Critical Pedagogy: Possibilities for Moving from Theory to Practice in Urban Schools*. New York: Peter Lang.

Gándara, Patricia, and Frances Contreras. 2009. *The Latino Education Crisis: The Consequences of Failed Social Policies*. Cambridge, MA: Harvard University Press.

Hancock Productions. 1998. *Off-Track: Classroom Privilege for All*. Video. New York: Teachers College Press.

Harklau, Linda. 2000. From the "good kids" to the "worst": Representations of English language learners across educational settings. *TESOL Quarterly* 34: 35–68.

Helms, Janet E. 1992. Why is there no study of cultural equivalence in standardized cognitive ability testing? *American Psychologist* 47: 1083–1101.

Hosp, John L., and Daniel J. Reschly. 2004. Disproportionate representation of minority students in special education: Academic, demographic, and economic predictors. *Exceptional Children* 70(2): 185–199.

Hu, Winnie. 2009. No longer letting scores separate pupils. *New York Times,* June 14, http://www.nytimes.com/2009/06/15/education/15stamford.html.

MacLeod, Jay. 2005. *Ain't No Makin' It: Aspirations and Attainment in a Low-Income Neighborhood,* 2nd ed. Boulder, CO: Westview.

Malgady, Robert G., Lloyd H. Rogler, and Giuseppe Costantino. 1987. Ethnocultural and linguistic bias in mental health evaluation of Hispanics. *American Psychologist* 42: 228–234.

Merton, Robert K. 1948. The self-fulfilling prophecy. *Antioch Review* 8: 193–210.

National Women's Law Center and Mexican American Legal Defense and Educational Fund (MALDEF). 2009. *Listening to Latinas: Barriers to High School Graduation*. Washington, DC.

Nieto, Sonia, and Patty Bode. 2008. *Affirming Diversity: The Sociopolitical Context of Multicultural Education*. Boston: Pearson.

Noguera, Pedro. 2001. Racial politics and the elusive quest for excellence and equity in education. *Education and Urban Society* 34(1): 18–41.

———. 2003. *City Schools and the American Dream: Reclaiming the Promise of Public Education*. New York: Teachers College Press.

Oakes, Jeannie. 2005. *Keeping Track: How Schools Structure Inequality,* 2nd ed. New Haven, CT: Yale University Press.

Oakes, Jeannie, and John Rogers, with Martin Lipton. 2006. *Learning Power: Organizing for Education and Justice*. New York: Teachers College Press.

Ogbu, John. 1978. *Minority Education and Caste: The American System in Cross-Cultural Perspective*. New York: Academic Press.

Valenzuela, Angela. 1999. *Subtractive Schooling: U.S.-Mexican Youth and the Politics of Caring*. Albany: State University of New York Press.

Wright-Castro, Rosina, Rosita Ramirez, and Richard Duran. 2003. *Latino Sixth-Grade Student Perceptions of School Sorting Practices*. ERIC document number ED477546. Battle Creek, MI: Kellogg Foundation.

CHAPTER 9

Associated Press. 2007. More blacks, Latinos in jail than college dorms: Civil rights advocates say Census Bureau figures are startling. MSNBC, September 27, http://www.msnbc.msn.com/id/21001543/.

Black, Timothy. 2009. *When a Heart Turns Rock Solid: The Lives of Three Puerto Rican Brothers*. New York: Pantheon.

Brown, Tara. 2007. Lost and turned out: Academic, social, and emotional experiences of students excluded from school. *Urban Education* 42(5): 432–455.

Children's Defense Fund. 1975. *Out-of-School Suspensions: Are They Helping Children?* Cambridge, MA: Children's Defense Fund.

Christle, Christine, Kristine Jolivette, and C. Michael Nelson. 2005. Breaking the school-to-prison pipeline: Identifying school risk and protective factors for youth delinquency. *Exceptionality* 13: 69–88.

Drakeford, William. 2004. Racial disproprotionality in school disciplinary practice. *National Center for Culturally Responsive Educational Systems*. Practitioner Brief, 1–8.

Edelman, Marian Wright. 2007. The cradle-to-prison pipeline: An American health crisis. *Preventing Chronic Disease* 4(3): 1–2.

Fields, Gary. 2008. The high school dropout's economic ripple effect. *Wall Street Journal*, October 21.

Lopez, Mark Hugo, and Gretchen Livingston. 2009. *Hispanics and the Criminal Justice System: Low Confidence, High Exposure*. Washington, DC: Pew Hispanic Center.

Mendez, Linda M. 2003. Predictors of suspension and negative school outcomes: A longitudinal investigation. *New Directions for Youth Development* 99: 17–33.

Monroe, Carla R. 2005. Why are 'bad boys' always black? Causes of disproportionality in school discipline and recommendations for change. *Clearing House: A Journal of Educational Strategies, Issues and Ideas* 79(1): 45.

No Child Left Behind Act of 2001. 2002. Public Law 107–110, 107th Cong., 1st sess., January 8.

Noguera, Pedro. 2003. *City Schools and the American Dream: Reclaiming the Promise of Public Education*. New York: Teachers College Press.

Skiba, Russell J., Robert S. Michael, Abra Carroll Nardo, and Reece L. Peterson. 2002. The color of discipline: Sources of racial and gender disproportionality in school punishment. *Urban Review* 34(4): 317–342.

Wald, Johanna, and Daniel J. Losen. 2003. Defining and redirecting a school-to-prison pipeline. *New Directions for Youth Development* 99: 9–15.

PART 4 INTRODUCTION

Freire, Paulo. 1970/2000. *Pedagogy of the Oppressed.* New York: Herter and Herter.

Torre, María Elena. 2005. The alchemy of integrated spaces: Youth participation in research collectives of difference. In *Beyond Silenced Voices,* ed. Lois Weis and Michelle Fine, 251–266. Albany: State University of New York Press.

Torre, María Elena, and Jennifer Ayala. 2009. Envisioning participatory action research. *Entremundos: Feminism and Psychology* 19(3): 387–393.

CHAPTER 10

Cammarota, Julio. 2008. *Sueños Americanos: Barrio Youth Negotiate Social and Cultural Identities.* Tucson: University of Arizona Press.

Fine, Michelle. 1991. *Framing Dropouts: Notes on the Politics of an Urban Public High School.* Albany: State University of New York Press.

MacLeod, Jay. 2005. *Ain't No Makin' It: Aspirations and Attainment in a Low-Income Neighborhood,* 2nd ed. Boulder, CO: Westview.

Treschan, Lazar. 2010. *Latino Youth in New York City: School, Work, and Income Trends for New York's Largest Group of Young People.* New York: Community Service Society.

U.S. Census Bureau. 2007. *Educational Attainment in the United States.* Washington, DC.

U.S. Department of Education, National Center for Education Statistics. 2009. *The Condition of Education, 2009.* Washington, DC

CHAPTER 11

Ahlquist, Roberta. 1991. Position and imposition: Power relations in a multicultural foundations class. *Journal of Negro Education* 60(2): 158–169.

Assaf, Lori C., and Caitlyn M. Dooley. 2006. "Everything they were giving us created tension": Creating and managing tension in a graduate-level multicultural course focused on literacy methods. *Multicultural Education* 14(2): 42–49.

Banks, James A., and Cherry A. McGee Banks, eds. 2004. *Multicultural Education: Issues and Perspectives.* Boston: Allyn and Bacon.

Clark, Christine. 1999. The secret: White lies are never little. In *Becoming and Unbecoming White: Owning and Disowning a Racial Identity,* ed. Christine Clark and James O'Donnell, 92–110. Westport, CT: Bergin and Garvey.

Clark, Christine, and James O'Donnell, J. 1999. Rearticulating a racial identity: Creating oppositional spaces to fight for equality and social justice. In *Becoming and Unbecoming White: Owning and Disowning a Racial Identity,* ed. Christine Clark and James O'Donnell, 1–10. Westport, CT: Bergin and Garvey.

Delpit, Lisa. 1995. *Other People's Children: Cultural Conflict in the Classroom.* New York: New Press.

Finn, Patrick. 1999. *Literacy with an Attitude: Educating Working-Class Students in Their Own Self-Interest.* Albany: State University of New York Press.

Freire, Paulo. 1970/2000. *Pedagogy of the Oppressed.* New York: Herter and Herter.

Galman, Sally. 2006. "Rich white girls": Developing critical identities in teacher education and novice teaching settings. *International Journal of Learning* 13(3): 47–55.

Gay, Geneva. 2000. *Culturally Responsive Pedagogy. Theory, Research, and Practice.* New York: Teachers College Press.

Gillespie, Diane, Leslie Ashbaugh, and JoAnn DeFiore. 2002. White women teaching white women about white privilege, race cognizance and social action: Toward a pedagogical pragmatics. *Race, Ethnicity, and Education* 5(3): 237–253.

Gutiérrez, Kris D. and Barbara Rogoff. 2003. Cultural ways of learning: Individual traits or repertoires of practice. *Educational Researcher* 32(5): 19–25.

Howard, Gary R. 1999. *We Can't Teach What We Don't Know: White Teachers, Multiracial Schools.* New York: Teachers College Press.

Irizarry, Jason G. 2009. Representin': Drawing from urban youth culture to inform teacher preparation. *Education and Urban Society* 41(4): 489–515.

Irizarry, Jason G., and René Antróp-González. 2007. RicanStructing the discourse and promoting school success: Extending a theory of culturally responsive pedagogy to DiaspoRicans. *Centro Journal for Puerto Rican Studies* 20(2): 36–59.

Irvine, Jacqueline J. 2003. *Educating Teachers for Diversity: Seeing with a Cultural Eye.* New York: Teachers College Press.

Kohl, Herbert. 1994. *I Won't Learn from You and Other Thoughts on Creative Maladjustment.* New York: New Press.

Kozol, Jonathan. 1992. *Savage Inequalities: Children in America's Schools.* New York: Crown.

Ladson-Billings, Gloria. 1994. *The Dreamkeepers: Successful Teachers of African American Children.* San Francisco: Jossey-Bass.

———. 1996. Silences as weapons: Challenges of a black professor teaching white students. *Theory into Practice* 35(2): 79–85.

LaDuke, Aja E. 2009. Resistance and renegotiation: Preservice teachers' interactions with and reactions to multicultural education course content. *Multicultural Education* 16(3): 37–44.

Lee, Enid, Deborah Menkart, and Margo Okazawa-Rey, eds. 1998. *Beyond Heroes and Holidays: A Practical Guide to K–12 Anti-racist, Multicultural Education and Staff Development.* Washington, DC: Network of Educators on the Americas.

Maxwell, Kelly. 2004. Deconstructing whiteness: Discovering the water. In *Identifying Race and Transforming Whiteness in the Classroom,* ed. Virginia Lea and Judy Helfand, 153. New York: Peter Lang.

McIntosh, Peggy. 1989. White privilege: Unpacking the invisible knapsack. *Peace and Freedom* (July–August): 10–12.

Milner, H. Richard. 2006. Preservice teachers' learning about cultural and racial diversity: Implications for urban education. *Urban Education* 41(4): 343–375.

Moll, Luis C., Cathy Amanti, Deborah Neff, and Norma González. 1992. Funds of knowledge for teaching: Using a qualitative approach to connect homes and classrooms. *Theory into Practice* 31(2): 132–141.

Nieto, Sonia. 2000. Puerto Rican students in U.S. schools: A brief history. In *Puerto Rican Students in U.S. Schools,* ed. Sonia Nieto, 5–39. Mahwah, NJ: Lawrence Erlbaum.

No Child Left Behind Act of 2001. 2002. Public Law 107–110, 107th Cong., 1st sess., January 8.

Ogbu, John U. 1992. Understanding cultural diversity and learning. *Educational Researcher* 21(8): 5–14.

Raible, John, and Jason G. Irizarry. 2007. Transracialized selves and the emergence of post–white teacher identities. *Race, Ethnicity, and Education* 10(2): 177–198.

Rodríguez, Louie F. 2008. "I've never heard of the word pedagogy before": Using liberatory pedagogy to forge hope for new teachers in our nation's public schools. *InterActions: UCLA Journal of Education and Information Studies* 4(2), http://repositories.cdlib.org/gseis/interactions/vol4/iss2/art2.

Ryan, Ann M. 2006. The role of social foundations in preparing teachers for culturally relevant practice. *Multicultural Education* 13(3): 10–13.

Sleeter, Christine E. 2001. Preparing teachers for culturally diverse schools: Research and the overwhelming presence of whiteness. *Journal of Teacher Education* 52(2): 94–106.

Solórzano, Daniel. 2001. Critical race theory, racial microaggressions, and campus racial climate: The experiences of African-American college students. *Journal of Negro Education* 69: 60–73.

Valenzuela, Angela. 1999. *Subtractive Schooling: U.S.-Mexican Youth and the Politics of Caring.* Albany: State University of New York Press.

Weiler, Karen. 1988. *Women Teaching for Change: Gender, Class, and Power.* South Hadley, MA: Bergin and Garvey.

Wise, Tim. 2005. *White Like Me: Reflections on Race from a Privileged Son.* Brooklyn, NY: Soft Skull Press.

———. 2009. *Between Barack and a Hard Place: Racism and White Denial in the Age of Obama.* San Francisco, CA: City Lights Books.

Yosso, Tara. 2005. Whose culture has capital? A critical race theory discussion of community cultural wealth. *Race, Ethnicity, and Education* 8(1): 69–91.

EPILOGUE

Appadurai, Arjun. 2006. The right to research. *Globalisation, Societies, and Education* 4(2): 167–177.

Cammarota, Julio, and Michelle Fine, eds. 2008. *Revolutionizing Education: Youth Participatory Action Research in Motion.* Routledge: London.

Cammarota, Julio, and Augustine Romero. 2006. A critically compassionate pedagogy for Latino/a youth. *Latino/a Studies* 4(3): 305–312.

Duncan-Andrade, Jeffrey, and Ernest Morrell. 2008. *The Art of Critical Pedagogy: Possibilities for Moving from Theory to Practice in Urban Schools.* New York: Peter Lang.

Fine, Michelle, and María Elena Torre. 2006. Intimate details: Participatory action research in prison. *Action Research* 4(3): 253–269.

Freire, Paulo. 1970/2000. *Pedagogy of the Oppressed.* New York: Herter and Herter.

Gutiérrez, Kris D., and Barbara Rogoff. 2003. Cultural ways of learning: Individual traits or repertoires of practice. *Educational Researcher* 32(5): 19–25.

McIntyre, Alice. 2009. Constructing meaning about violence, school, and community: Participatory action research with urban youth. *Urban Review* 32(2): 123–154.

Moll, Luis C., Cathy Amanti, Deborah Neff, and Norma González. 1992. Funds of knowledge for teaching: Using a qualitative approach to connect homes and classrooms. *Theory into Practice* 31(2): 132–141.

Morrell, Ernest. 2004. *Becoming Critical Researchers: Literacy and Empowerment for Urban Youth.* New York: Peter Lang.

O'Leary, Zina. 2004. *The Essential Guide to Doing Research.* London: SAGE Publications.

Payne, Yasser A., and Hanaa A. Hamdi. 2009. "Street love": How street life–oriented U.S.-born African men frame giving back to one another and the local community. *Urban Review* 41(1): 29–46.

Solórzano, Daniel G., and Dolores Delgado Bernal. 2001. Examining transformational resistance through a critical race and LatCrit theory framework: Chicana and Chicano students in an urban context. *Urban Education* 3: 308–342.

Torre, María Elena, and Jennifer Ayala. 2009. Envisioning participatory action research *Entremundos. Feminism and Psychology* 19(3): 387–393.

Torre, Elena, and Michelle Fine, with Natasha Alexander, Amir Bilal Billups, Yasmine Blanding, Emily Genao, Elinor Marboe,Tahani Salah, and Kendra Urdang. 2008. Participatory action research in the contact zone. In *Revolutionizing Education: Youth Participatory Action Research in Motion,* ed. Julio Cammarota and Michelle Fine, 23–43. New York: Routledge.

Torres-Guzmán, María. 2009. *Freedom at Work: Language, Professional, and Intellectual Development in Schools.* Boulder, CO: Paradigm.

Valenzuela, Angela. 1999. *Subtractive Schooling: U.S.-Mexican Youth and the Politics of Caring.* Albany: State University of New York Press.

INDEX

↤

Academic achievement of Latinos: blaming home language use for lack of, 127; data on Latino students, 5; deficit perspective, 42–49; educators' ignoring students' plight, 190–191; ethnic studies programs, 30; financial and social goals, 181–182; impact of disciplinary behavior on, 161–162; Latinocentric curriculum prompting student engagement, 62; poverty and, 41; Project FUERTE goals, 7; public school and magnet schools, 176, 178–180; Puerto Rican urban youth, 172; in Puerto Rico, 178–179; research linking multilingualism to, 124; school as equalizer, 179–180; schools as borderlands, 36; students' perception of, 2–3, 10–11, 40–41; teacher training as site of resistance, 62–65; YPAR as strategy to improve, 200. *See also* Expectations

Academic apartheid, 139

Achievement gap, 41, 61–62

Action Research and Social Change class, 7–8, 60, 185

African American Language (AAL), 36, 88, 91–92

African Americans, 61; color-based discipline, 156–157; diversity of whites and people of color, 79; multiracial identity, 70, 77; N-word use, 96–97; Obama's influence and example, 81; school-to-prison pipeline, 163–164

Ain't No Makin' It: Aspirations and Attainment in a Low-Income Neighborhood (MacLeod), 40, 177

Alvarez v. Lemon Grove School Districts, 28

Anti-immigrant climate, 27–28, 116

Anzaldúa, Gloria, 35–36

Apartheid, academic, 139

Arizona: anti-bilingualism, 18, 29, 116, 126; anti-immigration violence, 27; eliminating ethnic studies programs, 8, 30; State Bill 1070, 4, 109, 194

Articles of Confederation, 129

ASPIRA, 175

Assimilationism, 30, 33, 102

Aztlán, 25

Bardwell, Keith, 75

Bilingualism: as asset, 107; curbing Latinization through suppression of, 29–30; defending home language, 121–122; maintaining home language while learning English, 127–129;

ABOUT THE AUTHOR

Jason G. Irizarry is Assistant Professor of Multicultural Education in the Department of Curriculum and Instruction and Faculty Associate in the Institute for Puerto Rican and Latino Studies at the University of Connecticut.